WOMEN IN

Women in the Holocaust

A Feminist History

ZOË WAXMAN

OXFORD
UNIVERSITY PRESS

OXFORD
UNIVERSITY PRESS

Great Clarendon Street, Oxford, OX2 6DP,
United Kingdom

Oxford University Press is a department of the University of Oxford.
It furthers the University's objective of excellence in research, scholarship,
and education by publishing worldwide. Oxford is a registered trade mark of
Oxford University Press in the UK and in certain other countries

© Zoë Waxman 2017

The moral rights of the author have been asserted

First published 2017

Published in the United States of America by Oxford University Press
198 Madison Avenue, New York, NY 10016, United States of America

British Library Cataloguing in Publication Data
Data available

Library of Congress Control Number: 2016947626

ISBN 978-0-19-960868-3

Links to third party websites are provided by Oxford in good faith and
for information only. Oxford disclaims any responsibility for the materials
contained in any third party website referenced in this work.

For Nahum, Jacob, and William

Acknowledgements

I started this book an embarrassingly long time ago and have accumulated debts to numerous long-suffering colleagues, friends, and family along the way. It was begun whilst I was at Royal Holloway, University of London. I am grateful to my colleagues at the time, especially Dan Stone, Robert Eaglestone, Peter Longerich, and the late David Cesarani for their critical engagement in the early stages of the project. One of the great pleasures of working in Oxford has been being part of the vibrant community of Jewish scholars. It has been a great privilege as well as a great pleasure to work with David Rechter and Abigail Green. The wider community of scholars here working on gender have also been an inspiration. I especially thank Mara Keira for her encouragement and friendship. Cathryn Steele has been an incredibly patient, wise, and supportive editor. I owe her a great deal of gratitude. I am grateful to my copy-editor Virginia Catmur, whose brilliant interventions have helped to transform this book. Beyond Oxford, I must also thank Deborah Finding and Josie McLellan, whose generosity is unparalleled and feminist credentials unimpeachable. I have recently received the great honour and privilege of being elected a trustee of the Wiener Library in London. It is a delight to be able to thank the director, Ben Barkow, for his support.

I am also fortunate to have many other wise and generous friends whom I greatly appreciate. They are too numerous to mention but I hope you know who you are. A special thank you goes to my feminist book group.

My children Nahum and Jacob are constant reminders of how wonderful life can be. They, and I, owe much to our wider family: to my amazing parents Denis and Carole Waxman, for all their love; to Dov Waxman; and to Bill and Marian Whyte.

William Whyte is quite simply not only the best husband in the world; he's not a bad historian either. Both qualities have been essential to the writing of this book. I therefore dedicate it to him with all my love.

Oxford, 24 June 2016

Contents

Introduction

Some years ago, as a relatively young researcher, I gave a paper at a conference on the Holocaust. My talk addressed the subject of rape and sexual abuse. I was the only woman on the panel; indeed, I was one of only a handful of women at the conference. My research was at a preliminary stage and I was therefore eager for feedback from my more established colleagues. The first question I was asked after citing testimonies from women who had experienced sexual molestation in the ghettos, concentration camps, and in hiding was 'So what? Is this really worth discussing?' Over the subsequent years this question has continued to plague me and—increasingly—to enrage me.

My experience is not unique. Despite the development of women's studies in the 1970s and an increasing awareness of the importance of women in history, Holocaust scholars remained—until recently—largely hostile to the subject. When the feminist historian Joan Ringelheim, one of the earliest scholars to devote herself to women's Holocaust experiences, proposed a conference dedicated to women and the Holocaust, she received a letter from Cynthia Ozick which said:

> I think you are asking the wrong question. Not simply the wrong question in the sense of not having found the right one; I think you are asking a morally wrong question, a question that leads us still further down the road of eradicating Jews from history. You are—I hope inadvertently—joining up with the likes of [the Revisionists] who [say] that if it happened to the Jews it never happened. You insist that it didn't happen to 'just Jews'. It happened to women, and it is only a detail that the women were Jewish. It is not a detail. It is everything, the whole story.[1]

Ringelheim stood accused of appropriating the Holocaust to further her feminist goals by turning the Holocaust from a Jewish tragedy into another example of female oppression by a patriarchal society. Ozick insisted that 'The Holocaust happened to victims who were not seen as men, women,

---

[1] Cynthia Ozick, quoted in Joan Ringelheim, 'The Split between Gender and the Holocaust', in Dalia Ofer and Lenore J. Weitzman (eds.), *Women in the Holocaust* (New Haven, CT: Yale University Press, 1998), 348–9.

or children, but *as Jews*.'[2] Despite—or because of—such opposition
Ringelheim stood firm and the first major conference on women and
the Holocaust was held at Stern College in New York in 1983, bringing
together over four hundred survivors, academics, and children of survivors.[3] Amongst them was Vera Laska, a survivor who was already
concerned about the potential marginalization of women's wartime
experiences when she was liberated at the end of the war.[4] Out of the
conference came Ringelheim's pioneering article 'The Unethical and
the Unspeakable: Women and the Holocaust', in which she observed
that women were largely absent from the history of the Holocaust and
argued passionately for a reassessment of 'all generalizations and gender-
neutral statements about survival, resistance, the maintenance or collapse
of moral values, and the dysfunction of culture in the camps and ghettos'.[5]
In other words, Ringelheim demanded a women-centred approach to
Holocaust studies that paid particular attention to the specific nature of
women's survival strategies in extremity. She argued that women survived
in the concentration camps by forming mutually caring and supportive
relationships with other prisoners, whereas men tended to survive alone:
'Women's culture (not their biology) provides women with specific and
different conditions in which to make moral choices and act meaningfully.'[6]

　　Sybil Milton was similarly influential in suggesting that women were in
many ways more able to survive the horrors of the Holocaust than their
menfolk.[7] The publication of *Different Voices: Women and the Holocaust*

---

　　[2] Ibid., 349.
　　[3] See Esther Katz and Joan Miriam Ringelheim (eds.), *Proceedings of the Conference:
Women Surviving the Holocaust* (New York: Occasional Papers from The Institute for
Research in History, 1983).
　　[4] See Vera Laska (ed.), *Women in the Resistance and in the Holocaust: The Voices of
Eyewitnesses* (Westport, CT: Greenwood Press, 1983). Some of the earliest work on the
experiences of Jewish women and children appeared in the immediate post-war period.
Denise Dufournier produced a study of the women's camp at Ravensbrück as early as
1948. See idem, *Ravensbrück: The Women's Camp of Death* (London: Allen & Unwin,
1948). Several testimonies written by women were also published in the early years after
the war: Mary Berg, *Warsaw Ghetto: A Diary*, trans. Norbert Guterman and Sylvia Glass,
ed. S. L. Shneiderman (New York: Fischer, 1945); Seweryna Szmaglewska, *Smoke over
Birkenau*, trans. Jadwiga Rynas (New York: Henry Holt, 1947); *Prisoners of Fear* (London:
Gollancz, 1948) by Ella Lingens-Reiner, a non-Jewish Austrian doctor incarcerated in
Ravensbrück and Auschwitz-Birkenau; and Gisella Perl's *I Was a Doctor in Auschwitz*
(New York: International Universities Press, 1948).
　　[5] Joan Ringelheim, 'The Unethical and the Unspeakable: Women and the Holocaust',
Simon Wiesenthal Center Annual, 1 (1984), 69.
　　[6] Ibid.
　　[7] Sybil Milton, 'Women and the Holocaust: The Case of German and German-Jewish
Women', in Renate Bridenthal, Atina Grossmann, and Marion Kaplan (eds.), *When Biology
Became Destiny: Women in Weimar and Nazi Germany* (New York: Monthly Review Press,
1984), 297–323.

in 1993, the first English-language anthology focusing specifically on women's Holocaust experiences, was also based on this premise.[8] In their introduction Carol Rittner and John K. Roth argued that:

> It is fair to say that Holocaust memory has been shaped most decisively, and Holocaust scholarship has been influenced most frequently, by men. Remembering the Holocaust is an incomplete act, however, if the voices heard, and the silences commemorated are predominantly male ... What women and men remember is not identical ...

Exploration and emphasis, they argued, should occur not because women's voices are necessarily clearer or better than men's—though in many individual cases they are—but because they are women's voices reflecting on their own particular experience in ways that no one else can do for them. The need, however, is not just to let women speak for themselves. Of equal, if not greater, importance is the need for them to be heard.[9]

During the late 1980s and 1990s publications emerged focusing on women's roles as 'mothers' or 'caregivers'; for example, in an edited collection of oral testimonies of twenty-three Jewish women and two non-Jewish women who survived the Holocaust entitled *Mothers, Sisters, Resisters*—the editor, Brana Gurewitsch, states that 'all of the women here resisted their fates. They supported each other like sisters and nurtured each other like mothers'; and indeed, the front cover has a photograph taken in 1945 of five women holding their babies.[10] Judith Tydor Baumel's *Double Jeopardy: Gender and the Holocaust*, whilst also concerned to offer a positive account of women's responses to extremity, presented a more nuanced approach by taking into account such factors as religiosity and political affiliation when looking at how Jewish women experienced the Holocaust.[11] Tydor Baumel's work is careful to stress the differences as well as similarities between different women of different backgrounds.

Then, Dalia Ofer and Lenore Weitzman's edited collection *Women in the Holocaust*, published in 1998, containing essays by scholars such as Marion Kaplan, Myrna Goldenberg, Sarah Horowitz, Joan Ringelheim, and Paula Hyman as well as survivor writers such as Felicja Karay and Ruth Bondy, marked a significant landmark in the developing field of

---

[8] See Carol Rittner and John K. Roth (eds.), *Different Voices: Women and the Holocaust* (New York: Paragon House, 1993).

[9] Ibid., 38.

[10] Brana Gurewitsch (ed.), *Mothers, Sisters, Resisters: Oral Histories of Women Who Survived the Holocaust* (Tuscaloosa, AL: University of Alabama Press, 1998), xii. Cited in Anna Hardman, 'Women and the Holocaust', *Holocaust Educational Trust Research Papers*, 1/3 (1999–2000), 11.

[11] Judith Tydor Baumel, *Double Jeopardy: Gender and the Holocaust* (London: Vallentine Mitchell, 1998).

gender and the Holocaust by opening up important areas of women's experiences such as life in pre-war western and eastern Europe, in the ghettos, as partisans, passing as Aryans, and in forced labour camps. Their book—which grew out of a conference organized by Ofer and Weitzman at the Hebrew University in Jerusalem in 1995—was premised on the simple belief that 'questions of gender lead us to a richer and more finely nuanced understanding of the Holocaust'.[12] Unsurprisingly the book generated a great deal of publicity and influenced a generation of scholars—myself amongst them.

This small but increasingly significant literature was enough, however, to provoke a backlash, as other—more mainstream—scholars resisted any attempt to use gender or, more particularly, women's experiences as a particular category of analysis. Stressing the uniqueness of the Holocaust as an unparalleled historical event, these scholars and many Holocaust survivors refused even to engage with notions of gender, much less consider how women's experiences might differ—and differ significantly—from those of men. Lawrence Langer, a literary scholar who has written extensively on Holocaust testimony—and in Ofer and Weitzman's own volume—argued that to look specifically at women's Holocaust experiences was to attempt to establish 'a mythology of comparative endurance' in a 'landscape of universal destruction'.[13] He writes:

> [I]t seems to me that nothing could be crueller or more callous than the attempt to dredge up from this landscape of universal destruction a mythology of comparative endurance that awards favours to one group of individuals over another...All efforts to find a rule of hierarchy in that darkness, whether based on gender or on will, spirit or hope, reflect only our own need to plant a life sustaining seed in the barren soil that conceals the remnants of two thirds of European Jewry.[14]

His call was amplified—and, again, in the same volume—by a number of women who had actually experienced the Holocaust and were shocked at attempts to explore issues of gender rather than focusing exclusively on race. Ruth Bondy, a survivor of Theresienstadt and Auschwitz, fundamentally disagreed with Ofer and Weitzman. She allowed her essay to be included in their volume only on strictly empirical grounds, because she felt that the experiences of women in Theresienstadt should not be omitted.

---

[12] Lenore J. Weitzman and Dalia Ofer, 'The Role of Gender in the Holocaust', in Dalia Ofer and Lenore J. Weitzman (eds.), *Women in the Holocaust* (New Haven, CT: Yale University Press, 1998), 1.

[13] Lawrence Langer, 'Gendered Sufferings? Women in Holocaust Testimonies', in Ofer and Weitzman (eds.), *Women in the Holocaust*, 362.

[14] Cited in Hardman, 'Women and the Holocaust', 33.

Helen Fagin, also a Holocaust survivor and scholar, has likewise suggested that the importance of the Holocaust is somehow trivialized by a feminist agenda.[15] Gabriel Schoenfeld, a senior editor of the right-wing journal *Commentary*, has argued along the same lines, suggesting that a focus on gender was not really driven by the desire to achieve a deeper understanding of the events of the Holocaust but was essentially 'ideological'. He explained:

> That feminist scholarship on the Holocaust is intended explicitly to serve the purposes of consciousness raising—i.e. propaganda—is, as it happens, something its practitioners proudly admit, just as they are proud of their use of the Holocaust as a means of validating feminist theory itself. Unfortunately, in order to find these statements of intent, one has to be willing to subject oneself to their prose—the general execrableness of which, let it be said, easily surpasses that of their male colleagues, while adding its own special notes of querulousness and righteous self-regard.[16]

Such an accusation was, of course, premised primarily on an opposition to feminist scholarship and thus to the very study of gender and the Holocaust itself rather than on any meaningful dialogue with the content of the research.

Remarkably it was Ringelheim herself—and not her critics—who took on the challenge of seriously critiquing her own work. She did not deny the importance of gender or resile from a feminist agenda but, questioning her own 'cultural feminism', she challenged her tendency to homogenize women's experiences during the Holocaust: 'these aspects of women's daily lives—vulnerability to rape, humiliation, sexual exchange, not to speak of pregnancy, abortion and fear for one's children—cannot simply be universalized as true for all survivors'.[17] From this Ringelheim was also able to relativize her previous idealized assumptions that women behaved in especially moral or noble ways or had superior coping strategies to men.

Ringelheim's challenge—to write gender back into the Holocaust, but to do so without homogenizing or valorizing women's experiences—has been taken up by a generation of feminist scholars. To be sure, as Atina Grossmann observed a little over a decade ago, it remains the case that

[15] Cited in Joan Ringelheim, 'Thoughts about Women and the Holocaust', in Roger S. Gottlieb (ed.), *Thinking the Unthinkable: Meanings of the Holocaust* (New York: Paulist, 1990), 143.

[16] Gabriel Schoenfeld, 'Auschwitz and the Professors', *Commentary* 105/6 (June 1998), 42–6. Cf. the attack on a feminist approach to the writing of Jewish history by Hillel Halkin in 'Feminizing Jewish Studies', *Commentary*, 105/2 (1998), 39–45.

[17] Joan Ringelheim, 'Women and the Holocaust: A Reconsideration of Research', *Signs: Journal of Women in Culture and Society*, 10/4 (February 1998), 745.

these writers 'still operate on the defensive'.[18] The mainstream of historical research—as my opening anecdote suggests—has not taken on board the insights of women's or gender history, much less acknowledged the importance of insights derived from feminist theory. Recent major works on the subject still assume that the Holocaust was somehow gender-neutral or—worse still—that women's experiences are somehow a sideline, a distraction even from the main event. Tellingly, for example, a major recent study by a distinguished former colleague includes a separate index entry on 'women', but no entry headed 'men'.[19] This assumption, that men's experiences were normative and that women were either an addendum or that their specific experiences can shed no broader light onto the Holocaust, has proved surprisingly long-lasting.

In writing this book I have sought to challenge this status quo. Drawing on the work of a new generation of scholars such as Atina Grossmann, Kirsty Chatwood, Monika Flaschka, Rochelle Saidel, and Helene Sinnreich, I hope to contribute to this deeper understanding of women's experiences both in and after the Holocaust by exploring different layers of gender. Perhaps because we are now approaching a time when there will no longer be any living witnesses to the Holocaust, areas of research that have hitherto been avoided are now opening up. In 2010 Sonja Hedgepeth and Rochelle Saidel published an interdisciplinary anthology by a group of international scholars on subjects such as rape, forced prostitution, and forced sterilization and abortion during the Holocaust.[20] My book, which will attempt to develop

---

[18] Atina Grossmann, 'Women and the Holocaust: Four Recent Titles', *Holocaust and Genocide Studies*, 16 (Spring 2002), 94.

[19] See David Cesarani, *Final Solution: The Fate of the Jews 1933–1949* (London: Macmillan, 2016), and Zoë Waxman, 'Towards an Integrated History of the Holocaust: Masculinity, Femininity, and Genocide', in Christian Wiese and Paul Betts (eds.), *Years of Persecution, Years of Extermination: Saul Friedländer and the Future of Holocaust Studies* (London: Continuum, 2010), 311–21.

[20] Sonja M. Hedgepeth and Rochelle G. Saidel (eds.), *Sexual Violence against Jewish Women during the Holocaust* (Waltham, MA: Brandeis University Press, 2010). Cf. Annabelle Baldwin, 'Sexual Violence and the Holocaust: Reflections on Memory and Witness Testimony', *Holocaust Studies: A Journal of Culture and History*, 16/3 (2010), 112–34; Doris L. Bergen, 'Sexual Violence in the Holocaust: Unique and Typical?', in Dagmar Herzog (ed.), *Lessons and Legacies VII: the Holocaust in International Context* (Evanston, IL: Northwestern University Press, 2006), 217–28; Myrna Goldenberg, 'Rape during the Holocaust', in Zygmunt Mazur, Jay T. Lees, Arnold Krammer, and Władysław Witalisz (eds.), *The Legacy of the Holocaust: Women and the Holocaust* (Kraków: Jagiellonian University Press, 2007), 159–69; Regina Mühlhäuser, *Eroberungen. Sexuelle Gewalttaten und intime Beziehungen deutscher Soldaten in der Sowjetunion, 1941–1945* (Hamburg: Hamburger Edition, 2010); Na'ama Shik, 'Sexual Abuse of Jewish Women in Auschwitz-Birkenau', in Dagmar Herzog (ed.), *Brutality and Desire: War and Sexuality in Europe's Twentieth Century* (Basingstoke: Palgrave Macmillan, 2009), 221–47; and Helene J. Sinnreich, ' "And It Was Something We Didn't Talk About": Rape of Jewish Women during the Holocaust', *Holocaust Studies: A Journal of Culture and History*, 14/2 (2008), 1–22.

some of these discussions, is indebted, to the rich—if still slender—seam of scholarship on women's Holocaust experiences that has preceded it.

Beyond Holocaust history, gender is now an established—indeed, a widely respected—subfield. Most historians accept that understanding gender is essential to understanding human experience. In a field-defining essay, Joan Wallach Scott defines gender as 'a constitutive element of social relationships based on perceived differences between the sexes' and emphasizes that 'gender is a primary way of signifying relationships of power', and operates in ways which are often unspoken.[21] In other words, the differences between men and women are interpreted socially and culturally rather than in biological terms.[22] To cite Simone de Beauvoir: 'One is not born, but rather becomes, a woman.'[23] From there, one's gendered identity becomes the basis on which one's life is lived.[24] True enough, the concept of woman as a universal category of analysis has been widely critiqued on the basis of its ethnocentrism and essential biological determinism.[25] But, although I would concur that gender operates and is understood by its agents differently in different times and places, I follow Scott and most mainstream scholars in maintaining its importance in understanding lived experience.

This book, though, is not only written on the premise that gender is culturally constructed and conditioned. It is also, quite explicitly, a feminist history. In other words, it is predicated on the assumption that feminists are right to see gender not only as universal but as a system of oppression—a system that operates to subordinate women. I follow Naomi Seidman in arguing that the historical position of women—in

[21] Joan Wallach Scott, *Gender and the Politics of History* (New York: Columbia University Press, 1988), 42. Cf. Ann Taylor Allen, 'The Holocaust and the Modernization of Gender: A Historiographical Essay', *Central European History*, 30/3 (1997), 350.

[22] The debate over sexual versus social/cultural differences is ongoing. See, for example, Monique Wittig, 'One is Not Born a Woman', in *The Straight Mind* (Hemel Hempstead: Harvester Wheatsheaf, 1992), 9–20; Julia Kristeva, 'Women's Times', *Signs: Journal of Women in Culture and Society*, 7/1 (1981), 13–35; Luce Irigary, *This Sex Which is Not One* (Ithaca, NY: Cornell University Press, 1985); Hélène Cixous and Catherine Clément, 'Sorties', in *The Newly Born Woman* (Minneapolis, MN: University of Minnesota Press, 1986); Judith Butler, *Gender Trouble: Feminism and the Subversion of Identity* (New York: Routledge, 1990); and Denise Riley, *Am I That Name? Feminism and the Category of 'Women' in History* (Minneapolis, MN: University of Minnesota Press, 1988).

[23] Simone de Beauvoir, *The Second Sex* (New York: Vintage, 1973), 301.

[24] See Gerda Lerner, *The Creation of Patriarchy* (Oxford: Oxford University Press, 1986).

[25] See Michele Barrett and Anne Phillips, *Destabilizing Theory: Contemporary Feminist Debates* (Cambridge: Polity Press, 1992).

this case Jewish women—is dependent on a patriarchal system of hierarchies and misogynies.[26]

Gender, as Adam Jones has argued, becomes especially important in
times of war and upheaval.[27] Rather than being relegated to the realm of
social history, under Nazism gender needs to be understood as 'a central
political category'.[28] For a feminist historian, therefore, the experience of
women in the Holocaust is especially important and particularly revealing.
Women's lives in the Holocaust were different—and they were different
because they were women. Such an insight has two consequences. In the
first place, it means that we have to reassess what we mean by the
Holocaust, acknowledging that it was not a totalizing event, but was
rather a series of different—and differently experienced—events. In the
second place, it means that we should understand the Holocaust as one—
uniquely terrible, but nonetheless comprehensible—example of gendered
hierarchies at work. Indeed, a feminist history exposes the Holocaust as an
especially revealing example of gender in action.

The aim of this book, therefore, is threefold. In the first place, it builds
on existing work which draws attention to distinctive experiences of men
and women. In the second place, it is an attempt to explore the 'female
voice' as an antidote to what remains an overwhelmingly male narrative;
an approach which throws light on experiences which might hitherto have
gone ignored such as sexual abuse, pregnancy, amenorrhea and sterility,
and childbirth. While men also experienced sexual violence, for example,
much of the sexualized abuse was specifically directed at women because
of their biological role of bearer of future generations. Above all, however,
I believe—thirdly—that writing a specifically feminist history of the
Holocaust means using the testimony of the women themselves to give
voice to their own experiences and disempowerment before, during, and
after the Holocaust.

It is undeniable, of course, that race rather than gender was of primary
importance to both the Nazi world view and its politics. Nonetheless,
this does not mean that gender can be—or was—disregarded. Developing
a feminist approach to women's lives during the Holocaust involves
re-examining and reconceptualizing pregnancy, abortion, menstruation,
consensual sex, coerced sex, sexual molestation, and familial relationships.
What I seek to demonstrate is that by reducing women to their biological

[26] See Naomi Seidman, 'Theorizing Jewish Patriarchy in Extremis', in Miriam Peskowitz and Laura Levitt (eds.), *Judaism since Gender* (New York: Routledge, 1997), 40–9.

[27] Adam Jones, *Gendercide and Genocide* (Nashville, TN: Vanderbilt University Press,
2004).

[28] Sara R. Horowitz, 'Gender, Genocide and Jewish Memory', *Prooftexts*, 20/1&2
(Winter/Spring 2000), 181.

functions—rape, pregnancy, childbirth, motherhood, and so on—the Nazis were specifically targeting Jewish women as a distinct biological and racial group.[29] National Socialism, whilst premised on a monolithic hatred of the Jews, nevertheless saw Jewish women as being separate from Jewish men and persecuted them accordingly. Raul Hilberg sums it up when he states, 'the Final Solution was intended by its creators to ensure the annihilation of all Jews ... yet the road to annihilation was marked by events which specifically affected men as men and women as women'.[30]

The institutionalized and genocidal patriarchy of the Nazis regulated the lives of both non-Aryan and German women. The oft-stated words 'The Nazi Revolution will be an entirely male event'[31] referred to a dominant male Aryan race. Aryan women were encouraged to aspire to be the 'mothers of the Race' and therefore abortions, sterilizations, and contraceptives were banned.[32] Whilst Elizabeth Heineman correctly points out that single German women of appropriate racial and genetic origin did have a larger role to play as long as they contributed to the *Volksgemeinschaft*, married women were told that their place was in the home and were guided by the traditional principles of *Küche, Kinder und Kirche* (kitchen, children, and church).[33] In 1933, Professor Wagner, director of the women's clinic of Berlin's Charité Hospital, declared women's ovaries to be 'a national resource and property of the German state' and called for 'mandatory care for these vital organs, vital not only for the individual but for the health and future of the entire Volk'.[34] Marriage loans introduced in June 1933 allowed a newly married couple to apply for an interest-free loan of up to RM 1,000. Twenty-five per cent of the loan would be written off after the birth of each child. Not only did

---

[29] Although the Nazis overwhelmingly—and specifically—targeted the Jews for persecution and murder, a different history could be written about each one of the other groups singled out for persecution under the Nazi regime, such as the Sinti (German Gypsies), the Roma (Gypsies of eastern Europe), and the Jehovah's Witnesses.

[30] Raul Hilberg, *Perpetrators, Victims, Bystanders: The Jewish Catastrophe, 1933–1945* (London: HarperCollins, 1993), 126.

[31] Adolph Hitler, 9 September 1934. Cited in Benjamin C. Sax and Dieter Kunz (eds.), *Inside Hitler's Germany: A Documentary History of Life in the Third Reich* (Lexington, KY: D.C. Heath, 1992).

[32] The *Verordnung zum Schutz von Ehe, Familie und Mutterschaft* (Decree for the Protection of Marriage, Family, and Motherhood) meant that a German woman could be put to death for having an abortion.

[33] See Elizabeth D. Heineman, *What Difference Does a Husband Make? Women and Marital Status in Nazi and Postwar Germany* (Berkeley, CA: University of California Press, 1999).

[34] Cited in Tessa Chelouche, 'Doctors, Pregnancy, Childbirth and Abortion during the Third Reich', in *Israel Medical Association Journal*, 9 (2007), 203.

the prospective couple have to undergo a physical examination but they also had to supply a detailed family history to rule out any genetic flaws and demonstrate the desirability of their union. Increased taxes paid by single people financed the scheme.[35]

In 1935 the Nuremberg racial laws prohibited marriage between Aryans and non-Aryans. The *Lebensborn* (Spring of Life) programme introduced by Heinrich Himmler on 12 December 1935 promoted the principles of racial hygiene by encouraging accelerated birth rates by those deemed racially and hereditarily superior. The aim was to produce physically superior blonde-haired and blue-eyed children. In 1939 the programme was extended to include the removal of suitable children from German-occupied Europe and their relocation to German families. Some of these children were literally snatched from playgrounds and schools whilst other families were persuaded that their children were being temporarily relocated to safer places. At the same time the *Gesetz zur Verhütung erbkranken Nachwuchses* (Law for the Prevention of Genetically Diseased Offspring), passed in July 1933, dictated that German citizens deemed to be suffering from so-called disorders such as schizophrenia, manic depression, congenital feeble-mindedness, and chronic alcoholism were restricted from marrying, forcibly sterilized, or given abortions. Unmarried mothers and unskilled workers were also vulnerable.[36] Women who were judged to be sexually deviant in some way—for example, if they had engaged in prostitution or had lesbian relationships or were found to have sexually transmitted diseases—were labelled 'feeble-minded' and sterilized. While both men and women were subject to sterilization—through radium and X rays for women and vasectomy for men—women who were already pregnant were in particular danger. What is more, the female procedures were more complicated and 90 per cent of fatalities resulting from sterilizations were female.[37] Inevitably, those men and women who had been labelled non-Aryan, genetically inferior, or asocial were placed at great risk of institutionalization and even death as Germany entered total warfare.[38] Many non-Jewish Germans incarcerated in workhouses and mental institutions were later deported to the concentration camps. Indeed, approximately two-thirds of the 110,000 non-Jewish Germans sent to concentration camps by 1943 bore the label 'asocial'.[39]

[35] Heineman, *What Difference Does a Husband Make*, 22?

[36] For a discussion of Nazi distinctions between married and single women, see Heineman, *What Difference Does a Husband Make?*, 17–44.

[37] Atina Grossmann, 'Feminist Debates about Women and National Socialism', *Gender and History*, 3/3 (1991), 352.

[38] Heineman, *What Difference Does a Husband Make?*, 18–26.

[39] Ibid., 31.

Two of the first major studies of women's experiences under National Socialism focused on the contradictions of modernity and tradition at the heart of the Nazi view of women.[40] For both Aryan and non-Aryan women, the totalitarianism and violent misogyny of National Socialism meant that the state was to have total monopoly over their reproductive rights. Women were no longer in control of their own bodies. Whilst suitable Aryan women were encouraged to give birth to as many racially pure children as possible, 'racially inferior' women—*gemeinschaftsfremd* (alien to the communal body)—such as the Roma and Sinti, eastern European women working as forced labourers in Germany, Jehovah's Witnesses, and Jews, were stopped from bearing children. Their potential children were deemed as dangerous and impure and the women were subjected to forced abortions—which, often crudely carried out, gave rise to infections and permanent damage—and sterilizations.

Jewish women were in a particularly vulnerable position. From the very start it would seem that German women understood this and separated themselves accordingly. Allison Owings' study of twenty-nine German women who lived through Nazism shows that German women were terrified of being seen to associate with Jews. She interviewed a woman named Frau Liselotte Otting who would not even let a Jewish woman water her plants while she was away at a spa for fear of being seen to fraternize with the enemy.[41] Claudia Koonz's book *Mothers in the Fatherland: Women, the Family and Nazi Politics* looked more explicitly at the question of the collective guilt of German women, showing that the experience narrated by Frau Otting was an almost universal one.[42]

Without doubt, Jewish women were isolated from civil society. For women of childbearing age the situation was especially dangerous. Jewish children were regarded as enemies of the Reich which meant that being pregnant was a criminal offence. Simply put, for Jewish women becoming a mother became a violation of Nazi law. Realizing this, throughout Nazi Germany desperate Jewish women sought out illegal abortions. Then, in 1938, abortion was made legal for Jewish women.[43] No more Jewish

---

[40] See Jill Stephenson, *Women in Nazi Society* (New York: Routledge, 1975), and Leila J. Rupp, *Mobilizing Women for War: German and American Propaganda, 1939–1945* (Princeton, NJ: Princeton University Press, 1978). Cited in Allen, 'The Holocaust and the Modernization of Gender', 355.

[41] Alison Owings, *Frauen: German Women Recall the Third Reich* (London: Penguin, 1993), 76.

[42] See Claudia Koonz, *Mothers in the Fatherland: Women, the Family and Nazi Politics* (London: Jonathan Cape, 1987). Cf. Gisela Bock's critique of Koonz in the *Bulletin of the German Historical Institute London*, 11/1 (1989), 16–24.

[43] Robert N. Proctor, *Racial Hygiene: Medicine under the Nazis* (Cambridge, MA: Harvard University Press, 2002), 123.

babies were to be born and before long all living Jewish children were to be murdered. Approximately a million to a million and a half Jewish children under the age of sixteen lost their lives during the Holocaust.[44]

The Nazis identified Jewish men and Jewish women by their sex, renaming them either Israel or Sara. They then proceeded to treat men and women differently at each stage of their persecution, resulting in gender-specific experiences. However, it is important to point out that gender was not a category invented by the Nazis. Gender also played a central role in pre-war Jewish family life. Scholars such as Paula Hyman have contributed greatly to our knowledge and understanding of the lives of Jewish women in the late nineteenth and early twentieth century. For example, in both eastern and western Europe, family life prior to the outbreak of World War II revolved around specific gender roles. Whilst the major social developments of the nineteenth century—emancipation, industrialization, mass migration, urbanization, assimilation—certainly impacted on traditional Jewish family life, women's roles as guardians of the family remained relatively unchanged.[45] As feminist scholars argue, it is not until marriage and the family undergo serious transformations that traditional gendered roles can really be altered. Until the twentieth century Jewish women were excluded from active participation in Jewish community life when it came to both civil and religious matters. Their contributions were concentrated in the domestic, educational, and benevolent spheres through Jewish women's organizations which looked after the ill and impoverished members of the community.

The rapid social mobility of the late nineteenth and early twentieth century thus transformed western European Jewish life, without seriously challenging long-standing gendered roles and norms. Many Jewish women no longer needed to help out economically, but they nevertheless mostly followed the bourgeois model, focusing on the domestic sphere and particularly the rearing of children. Whilst many middle-class Jewish families employed cooks, maids, and nannies, it was Jewish women—as housewives—who managed them. This allowed men to participate in economic and professional life.[46] However, this was not necessarily the

---

[44] For a ground-breaking study of children's experiences under Nazism, see Nicholas Stargardt, *Witnesses of War: Children's Lives under the Nazis* (London: Jonathan Cape, 2005).

[45] Paula E. Hyman, 'The Modern Jewish Family: Image and Reality', in David Kraemer (ed.), *The Jewish Family: Metaphor and Memory* (Oxford: Oxford University Press, 1989), 180.

[46] Paula E. Hyman, *Gender and Assimilation in Modern Jewish History: The Roles and Representation of Women* (Seattle, WA: University of Washington Press, 1995). Cf. Joan B. Landes, 'The Public and the Private Sphere: A Feminist Reconsideration', in Johanna Meehan (ed.), *Feminists Read Habermas: Gendering the Subject of Discourse* (New York: Routledge, 1993), 91–116.

case in the less prosperous eastern Europe—in countries such as Poland, Russia, Ukraine, Belarus, Lithuania, and Latvia—where Jewish women were more likely to need to find work outside the home in order to support their families. Here women continued to labour in the traditional Jewish trades of peddling and small shop-keeping. In religious families too, women took on financial responsibilities to allow their men to pursue full-time Torah studies and communal responsibilities.[47] Crucially, this bestowed on women a certain authority—even if they could never aspire to become scholars (by far the more important role), they were responsible for the economic wellbeing of their families. It also gave them a greater understanding of the world outside the home. Moreover, whilst their sons were sent to traditionalist Jewish schools, their daughters were often educated at secular public institutions. During the German occupation of Europe this was to take on critical significance.

Nevertheless, uniting European Jewish family life, whether middle- or working class, urban or *shtetl*, secular or religious, was the fact that women's primary roles were as wives and mothers.[48] Where women gained more status through activities outside the home, they paid the price with their own labour.[49] Importantly, it was women who were chiefly responsible for the transmission of traditional Jewish cultural, social, and religious values—through education, the rituals of Jewish life, and the observance and celebration of Jewish festivals—and therefore were blamed for any failings. Furthermore, in times of dramatic social, economic, and political upheaval, it was women who needed to oversee and protect the fundamental relationships between parent and child and husband and wife. When economic hardship and rising anti-Semitism threatened the future of European Jewish existence, women's devotion to their families and their communities was crucial. Nevertheless, the fact remained that whilst the importance of women's contribution to the domestic sphere was widely acknowledged, women were still regarded as inferior to men.

It was through this well-established structure of meanings, roles, and experiences that the gendered nature of Jewish life was lived. It was also to lay the foundations for the different ways in which the Holocaust was to

---

[47] Paula E. Hyman, 'Gender and the Jewish Family in Modern Europe', in Ofer and Weitzman (eds.), *Women in the Holocaust*, 25–34. Cf. Antony Polonsky, *The Jews in Poland and Russia*. vol. 3: *1914–2008* (London: The Littman Library of Jewish Civilization, 2012).

[48] Margarete Myers Feinstein, 'Absent Fathers, Present Mothers: Images of Parenthood in Holocaust Survivor Narratives', *Nashim: A Journal of Jewish Women's Studies and Gender Issues*, 13 (2007), 161.

[49] See Susan A. Glenn, *Daughters of the Shtetl: Life and Labor in the Immigrant Generation* (Ithaca, NY: Cornell University Press, 1995), 11–12.

be experienced.[50] In order to understand how the Jews responded to the destruction they were forced to endure and to appreciate the heterogeneity of the victims of the Holocaust, we need to comprehend the various factors which influenced that response. This is not of course limited to gender. Social, cultural, economic, and political differences all had an impact on the experiences of Jews during the Holocaust, as did age and familial circumstances. The Jewish victims cannot be treated as a homogenous entity. Some were religious, some secular, some Zionist, Communist, or politically uninterested. While some Jews were poor and lived in small villages, others were more prosperous and lived in major cities. Nonetheless, as we shall see, overlying and underpinning these distinctions, gender was inescapable—and became ever more important as the catastrophe went on.

All Jews, regardless of who they were, were intended to die. As the following chapters will show, both men and women were forced to endure the acute deprivations and degradation of the ghettos, the uncertainties and fear of life in hiding, and the appalling suffering of the concentration and death camps. They were also powerless to stop the anguish of their loved ones—their children, their husbands, their wives, their parents—and ultimately were forced to accept their almost inevitable deaths whether in the disease-ridden ghettos of eastern Europe, the killing fields of Belarus, Ukraine, Latvia, Estonia, Lithuania, and Yugoslavia, or the gas chambers of places such as Auschwitz-Birkenau, Chełmno, Bełżec, Sobibór, Treblinka, and Majdanek. Approximately 6 million Jews—two-thirds of European Jewry and one-third of the world's Jewish population at the time—were murdered.[51]

In Germany the first mass arrest of Jews following *Kristallnacht* (the Night of Broken Glass) on 9–10 November 1938 was exclusively focused on men. As Jewish men were presumed to constitute the greatest threat they were initially more likely to be arrested and imprisoned. Jewish men, especially the Haredi—or the so-called ultra-Orthodox—with their beards, side locks, and traditional clothing, were especially easily identifiable. Around 30,000 Jewish men were arrested throughout Germany and deported to concentration camps at Dachau, Sachsenhausen, and Buchenwald, leaving their women and children to face the worsening situation in Germany alone.[52] In the ghettos of eastern Europe the Nazis also clearly distinguished between men and women. Haredi men suffered

---

[50] Waxman, 'Towards an Integrated History of the Holocaust: Masculinity, Femininity, and Genocide', 313.

[51] Michael Marrus, *The Holocaust in History* (Harmondsworth: Penguin, 1993), 195.

[52] There were also pogroms in Austria and Bohemia.

some of the first attempts at public humiliation during the so-called 'beard actions', where their facial hair was publicly—and painfully—shaved off. They were then murdered as part of the systematic targeting of community leaders. Raul Hilberg used ghetto statistics and *Einsatzgruppen* (SS death squads) records to show that in the early years of the war more men were killed than women. In the Łódź ghetto, for example, with the exception of Chaim Rumkowski,[53] all the original members of the *Judenrat* (Jewish Council) were killed in this way. This resulted in what Hilberg has called a 'newly isolated community' consisting of 'men without power and women without support'.[54] However, the German invasion of the Soviet Union in 1941 soon meant that not just men, but women and children also, were targeted and murdered.

The first chapter of this book, on women in the ghettos, explores how gendered relationships, interfamilial dynamics, and religious communities were challenged by the Holocaust. The family unit was being violently dismantled. For example, women were not allowed to give birth and nor were they allowed to raise any existing children to adulthood. This was in direct opposition to Jewish law which permits abortion only when there is a direct threat to the life of the mother either by carrying the foetus to term or through the act of childbirth. Jewish men were unable to protect their wives or children. Despite—or because—of this, both men and women clung on to pre-war roles and behaviours. Not only did men and women struggle against all odds to perform their gendered roles—with women desperately trying to feed their families in the face of dwindling provisions—but the writings of the ghetto diarists clearly illustrate that gender continued to inform their understanding of what was happening to them, whether the diarist was male or female. The behaviour of women, for example, was scrutinized in ways which reinforced the inferiority of their position in relation to men. The fear and deprivations of the ghettos led to the breakdown of marriages, and an increase in illegitimate births, pre-marital sex, and even infanticide. It was women who were often blamed. At the same time, women increasingly took over the task of queuing for foodstuffs or engaging with the ghetto authorities, as it was widely assumed that it was only men who faced real danger. Women, though, were constantly reminded that the situation was temporary and born out

---

[53] Chaim Rumkowski was appointed head of the Łódź *Judenrat* by the Nazis in 1939. He was beaten to death by Jewish inmates of Auschwitz in 1944 in revenge for his complicity with Nazism.
[54] Hilberg, *Perpetrators, Victims, Bystanders*, 127.

of extraordinary circumstances.[55] In the event that they survived the war traditional gendered mores would return. Moreover, of course, this transformation of domestic-patriarchal power could never be liberating, as women remained responsible for the domestic sphere too. This, together with the fact that inevitably they were hardly more able than their menfolk to protect their children, their parents—and indeed their husbands—in any meaningful ways, reinforced the vulnerability and suffering of Jewish women under Nazism.

Chapter 2 looks at the women who survived at the periphery of the Nazi genocide—by hiding in the countryside, towns, and cities of German-occupied countries such as Poland, Lithuania, Latvia, and Ukraine. Forced to leave their homes, families had to decide whether to try to stay together or to go into hiding separately and hope against all odds to be reunited after the war. Research on the experiences of women in hiding is still in its infancy. That which exists on Jews in hiding typically focuses on the partisan groups who hid in the forests rather than on individual experiences of hiding. What Gunnar S. Paulsson terms 'evasion' as a means of survival has for the most part been neglected. Paulsson suggests that this neglect can be partly explained by the 'stigma attached to flight' as well as to the consequent 'survivors' guilt' for abandoning relatives.[56] As Lenore Weitzman—whose research is largely responsible for bringing this important topic to light—has shown, this neglected area of Holocaust research is particularly significant for women, especially in Poland, where the majority of Jews who survived by passing themselves as 'Aryan' were women. Whilst in hiding for their lives most women also had to bear the agony of being separated from their children. In this chapter I will explore the issue of separation from children and the impact it had on both parents and children alike. It will also explore some of the other issues faced by women in hiding, such as the risk of rape and sexual abuse. In recent years important research has been carried out into the sexual violence committed by the *Wehrmacht* in the East, but far less exists on the sexual exploitation of women at the hands of individual 'rescuers'.[57]

---

[55] On the reversal of men's and women's roles during the Holocaust, see Sara R. Horowitz, 'Memory and Testimony of Women Survivors of Nazi Genocide', in Judith R. Baskin (ed.), *Women of the Word: Jewish Women and Jewish Writing* (Detroit, MI: Wayne State University Press, 1994), 258–82, and Horowitz, 'Gender, Genocide and Jewish Memory'.

[56] See Gunnar S. Paulsson, *Secret City: The Hidden Jews of Warsaw, 1940–1945* (New Haven, CT: Yale University Press, 2002), 10. Cf. Michal Borwicz's classic study, *Arishe papirn* [Aryan Papers], 3 vols. (Buenos Aires: Tsentral-Farband fun Poylishe Yidn, 1955).

[57] See for example: Birgit Beck, *Wehrmacht und sexuelle Gewalt. Sexualverbrechen vor deutschen Militärgerichten 1939–1945* (Paderborn: Schöningh, 2004); David Raub Snyder,

Tracing the history of those deported to the death camps, much less determining the continued experience of gender on their lives—and deaths—is made difficult by a paucity of evidence. Testimony from Treblinka as well as from the other death camps at Chełmno, Bełżec, and Sobibór is extremely rare, as very few prisoners survived, and most of the documentation was destroyed by the Nazis. It is not, however, impossible to uncover what happened. Careful sifting of the evidence, and the testimony of those in other camps—not least the enormous Auschwitz-Birkenau complex, which combined aspects of a concentration and death camp—enables us to see that even in the extremity of the extermination process, gender was still present, still real, and still formative of men's, women's, and children's lives.

Chapter 3 looks at the distinctive experiences of women in the concentration camps. Not only were men separated from women, but women accompanied by children under the age of 14 were sent straight to their deaths.[58] Being visibly pregnant also meant an immediate death sentence.[59] In the camps, women's experiences—their treatment by concentration camp guards, their relationships with other prisoners, and even their very chances of survival—were different to those of men. Before the war conditions for men were much worse than they were for female concentration camp inmates. They experienced both far higher levels of brutality and were subjected to particularly gruelling physical labour, from the useless 'digging for the sake of digging' to contributing to the German war effort. However, by early 1939 the first camp specifically for women was in operation at Ravensbrück, and by the spring of 1942 a women's camp was opened in Auschwitz to relieve the overcrowding there. Jewish women were then forced into forms of labour just as appalling to that of their menfolk and were subjected to similar levels of brutality. What is interesting is that women's testimonies document how many women went to great lengths to hold on to something of their past lives. For some this meant forming loving and nurturing relationships, for others finding ways to continue to practise

Sex Crimes under the Wehrmacht (Lincoln, NE: University of Nebraska Press, 2007); and Mühlhäuser, *Eroberungen.*

[58] Danuta Czech's data on Auschwitz suggests that more women than men were immediately sent to the gas chambers on arrival at Auschwitz-Birkenau. See Danuta Czech, *Auschwitz Chronicle, 1939–1945: From the Archives of the Auschwitz Memorial and the German Federal Archives,* trans. Barbara Harshav, Martha Humphreys, and Stephen Shearier (New York: Henry Holt, 1990).

[59] Ellen Fine writes: 'Being a mother directly affected the chances for survival; being a father did not'; see Ellen Fine, 'Women Writers and the Holocaust: Strategies for Survival', in Randolph L. Braham (ed.), *Reflections of the Holocaust in Art and Literature* (New York: City University of New York Press, 1990), 82.

their religion. Whilst some women did change dramatically, it appears that gendered behaviours and pre-war morality still mattered.

The final chapter explores Jewish life in the Displaced Persons (DP) camps. It has not been until relatively recently that scholarly research has looked at the experiences of the DPs as part—rather than as the aftermath—of the Holocaust. The chapter draws on the pioneering work of scholars such as Atina Grossmann and Judith Tydor Baumel to look specifically at women's responses to liberation and the years that followed. Grossmann, in particular, has been instrumental in looking at the experiences of the Jewish survivors in relation to sexuality and reproduction. She explains that 'the experience of liberation (and the prospect of future heterosexual relations) may have been profoundly different for women and men precisely because so many women found themselves having to fear or, indeed, undergo, renewed attack, this time from those they had welcomed as liberators'.[60] Whilst the Nazis had plunged everything into the wholescale murder of every Jewish man, woman, and child, they did not in the end succeed. Between 1945 and 1948 tens of thousands of Jews emerged from the concentration and labour camps, and from hiding. Whilst many were desperate to go home, a large number were forced to gather in the DP camps of Austria, Germany, and Italy, waiting for life to begin again. For many women this was a particularly vulnerable time and they quickly sought protection from Jewish men.

In fact both men and women needed each other. After such a sustained period of enforced passivity and suffering, the Jewish DPs were desperate to begin rebuilding their shattered lives. At the same time the extremity and magnitude of the Holocaust cast considerable obstacles in their way. Whilst they had survived, millions of others—their families included—had not. Hence, there was little joy to be found in survival. Stranded in the primitive and often punitive half-world of the DP camps—somewhere between the lives they had left behind and the uncertainties of the future—many survivors were desperate to start families. The extraordinary number of weddings and the sudden baby boom in the DP camps is testament to this. Many of the DPs wanted to have as many children as they possibly could, as quickly as they possibly could. Not only would this rebuild the Jewish population that the Nazis had sought to extinguish, but it returned them to the life they had expected to live before they had been so violently expelled from it. For many, this meant reclaiming their domestic and

[60] Atina Grossmann, 'Victims, Villains, and Survivors: Gendered Perceptions and Self-Perceptions of Jewish Displaced Persons in Occupied Postwar Germany', *The Journal of the History of Sexuality*, 11/1–2, Special Issue: Sexuality and German Fascisms (January/April 2002), 307.

reproductive roles. Both women and men saw motherhood and fatherhood as defining features of their re-entry into the world. Men were eager to take up once more their roles as providers and protectors of their wives and children, while mothers were desperate once more to provide love and nurture. Whilst the Nazis had sought to destroy the Jews of Europe and all they stood for, the survivors of the Nazi genocide clung to the values and gendered roles that the Nazis had tried to obliterate. Not only did gender matter before the war, it continued to matter during the war, and went on to structure the lives of its survivors and their descendants after the war.

1

Women in the Ghettos

The historian of the future will have to devote a fitting chapter to the
role of the Jewish woman during the war. It is thanks to the courage
and endurance of our women that thousands of families have been
able to endure these bitter times.

Ringelblum, *Notes from the Warsaw Ghetto*[1]

Hundreds of ghettos were created throughout German-occupied eastern
Europe, beginning in December 1939 with a ghetto in Radomsko and
culminating with the liquidation of the Łódź ghetto in 1944. Some
ghettos—such as Łódź—were completely closed, and others—including
Radom, Kielce, and Warsaw—partially open. Certain ghettos were in
existence for just a few days, others much longer. At its height, more
than 400,000 people were imprisoned in the Warsaw ghetto, while some
of the smaller ghettos held just a few thousand Jews. The ghettos were not
confined to Poland. Following Hitler's attack on the Soviet Union in June
1941 a policy of ghettoization was pursued in the Soviet Union and the
Baltic territories.[2] Not only this but each ghetto was very different, not just
in terms of its geography and design but also in terms of Nazi policies and
its own internal leadership. What they had in common, however, was their

---

[1] Emanuel Ringelblum, *Notes from the Warsaw Ghetto: The Journal of Emanuel Ringelblum*, ed. and trans. Jacob Sloan (New York: Schocken, 1974), 294.

[2] The Center for Advanced Holocaust Studies (CAHS) at the United States Holocaust
Memorial Museum has compiled a comprehensive encyclopaedia of more than 1,150
ghettos throughout the towns and villages of Poland and the Soviet Union. See Martin
Dean and Geoffrey P. Megargee (eds.), *Ghettos in German-Occupied Eastern Europe* (vol. 2
of Center for Advanced Holocaust Studies, *The United States Holocaust Memorial Museum
Encyclopedia of Camps and Ghettos, 1933–1945*) (Bloomington, IN: Indiana University
Press, 2012). On the difficult task of deciding what can be defined as a ghetto, Martin
Dean states: 'three critical elements form necessary prerequisites: the resettlement of Jews
into a clearly defined residential area, their physical separation from the surrounding
population, and some threatened punishment for leaving their confined space'. See Martin
Dean, 'Life and Death in the "Gray Zone" of Jewish Ghettos in Nazi-Occupied Europe:
The Unknown, the Ambiguous, and the Disappeared', in Jonathan Petropoulos and John
K. Roth (eds.), *Gray Zones: Ambiguity and Compromise in the Holocaust and its Aftermath*
(New York: Berghahn, 2005), 209.

enforced segregation from the outside population and their subordination
to the German authorities. The ghettos have long been regarded as just a
stepping stone on the way to the death camps; yet they also constitute a
significant chapter of Jewish history. As they could not know their fate,
at least at the beginning, many Jews—particularly the Orthodox and
the Haredi—thought that the ghettos might give them a future; they
offered, to a degree, self-administration and protection for their Jewish
inhabitants.[3]

Piecing together their story is difficult. Many ghettos left behind almost
nothing. Recovering the quotidian reality of life within even the largest
and longest-lasting ghetto is very hard. Nevertheless, despite the confusion, fear, and lack of precise information available, hundreds of Jewish
men, women, and children kept diaries in the ghettos. In many of the
ghettos large-scale clandestine documentary projects were in operation to
record the suffering and destruction of the Jews.[4] In Łódź—the second
largest but most isolated of the ghettos—the Department of the Archives
of the Jewish Council compiled the *Łódź Ghetto Chronicle* to document
the life of the Jews of Łódź between January 1941 and January 1944.[5]
Further archives were set up in Białystok in north-east Poland, in the
Lithuanian capital Vilna,[6] in Kraków, in southern Poland, in Lvov in
eastern Galicia,[7] in Kovno in central Lithuania,[8] and in Theresienstadt in
north-east Czechoslovakia.

One particularly revealing—but not unproblematic—source comes
from the Warsaw ghetto, where the left-wing, secular, social historian

---

[3] Ibid., 204.

[4] For a discussion of the lack of accurate information, see Daniusz Stola, 'Early News of
the Holocaust from Poland', *Holocaust and Genocide Studies*, 11/1 (Spring 1997), 1–27.

[5] See Lucjan Dobroszycki (ed.), *The Chronicle of the Lodz Ghetto, 1941–1944*, trans.
Richard Lourie, Joachim Neugroschel, et al. (New Haven, CT: Yale University Press,
1984). Photographs taken by Mendel Grossman have also survived as part of the archive;
see Mendel Grossman, *With a Camera in the Ghetto*, ed. Zvi Szner and Alexander Sened
(New York: Schocken, 1977).

[6] On Vilna, see Herman Kruk, *The Last Days of the Jerusalem of Lithuania*, trans. Barbara
Harshav (New Haven, CT: Yale University Press, 2002), and David Fishman, *Embers
Plucked from the Fire: The Rescue of Jewish Cultural Treasures in Vilna* (New York: YIVO
Institute for Jewish Research, 2009). Vilna (German spelling Wilna) is now known as
Vilnius.

[7] Lvov is known as Lwów in Polish, and Lviv in transliterated Ukrainian. The old
German name Lemberg is sometimes used too.

[8] In Kovno the *Judenrat* commissioned artists to make a visual record of Jewish life. An
engineer by the name of Hirsh Kadushin became the photographic chronicler of the ghetto.
Using a small camera concealed in his clothing, he managed to film many aspects of ghetto
life. He obtained the film from a nurse who worked with him in the ghetto hospital.
Kadushin's photographs were discovered after the war, and can now be found in the United
States Holocaust Memorial Museum. Kovno is now known as Kaunas.

and teacher Emanuel Ringelblum initiated the Warsaw-based *Oneg Shabbat* ('Sabbath delight'—a code-name for the clandestine Sabbath afternoon gatherings) archives within a month of the German invasion of Poland in September 1939.[9] Conditions in the Warsaw ghetto were amongst the worst in Poland—and this was the largest of the ghettos. The sheer volume of people, particularly the large number of refugees, squeezed into the ghetto meant that hunger and disease were particularly rife. At the same time, however—in comparison with other ghettos—Jews in the Warsaw ghetto had a greater degree of autonomy. The Warsaw *Judenrat* (Jewish Council) did not insist on the control of relief activities—and for the most part—did not attempt to curtail cultural activities.

While this means that historians studying the Warsaw ghetto have a rich variety of sources, for a feminist historian there is a problem. Most of the staff of the archival projects were men, and unsurprisingly, there is tendency to represent women rather uncritically according to traditional gendered expectations;[10] in particular, to highlight women's domestic roles and nurturing qualities even under the extreme conditions they were experiencing. This focus on the domestic and the familial may have reflected many women's realities, but it was not necessarily representative of all women. Prior to the outbreak of the war women were gaining a strong presence in Jewish communal activism, and this was expected to continue despite wartime conditions. Indeed, it did, with women acting as air-raid wardens and fire-fighters and organizing relief work.

An integral part of this relief work was the running of the ghetto's soup kitchens—and it is through this that we gain access to one especially useful account written by a woman. Ringelblum asked Rachel Auerbach (in Yiddish, Rokhl Oyerbakh), a writer and editor of several literary magazines, to manage the soup kitchen at 40 Leszno Street, which she did until 1942, despite the urging of her family to join them in Soviet-occupied Lvov.[11] The soup kitchens were a vital part of the Jewish response to the

[9] The original documents of *Oneg Shabbat* are housed at the ŻIH (Jewish Historical Institute) in Warsaw. There are copies of most of the documents in the Yad Vashem Archives (YVA) in Jerusalem and the United States Holocaust Memorial Museum in Washington. On the history of *Oneg Shabbat* see Samuel Kassow, *Who Will Write Our History? Emanuel Ringelblum, the Warsaw Ghetto, and the Oyneg Shabes Archive* (Bloomington, IN: Indiana University Press, 2007). Cf. Zoë Waxman, *Writing the Holocaust: Identity, Testimony, Representation* (Oxford: Oxford University Press, 2006), Chapter 1.

[10] In the case of Warsaw there were several women who worked for the archive: Rachel Auerbach, Cecilya Ślepak, Henryka Lazowert, Gustawa Jarecka, and Bluma Wasser.

[11] On Rachel Auerbach, see Joseph Kermish, 'Daily Entries of Hersh Wasser', in *Yad Vashem Studies*, 15 (1983), 201–82. For her account of life in the Warsaw ghetto, see Rachel Auerbach, *Varshever tsavoes: Bagegenishn, aktivitetn, goyroles* [Warsaw Testaments: Meetings, Activities, Fates], *1933–1943* (Tel Aviv: Israel Book, 1974).

catastrophe that was unfolding. In addition to providing food, they also served as meeting points for clandestine schools, and the various youth movements which operated in the ghetto. The women who ran the soup kitchens were both envied and reviled. In particular, those distributing the subsidized meals were often accused of favouring family and friends. This was not entirely unfair. Ringelblum, for example, sent colleagues and people he wanted to support to the soup kitchen where Auerbach worked, with instructions to give her a password which would allow them soup without having to present a ticket.[12] Nevertheless, working in the soup kitchen allowed Auerbach to interact with a wide range of different people, including the ghetto's poorest inhabitants, and she carefully documented her observations for the *Oneg Shabbat* archives.[13] Like Ringelblum she was committed to the recording of Jewish history and she took pains to ensure that both her staff and customers would be remembered by future generations.

At least at the beginning of the German occupation, Ringelblum and Auerbach shared more than just a devotion to the recording of Jewish history. As well as being dedicated to active resistance against their German oppressors, they were radicals who also wanted to shape the Jewish future. Their emphasis on the importance of social history—collected by as many different people as possible—spoke to them of the possibility of a more united, less atomized people committed to a better future. By documenting the efforts of ordinary Jews they sought to undermine the power of the Jewish elites and sow the seeds for an increasingly influential secular Jewry. As the months went on, and Ringelblum and his colleagues began to realize the hopelessness of their predicament and the increasing inevitability of their fate, they worked even harder to document Jewish life and its destruction. Throughout his life Ringelblum remained faithful to the belief that the recording of history could hold the key to a better world. Stressing the importance of recording women's lives in the Warsaw ghetto, Ringelblum declared: 'The story of the Jewish woman will be a glorious page in the history of Jewry during the present war' (May 1942).[14] Although this statement refers to the courageous women who served as couriers for the resistance and spies throughout

---

[12] For Auerbach's reflections on her work in the soup kitchen, see ibid.

[13] Rachel Auerbach was to visit the Treblinka death camp on 7 November 1945 as part of an official delegation by the Main Commission of the Investigation of Hitlerite Crimes. She published a book about Treblinka, including a report of her visit in Yiddish, as *Oyf difelder fun Treblinke* [In the Fields of Treblinka] (Warsaw: Żydowska Komisja Historyczna, 1947). Cf. Samuel Kassow, 'Oyerbach Rokhl', in *The YIVO Encyclopaedia of Jews in Eastern Europe*, vol. 2 (New Haven, CT: Yale University Press, 2008), 1301–2.

[14] Ringelblum, *Notes from the Warsaw Ghetto*, 273–4.

occupied Poland, it is also illustrative of Ringelblum's larger tendency to present women in an almost heroic light.

Ringelblum's romantic vision of Jewish women in the ghetto was, however, only one vision. At the other end of the spectrum are the writings of Rabbi Shimon Huberband, who—quite contrary to Ringelblum's celebration of women's unselfish heroism—spends much time detailing his disappointment with Jewish women for failing to live up to the high moral standards he had set for them. Rather than acting in accordance with what he believed to be their innate qualities of charity and empathy, the Rabbi felt that they were behaving in selfish and self-serving ways, with many using the disorder of the time to further their own feminine but far from maternal interests. Nor was he alone. Strikingly, even at a time of such tremendous upheaval, several members of *Oneg Shabbat* recorded their disapproval of women for such seemingly innocuous behaviour as dressing immodestly. For example, referring to the women who were still able to wear fine clothes, teacher and diarist Abraham Lewin wrote: 'It pains me that Jewish women have so little sense of modesty and moderation.'[15]

Less censorious, but no less critical—and certainly more revealing of the very different experiences of different women—was the research carried out by Cecilya Ślepak, a young Jewish journalist and translator, also commissioned by Ringelblum to produce a study of women's responses to life under the German occupation. Ślepak, who began her work with the belief that 'Women are playing an important role in the positive trends of our life',[16] like Ringelblum wanted to reshape Jewish society. This belief emphasized the power and tenacity of women in the face of fear and suffering, and she suggested that it could lead to a rethinking of women's social and political roles in the post-war era.

Ślepak's research, part of *Oneg Shabbat*'s collective project 'A Year in the Life of the Ghetto—Two and a Half Years of Nazi Occupation', revolves around in-depth interviews with seventeen women from different economic, intellectual, and political backgrounds conducted during the winter of 1941 and up to the spring of 1942. With the exception of Bathia Temkin, a member of the Jewish underground who established a children's library in the ghetto, none of the women are named, and are identified only by an initial.[17] It covers the women's experiences in the

[15] Abráham Lewin, *A Cup of Tears: A Diary of the Warsaw Ghetto*, trans. Christopher Hutton, ed. Antony Polonsky (Oxford: Blackwell, 1988), 85.

[16] Cited in Kassow, *Who Will Write Our History?*, 243.

[17] See her diary, Bathia Temkin-Bermanowa, *Dziennik z podziemia* [Official from the Underground], eds. Anka Grupińska and Paweł Szapiro (Warsaw: Jewish Historical Institute, 2000). Temkin survived the war by passing herself off as an Aryan.

months prior to the outbreak of the war and during the German occupation. Ślepak was interested in what she called 'the rhythm of uprooted life'.[18]

The focus was the trauma of the move to the ghetto and the struggle for survival. Middle-class Jews were forced to move out of comfortable homes in elegant areas to relocate to ghettos which were usually situated in the poorest parts of the city, with no running water or electricity, making the maintaining of basic hygiene all but impossible. Unsurprisingly diseases such as typhus and tuberculosis became rife. Many women felt that they had become strangers in their own countries. As well as surrendering their homes, they were forced to leave behind any objects which might be of value such as furniture, jewellery, or even food.

They were then subjected to various confiscations. For example, the 'fur coat operation' between January and February 1942 set out to strip the Jews of their warm winter garments and redistribute the coats to the Reich. In Warsaw alone the *Judenrat* estimated that 690 men's fur coats, 2,451 women's fur coats, 4,441 men's and 4,120 women's quilted coats, 122 silver fox-fur scarves, 872 red fox scarves, 5,118 marten scarves, and 39,556 fur collars were seized.[19] As Stanisław Adler, a lawyer, who was amongst those recruited by the *Judenrat* to serve in the (Jewish) ghetto police, observed: 'For many scores of thousands of Jews, transfer to the ghetto meant complete financial ruin.'[20] The cost of living was extremely high in the ghettos, with black-market prices continually rising. However, as Raul Hilberg has observed, 'inequality was in evidence everywhere'.[21] While the more affluent were at least initially in a better position to endure the various hardships of ghetto life, as assets dwindled they too were often forced to join the ranks of the hungry.[22] In their place, the ghettos gave

[18] Ślepak's research can be found in the Ringelblum Archive at the YVA (JM/215/3). Dalia Ofer has produced two excellent articles on Ślepak's study: 'Gender Issues in Diaries and Testimonies of the Ghetto: The Case of Warsaw', in Dalia Ofer and Lenore J. Weitzman (eds.), *Women in the Holocaust* (New Haven, CT: Yale University Press, 1998), 143–69; and 'Her View through My Lens: Cecilia Slepak Studies Women in the Warsaw Ghetto', in Judith Tydor Baumel and Tova Cohen (eds.), *Gender, Place and Memory in the Modern Jewish Experience: Re-placing Ourselves* (London: Vallentine Mitchell, 2003), 29–50.

[19] Adam Czerniaków, *The Warsaw Ghetto Diary of Adam Czerniakow: Prelude to Doom*, eds. Raul Hilberg, Stanisław Staron, and Josef Kermisz (New York: Stein & Day, 1982), 310.

[20] Stanisław Adler, *In the Warsaw Ghetto 1940–1943: An Account of a Witness* (Jerusalem: Yad Vashem, 1982), 33. Adler committed suicide in 1946.

[21] Raul Hilberg, *The Destruction of the European Jews*, 3 vols. (Chicago, IL: Quadrangle, 1961), 171.

[22] See Lucjan Dobroszycki, 'Jewish Elites under German Rule', in Henry Friedlander and Sybil Milton (eds.), *The Holocaust: Ideology, Bureaucracy and Genocide* (New York: Kraus, 1980), 221–30.

birth to what might be dubbed a 'new elite', consisting of smugglers, blackmailers, and black-marketeers. These *nouveaux riches* were keen to frequent the various cafés, restaurants, and nightclubs that emerged. Ringelblum wrote that their motto was, 'eat, drink and be merry . . . for who knows how tomorrow will end',[23] and an unknown diarist of the Warsaw ghetto observed: 'the shop-windows are full of the best . . . It is characteristic for our time, that next to such a shop-window displaying bakery goods, children are lying dead, covered with paper.'[24] If you had the money you could even purchase one of the luxury satin bands with the Star of David embroidered in deep blue silk to separate you from the masses with their cheap paper armbands.[25]

Having money also led to other privileges: in the ghetto employment, housing, and even exemption from deportation could all be obtained at a price, albeit temporarily. Mary Berg, the 15-year-old daughter of a well-known Łódź art dealer, wrote in her diary whilst imprisoned in the Warsaw ghetto that 'only those who have large sums of money are able to save themselves from this terrible life'.[26] It was a temporary respite—but no less real or important for all that.

The Warsaw ghetto not only constituted a highly stratified society but, as we have begun to see, it also possessed an intricate social structure. This caused a great deal of friction. As Isaiah Trunk remarks: 'There was no social peace in the ghetto, because there was no equality among the inmates.'[27] The sudden influx of refugees from the provinces on to already overcrowded ghetto streets was one of the most obvious sources of conflict, as were the Jews married to Gentile Poles and the Jewish converts to Christianity, all of whom competed for limited resources. Fuelling this were the rumours that swarmed the ghettos which led the strong to believe that they would be protected at the cost of the very young, the old, and the

---

[23] Ringelblum, *Notes from the Warsaw Ghetto*, 279.

[24] Joseph Kermish (ed.), *To Live with Honor and Die with Honor! Selected Documents from the Warsaw Ghetto Underground Archives 'O.S.' ['Oneg Shabbath']* (Jerusalem: Yad Vashem, 1986), 537.

[25] See Janina David, *A Square of Sky: Memoirs of a Wartime Childhood* (London: Eland, 1992), 222.

[26] Mary Berg, *Warsaw Ghetto: A Diary*, trans. Norbert Guterman and Sylvia Glass, ed. S. L. Shneiderman (New York: Fischer, 1945), 32. The diary was first serialized in the Yiddish daily *Forverts* before being published as a book in February 1945 (before the end of the war). Reviews appeared in *The New York Times*, *The New Yorker*, *The Chicago Sunday Tribune*, and *The Saturday Review of Literature*.

[27] Isaiah Trunk, *Judenrat: The Jewish Councils in Eastern Europe under Nazi Occupation* (New York: Macmillan, 1972), 328.

infirm, who could not be of use to the Germans.[28] Ringelblum himself was drawn into this type of reasoning:

> The well-established fact is that people who are fed in the public kitchens are all dying out, subsisting as they do only on soup and dry rationed bread. So the question arises whether it might not be more rational to set aside the money that is available for the sole use of certain select individuals, those who are socially productive, the intellectual elite and the like. However, the situation is that, in the first place, the elite themselves constitute a considerable group and there wouldn't be enough to go around even for them; and, in the second place, why should labourers and artisans, perfectly deserving people who were productive in their home towns, and whom only the war and the ghetto existence have deprived of their productive capacity—why should they be judged worthless, the dregs of society, candidates for mass graves? Or are we to give full measure to a few, with only a handful having enough to survive?[29]

At the same time, the above quotation shows that the conditions of the ghetto had not managed to completely reverse pre-war values. The *nouveaux riches* might have been able to squeeze material rewards from an otherwise miserable existence, but they also had to suffer the scorn of their fellow Jews. Instead, it was the rabbis, scholars, and doctors who enjoyed the continued respect of the masses, although they also suffered greatly.[30]

The experiences of the women in Ślepak's research project reflect the massive inequalities and complexities of ghetto life.[31] Some of the women were university educated but others had practically no formal education. That the majority of the women can be roughly defined as middle class highlights the fact that it was the poorest people who were the first to be deported from the ghettos to the concentration and death camps. Among those who remained and whom Ślepak interviewed were: a middle-class mother who took on work as a cleaning woman to support her 10-year-old daughter; women who were engaged in prostitution before the war as well as bourgeois women who were forced to use sex as a means of survival as conditions in the ghetto worsened; beggars, smugglers, and women who

---

[28] See Nora Levin, *The Holocaust: The Destruction of European Jewry 1933–1945* (New York: Schocken, 1973), 223.

[29] Ringelblum, *Notes from the Warsaw Ghetto*, 181–2.

[30] See Lucy Dawidowicz, *The War against the Jews, 1933–1945* (New York: Holt, Rinehart & Winston, 1975), 213.

[31] For an early attempt to examine the complex social structure of the ghetto, see Samuel Gringauz, 'The Ghetto as an Experiment of Jewish Social Organization', *Jewish Social Studies*, 11/1 (1949), 3–20. Cf. idem, 'Some Methodological Problems in the Study of the Ghetto', *Jewish Social Studies*, 12/1 (1950), 65–72.

worked in the public kitchens and orphanages.[32] While the Nazis ordered that Jewish women be excluded from serving in the *Judenräte*, Ślepak's research reveals that women occupied important roles in health care, social welfare, and education.[33] They were particularly prominent in the 'house committees', which organized each building, negotiating evictions and assisting the needy in obtaining food and clothing. Indeed, Ringelblum noted that 'In many house committees women are replacing men who are leaving because they are burned out and tired.'[34] Women raised funds for charitable purposes—not least the soup kitchens—through a wide range of activities ranging from direct taxation to gambling parties.[35] Mary Berg wrote that in her building a kettle of soup was cooked every Friday for the children's hospital.[36] In the ghetto's hospitals too nurses and doctors— many of them women—battled against starvation and struggled, mostly without success, to contain the epidemics which plagued the ghetto, such as typhus, dysentery, and tuberculosis.[37]

While the refugees who arrived penniless from smaller communities or the western districts of Poland, and who, without contact, had little chance of employment, were often forced to turn to begging as their only source of sustenance, other women such as 'G', an upper-middle-class housewife, continued to enjoy comfortable housing and ample food. They were also able to employ household maids and maintain a rather genteel existence revolving around visits to cafés, the hairdresser, and the manicurist. These women had either managed to hold on to valuable assets such as dollars and jewellery, were married to members of the *Judenrat* or heads of the police, or, towards the lower end of the spectrum, were married to those who had jobs outside the ghettos. Ślepak herself,

---

[32] On the subject of prostitution in the Warsaw ghetto, see Katarzyna Person, 'Sexual Violence during the Holocaust—The Case of Forced Prostitution in the Warsaw Ghetto', *Shofar*, 33/2 (2015), 103–21. Cf. Anna Hájková's excellent article, 'Sexual Barter in Times of Genocide: Narrating the Sexual Economy of the Theresienstadt Ghetto', *Signs: Journal of Women in Culture and Society*, 38/3 (Spring 2013), 503–33.

[33] However, female secretaries to the *Judenräte* had contact with many powerful groups including the German authorities, the Jewish police, and the underground movements. In the Warsaw ghetto, Gustawa Jarecka, a mother of two, worked as a typist for the *Judenrat* and managed to secretly copy documents to smuggle to *Oneg Shabbat*.

[34] Cited in Kassow, *Who Will Write Our History?*, 239.

[35] See Michael Mazor, 'The House Committees in the Warsaw Ghetto', in Yehuda Bauer and Nathan Rotenstreich (eds.), *The Holocaust as Historical Experience* (New York: Holmes & Meier, 1981), 95–108.

[36] Cited in Dawidowicz, *The War Against the Jews*, 247.

[37] In the Warsaw ghetto a school for nurses was permitted, run by Luba Bilecka. See Charles G. Roland, 'An Underground Medical School in the Warsaw Ghetto', *Medical History*, 33 (1989), 399–419. The testimony of Luba Bilecka can be found in the Oral History Department, Institute of Contemporary Jewry, Hebrew University, Jerusalem (47), 10.

who was closely involved with the Yiddish literary elite and married to a successful engineer, maintained a comfortable home life for quite a time. Rachel Auerbach describes the regular Sunday afternoon coffee parties she attended during the first winter of the German occupation in the Ślepaks' comfortable apartment, the noodle cake she ate there, and the chamber music performed by the guests.[38]

However, regardless of their social status or economic position, women were without doubt in a particularly vulnerable position. Not only was ghettoization a significant stage in the persecution and murder of the Jews as a race, but it also marked the breakdown of the Jewish family and the destruction of networks of support and dependency. In November 1941, Ringelblum recorded: 'Jews have been prohibited from marrying and having children. Women pregnant up to three months have to have an abortion.'[39] From the German perspective, not only were children unable to contribute to the wartime economy but they also represented the possibility of a Jewish future. In the Vilna ghetto, Herman Kruk noted that 'Today [5 February 1942] the Gestapo summoned two members of the *Judenrat* and notified them: No more Jewish children are to be born. The order came from Berlin.'[40] Giving birth to a Jewish child meant death for mother and baby as well as the father and any Jewish midwife or doctor assisting in the birth.[41] Similarly, in the Shavli ghetto (Lithuania), pregnancy was explicitly forbidden on 4 March 1942. Dr Aharon Pick wrote at the time: 'Soon they will order us to sterilize the men and then their goal to exterminate the Jews will be completed. When this will happen the horrors of both men and women will be equal.'[42] And in 1942 in the Kovno ghetto women were forced to undergo compulsory abortions if found to be pregnant. Dr Aharon Peretz, a gynaecologist in the Kovno ghetto, testified:

[38] Cited in Ofer, 'Gender Issues in Diaries and Testimonies', 149. Cf. Auerbach, *Varshever tsavoes*, 53–60.

[39] Ringelblum, *Notes from the Warsaw Ghetto*, 230. Jewish women who were more than three months pregnant were deported to the camps.

[40] Herman Kruk, 'Diary of the Vilna Ghetto', trans. Shlomo Noble, *YIVO Annual of Jewish Social Sciences*, 13 (1965), 9–78. Cf. Herman Kruk, *Togebukh fon Vilner geto* [Diary of the Vilna Ghetto] (New York: YIVO, 1961), 20.

[41] Solon Beinfeld reports that children born after the decree were registered as having been born before it: see 'Health Care in the Vilna Ghetto', *Holocaust and Genocide Studies*, 12/1 (1998), 81.

[42] Cited in Lenore J. Weitzman and Dalia Ofer, 'Women in the Holocaust: Theoretical Foundations for a Gendered Analysis of the Holocaust', in Marcia Sachs Littell (ed.), *Women in the Holocaust: Responses, Insights and Perspectives (Selected Papers from the Annual Scholars' Conference on the Holocaust and the Churches 1990–2000)* (Merion Station, PA: Merion Westfield Press, 2001), 12–13.

Unwittingly, they would reach advanced stages of pregnancy . . . by an order of July 1942 pregnancy in the Kaunas ghetto was punishable with death to the father, the mother, and the infant . . . We had to start making abortions by the hundreds . . . yet there were many women who refused abortion, for all the danger it involved, and with great courage awaited the day of giving birth.[43]

For observant Jews the decision to abort their foetuses was particularly difficult. In Jewish law the greatest value is given to the preservation of life. However, when the life of an unborn child threatens the life of the mother, Jewish law dictates that the latter be given preference, and allows for abortion in certain cases.[44] In Kovno, rabbis actually decreed that as a result of the Nazi decree abortion was permissible without any medical indication.[45] Nevertheless, for women who would at other times have been joyful at the prospect of motherhood the necessity to abort their child was, needless to say, devastating. Added to this was the fear—rational or not—that abortion might result in permanent infertility.

Despite the prohibition on childbearing, many women continued to get pregnant in the ghettos. One of the reasons for this appears to be the suppression of menstruation, which gave women the impression that they would be unable to conceive.[46] In the Vilna ghetto as many as 75 per cent of women were estimated as being affected. Whether their amenorrhoea was due to endocrine changes, vitamin deficiencies, or psychological trauma—all of which were suggested at the time—the exact reasons were unclear. Once women had adjusted to life in the ghetto, however, menstruation usually reappeared—although it remained irregular, making it hard to distinguish the symptoms of pregnancy and to plan or prevent parenthood.[47] Whatever their condition, it was also hard to give up on the dream of new life—of a future. Solon Beinfeld further elaborates: 'Many—perhaps most—of the children born in the early period no longer had fathers; the desire for a remembrance of a victim . . . explains the risky decision of some women to carry their babies to term.'[48] Janina David's mother became pregnant in the Warsaw ghetto. She explained, 'when I see the destruction around us, I feel I want to have as many [children] as

[43] Gideon Hausner, *Justice in Jerusalem* (New York: Harper & Row, 1966), 213.

[44] On this subject, see Avraham Steinberg, 'Induced Abortion according to Jewish Law', *Journal of Halacha [Jewish Law] and Contemporary Society*, 1/1 (1981), 29–52.

[45] Charles G. Roland, *Courage under Siege: Starvation, Disease and Death in the Warsaw Ghetto* (Oxford: Oxford University Press, 1992), 66.

[46] See Leah Preiss, 'Women's Health in the Ghettos of Eastern Europe', in Dalia Ofer and Paula E. Hyman, *Jewish Women: A Comprehensive Historical Encyclopaedia* (Philadelphia, PA: Jewish Publications Society, 2007).

[47] Beinfeld, 'Health Care in the Vilna Ghetto', 88.   [48] Ibid., 81.

I can'.[49] At the same time she was terrified of raising a child in such conditions. Her cousin's child had died of starvation in front of his helpless mother, 'shrivelled and wrinkled, his head bent back, dribbling and smelling of death'.[50] She nevertheless asks:

> But if I do anything to prevent it being born, won't I be playing into Hitler's hands? Wasn't this precisely what he wanted to achieve? To destroy our race? Would I not be doing his work for him? After all, if the war ended soon there would be one new life already to compensate for those who have died?[51]

She miscarried shortly after.

Adina Blady-Szwajger, a 22-year-old Polish Jew, worked in the Warsaw Children's Hospital and was about to qualify as a doctor when the war broke out. She remembers: 'Children are always being born. Even in hiding places and in cellars.' However, she continues, 'But they often die, and it is not always possible to save them. You have only your own hands, but you also need medicines, and mother's milk, which in this case did not flow at all.'[52] A hospital in the Vilna ghetto even had a gynaecological ward whose main function was to perform abortions.[53] It is unclear how many of the women chose to abort their foetuses and how many were compelled to do so by the ghetto police.[54] Blady-Szwajger herself discovered she was pregnant whilst in hiding. A 'trusted' doctor performed an abortion for a large amount of money. She writes: 'It was not nice at all. And the very idea was not very nice either. The doctor was skilful, but terribly vulgar. Obviously he did the operation without anaesthetic, and it was a terrible experience for me.'[55] She also describes how she:

> [H]ad to take three other young girls for the same operation, each of whom might, as a consequence, never be able to have children. Especially as I couldn't guarantee them anything except the operation itself. There were no facilities for convalescence. But that was the way it had to be. Because who knew better than I that children had no right to be born? . . . I had to be present at each operation. I had to hold the girls by the hand and make sure they didn't scream. I did not like it all, I detest the thought to this day, but that was the way it had to be. We were involved in some cunning two-way blackmail with this doctor. He blackmailed me, saying that he knew who I was bringing and raised his fees accordingly, and I blackmailed him with the fact that he was carrying out illegal operations. It was disgusting![56]

[49] David, *A Square of Sky*, 179.   [50] Ibid.   [51] Ibid.
[52] Adina Blady-Szwajger, *I Remember Nothing More: The Warsaw Children's Hospital and The Jewish Resistance*, trans. Tasja Darowska and Danusia Stok (London: Collins Harvill, 1990), 137.
[53] Beinfeld, 'Health Care in the Vilna Ghetto', 81.   [54] Ibid.
[55] Blady-Swazjger, *I Remember Nothing More*, 148.   [56] Ibid., 148–9.

Macha Rolnikas, who was 14 years old when the Germans occupied her home town of Vilna, describes in her diary what happened when a woman was left alone to give birth just outside of the ghetto walls:

> A woman is crawling on all fours. Her hair is all tangled, her clothes dirty because of dragging herself along the ground, her eyes wide open, her face grimacing. Her bulging belly is resting on the ground. Covered with sweat, she stops every few minutes and, like an animal, pricks up her ears: is danger awaiting her somewhere? She is losing her strength. With every passing moment she feels a bit weaker. A great pain seizes her, shooting pains into her breast. She knows that her last moments are approaching, she is going to give birth.

> All night long, rolled up like a ball, exhausted, full of pain, she felt the approaching delivery. She continues to advance on all fours. She flops down in the middle of the street, very close to the entrance [of the ghetto], crawls to the sidewalk so as not to get run over. She won't ever get up again. She turns over and over in pain, in a kind of convulsion, writhing like a snake. She startles and death comes to interrupt her anguish at the same moment her little girl comes to this world of pain and shadows. She is found next to her and is taken into the ghetto and named Ghettala. Poor little girl.[57]

During the last days of the ghetto, when few Jews were left and deportation became increasingly inevitable, the plight of women and children became ever more desperate. Abraham Lewin observed that during the mass deportations in the summer of 1942 'women who were seized yesterday.... were freed if they sacrificed their children. To our pain and sorrow many women saved themselves in this way.'[58] In their anguish, other mothers left their children on the doorsteps of non-Jewish homes and Christian institutions in the hope that someone would take pity on their child.[59] Nurses working in ghetto hospitals describe smothering new-born babies after the mothers were deported. Dentists and other medics with access to arsenic and cyanide also provided desperate women with a means of ending their children's suffering. Indeed, Blady-Szwajger herself gave children and the elderly morphine during the last days of the ghetto. She writes:

> I took the morphine upstairs. Dr. Margolis was there, and I told her what I wanted to do. So we took a spoon and went to the infants' room. And just

---

[57] Laurel Holliday (ed.), *Children's Wartime Diaries: Secret Writings from the Holocaust and World War II* (London: Piatkus, 1995), 187–8. Macha survived the war and translated her diary herself from Yiddish into French. See Macha Rolnikas, *Je Devais le Raconter* (Paris: Les Éditeurs Français Réunis, 1966).

[58] Lewin, *A Cup of Tears*, 157.

[59] Dalia Ofer, 'Motherhood under Siege', in Esther Hertzog (ed.), *Life, Death and Sacrifice: Women and the Family in the Holocaust* (Jerusalem: Gefen, 2008), 58.

as during those two years of real work in the hospital, I bent down over the tiny little mouths. Only Dr. Margolis was with me. And downstairs there was screaming because the Szaulis [Lithuanian paramilitaries] and the Germans were already there, taking the sick from the wards to the cattle trucks. After that we went to the older children and told them that the medicine was going to make their pain disappear. They believed me and drank the required amount from the glass.[60]

Finally, some women threw their babies out of the cattle trucks on the way to the concentration and death camps.[61] This included women who had given birth on the trains.

Jewish family life was also attacked in other more insidious ways. For example, in January 1940 the Nazis closed the synagogues and *mikvehs* (ritual baths). This led many rabbis to stop performing weddings as the Jewish law of family purity demands that brides visit a *mikveh* for the preparatory bath prior to their nuptials.[62] The few *mikvehs* that remained were turned into an opportunity for further humiliation. On 12 May 1942, Adam Czerniaków, head of the Warsaw *Judenrat*, stated that: 'Avril [an SS officer] arrived with the film-makers and announced that they would shoot a scene at the ritual baths on Dzielna Street. They need 20 Orthodox Jews with ear-locks and 20 upper-class women.'[63] On 14 May the intention behind this demand was revealed:

> Both sexes were forced by means of intimidation and whiplashes to remove their clothes and remain naked; afterwards they were made to get into one [ritual bath] both together and were forced into lewd and obscene acts imitating the sexual behaviour of animals... While one Nazi cracked his whip over the heads of the captives, his partner set himself up in a corner with a camera. Henceforward all the world will know how low the Jews have fallen in their morals, that modesty between the sexes has ceased among them and that they practice sexual immorality in public.[64]

From the very beginning of the German occupation, the Jews were subject to religious persecution. The Haredi, as the most visible carriers

[60] Blady-Swazjger, *I Remember Nothing More*, 57.

[61] Ofer, 'Motherhood under Siege', 58.

[62] On religious leadership during the Holocaust, see Joseph Walk, 'Religious Leadership during the Holocaust', in Israel Gutman and Cynthia J. Haft (eds.), *Patterns of Jewish Leadership in Nazi Europe 1933–1945. Proceedings of the Third Yad Vashem International Conference* (Jerusalem: Yad Vashem, 1979), 377–91.

[63] Czerniaków, *The Warsaw Ghetto Diary of Adam Czerniakow*, 352–3. Cf. Lewin, *A Cup of Tears*, 71.

[64] Cited in David Patterson, *Along the Edge of Annihilation: The Collapse and Recovery of Life in the Holocaust Diary* (Seattle, WA: University of Washington Press, 1999), 110–11. Rachel Auerbach also writes about the German film crews. See Rachel Auerbach, *Bi'hutsot Varsha* [The Streets of Warsaw] (Tel Aviv: Israel Book, 1954), 31–2.

of Judaism, were the first to be persecuted.[65] Rabbi Shimon Huberband describes how men had to remove their beards and *peyos* (sidelocks). If caught, they risked having their beards torn or burnt off and at times were even forced to swallow their own shorn hair. The attack on women was even more pernicious. On occasion Jewish women were forced to shave off the beards of their male relatives: an act of humiliation for both parties.[66] In cities such as Zduńska Wola, Łuków, and Gorzkowice, Jewish women were prohibited from wearing wigs—an attack on their modesty and their marital status, for Haredi women were required by religious law to wear them, and believed it sexually scandalous not to do so.[67]

While religious life did continue—male collective prayer groups met in secret, underground religious education continued, people attempted to consume only kosher food, and women undertook difficult journeys to reach the few *mikvehs* that remained, such as in Rembertów or Pruszków[68]—it was extremely challenging. For orthodox Jewish women life was particularly difficult. The biblical Book of Proverbs depicts the ideal figure of a Jewish mother and wife as an *eschet chayil* (woman of valour), who is devoted to her children and husband. As the identity of religious women was dependent to a large extent on their ability to bear and raise Jewish children, the Nazi attack on the Jewish family was particularly brutal. Not only this, but their comparatively large number of children made them particularly vulnerable to the threat of deportation.

As they adjusted to the hardships of ghetto life, both men and women were forced to inure themselves to the suffering around them. It is unsurprising that generally accepted standards of normally appropriate behaviour slipped in the ghettos. Nevertheless traditional rabbis such as Shimon Huberband singled out women for particular criticism. In his

---

[65] On the subject of Jewish religious life during the Holocaust, see Dan Michman, 'Research on the Problems and Conditions of Religious Jewry under the Nazi Regime', in Israel Gutman and Gideon Greif (eds.), *The Historiography of the Holocaust Period* (Jerusalem: Yad Vashem, 1988), 737–48. Cf. Dan Michman, 'Le-Verur ha-Tnaim le-Kiyyum Chayim Datiyim Tachat ha-Shilton ha-Naz' [An Appraisal of the Conditions for Religious Life under the Nazi Regime], *Sinai*, 91/5–6 (August/September, 1982), 254–69.

[66] Shimon Huberband, *Kiddush Hashem* [Sanctification of the Name]: *Jewish Religious and Cultural Life in Poland during the Holocaust*, trans. David E. Fishman, ed. Jeffrey S. Gurock and Robert S. Hirt (Hoboken, NJ: Ktav, 1987), 189.

[67] It is the custom of Haredi men to maintain beards and *peyos* and for Haredi women to cover their hair with wigs and scarves.

[68] Huberband also reports four clandestine *mikvehs* in Warsaw. See idem, '*Mikvehs* and Jewish Family Purity', Chapter 16 in his *Kiddush Hashem*, 193–9.

essay—significantly entitled 'The Moral Decline of the Jewish Woman
during the War'—he describes the following scene:

> During the freezing cold days of winter 1941 and 1942, countless naked
> children lay on the streets of the Jewish quarter. Such children are visible on
> literally every street corner. Thousands upon thousands of Jewish women,
> elegantly dressed, wearing makeup and perfume, passed them by indiffer-
> ently. Only very rarely did a Jewish woman stop for a second to throw a
> groschen at the children. If one spotted a woman giving alms, it was usually a
> woman from the older generation.[69]

Rabbi Huberband is not alone in his singling out of women rather than
men for their lack of concern. Women—and in particular young
women—are criticized in many ghetto diaries for appearing frivolous in
the face of suffering, and indeed the image of women still concerned to
keep up with the latest fashions at such an awful time is certainly unsettling.[70] However, it also seems extraordinary that even in the ghettos men
were continuing to censor women's physical appearance. Abraham Lewin
too wrote in his Warsaw ghetto diary:

> The ghetto is most terrible to behold with its crowds of drawn faces with the
> colour drained out of them. Some of them have the look of corpses that have
> been in the ground a few weeks. They are so horrifying that they cause us to
> shudder instinctively. Against the backdrop of these literally skeletal figures
> and against the all-embracing gloom and despair that stares from every
> pair of eyes, from the packed mass of passers-by, a certain type of girl or
> young woman, few in number it must be said, shocks with her over-elegant
> attire... Walking down the street I observe this sickly elegance and am
> shamed in my own eyes.[71]

It is perhaps also important to point out here that well-dressed women
did not escape suffering but were in some ways particularly vulnerable
to harassment by the Germans. For example, 'upper-class' women were
specifically recruited for the atrocity committed at the ritual baths cited
above. Similarly there is evidence to suggest that attractive women were
more likely to be targeted for particularly demeaning forced labour such
as cleaning floors in their underwear. However, for diarists such as
Huberband, what is important is not that both men and women were
sometimes drawn into less than favourable behaviour in the ghettos, or
even that they both suffered, but that the position that Judaism accords

---

[69] Ibid., 240.
[70] In Kraków, however, Jewish women were banned from wearing short sleeves and
high-heeled shoes: Ringelblum, *Notes from the Warsaw Ghetto*, 37.
[71] Lewin, *A Cup of Tears*, 84.

women should have meant that women in particular should have been able to transcend their circumstances: 'if Jews in general have been called "the compassionate children of compassionate ones", then the Jewish women should be called by that appellation even more so'.[72]

As this suggests, the Jewish woman was charged with maintaining family life even under—perhaps especially under—wartime conditions. If Ringelblum's words are to be believed, 'It is thanks to the courage and endurance of our women that thousands of families have been able to endure these bitter times.' And no doubt many women did everything they could to hold their families together for as long they could. However, diaries written in the ghettos of eastern Europe also reveal the extent to which the hardships and uncertainties of ghetto life destroyed familial bonds. While it is important not to idealize pre-war Jewish families—no doubt they were subject to their own particular strains and frailties—wartime conditions made family life particularly difficult. Families became extended as relatives who lived outside the ghetto were forced to move in with those who lived inside the ghetto walls. At the same time, over-crowding in the ghettos also meant that people had to share their homes with strangers they didn't necessarily trust.

In the Łódź ghetto Sara Selver-Urbach describes hearing 'people fighting over bread, their screaming voices bursting out of the open window.'[73] Oblique references are made to both lodgers and family members stealing each other's food. Dawid Sierakowiak, who was 15 years old when he began his diary in Łódź, wrote that if his father and sister had not regularly eaten the food that should have gone to his mother she would not have grown so weak.[74] Sierakowiak, who was to die, aged 16, of tuberculosis and starvation, reserves particular scorn for his father, who not only steals his wife's bread but also that of his son and daughter. The hardships Dawid was forced to endure led him to challenge the traditional gendered hierarchies on which nuclear family life is so often based. On 22 November 1942 he writes:

> Today nearly resulted in a fight between Father and me. He drove me to the point where I threw a few radish slices at him because he wouldn't let me eat them in peace. You can't even suggest that he start working somewhere... He is still full of lice and doesn't even consider bathing to get rid of them. He sleeps in his street clothes and blows his nose on a dirty towel. Neither his

---

[72] Huberband, *Kiddush Hashem*, 240.

[73] Sara Selver-Urbach, *Through the Window of My Home: Recollections from the Lodz Ghetto*, trans. Siona Bodansky (Jerusalem: Yad Vashem, 1971), 77.

[74] Dawid Sierakowiak, *The Diary of Dawid Sierakowiak: Five Notebooks from the Łódź Ghetto*, trans. Kamil Turowski, ed. Alan Adelson (London: Bloomsbury, 1997), 220.

willingness to wash my shirt nor his speed in buying all kinds of food rations and allocations are able to mollify me. I don't even mention his thievery and childish cheating in portioning the food. As always, he fusses over every crumb and peel. In a word, he is a completely broken man.[75]

Also in the Łódź ghetto, an anonymous girl wrote in her diary: 'I ate all the honey. I'm selfish. . . . I'm not worthy of my mother who works so hard . . . I eat everything that lands near me.'[76] Hunger was a form of torture that dominated people's thoughts, dreams, and actions. A diarist in the Minsk ghetto wrote, 'We thought about nothing other than bread, both by day and in our dreams. We ate pieces of paper, scratched away the chalk from the stoves.'[77] In Warsaw, Emanuel Ringelblum recorded on 20 May 1941 that bread prices had increased to 15 zloty for a one kg loaf. At that price, the vast majority of the ghetto's inhabitants would starve.[78] Bajla Grinberg lived with her family in a refugee shelter in the Warsaw ghetto. Recording her testimony for *Oneg Shabbat*, she describes the terrible hunger she endured:

> Days went by, when I did not eat at all; not one, but many such days. The hunger is such that it is hard to remain standing, for lack of strength. I did not have the wherewithal to live, so I began to beg; the best area—that was Leszno. I was often ashamed, but hunger nagged.[79]

Rachel Auerbach observed the gradual degradation of the poor and hungry. Working in the soup kitchen allowed her to chart the downfall of people from a whole range of different backgrounds as they slowly became consumed by their own helplessness. She describes how one woman, Dama, succumbed to the filth around her. She had become like a grotesque parody of the richer women in the ghettos—or, indeed—of her former self. Auerbach writes:

> And so she has been wearing for many weeks a black georgette cocktail dress, dragged down at the bottom in uneven tails, the seams plastered with nits, on her head a cloth jockey cap, yellow with brown strips, perhaps from some

---

[75] Ibid., 231.

[76] Cited in Michal Unger, 'The Status and Plight of Women in the Łódź Ghetto', in Ofer and Weitzman (eds.), *Women in the Holocaust*, 134.

[77] Anna Krasnopërko, *Briefe meiner Erinnerung. Mein Überleben im jüdischen Ghetto von Minsk 1941/42* (Frankfurt: Villigst, 1991), 70.

[78] Cited in Ofer, 'Motherhood under Siege', 47. On starvation in the Warsaw ghetto, see Myron Winick (ed.), *Hunger Disease: Studies by the Jewish Physicians in the Warsaw Ghetto*, trans. Martha Osnos (New York: Wiley, 1979).

[79] Cited in Ruta Sakowska (ed.), *Archiwum Ringelbluma: Konspiracyjna Archiwum Getta Warszawy* [Ringelblum Archive: Underground Warsaw Ghetto Archive]. vol. 2: *Dzieci— tajne nauczanie w getcie warzawskim* [Children—Secret Education in the Warsaw Ghetto] (Warsaw: Jewish Historical Institute, 2000), 49–50.

skiing costume, and over her shoulders, weighing her down, inseparable collections of large bags and small handbags stuffed with what few possessions she has left.[80]

Inevitably Auerbach began to see herself as complicit in the suffering she witnessed:

> I have been slowly coming to the conclusion that the whole balance of this self-help activity is simply that people die more slowly. We must finally admit to ourselves that we can save nobody from death; we don't have the means to. We can only put it off, regulate it but we can't prevent it. In all my experience in the soup kitchen, I have not been able to rescue anybody, nobody! And nobody could accuse me of caring less than the directors of other soup kitchens.[81]

At times family members went so far as to denounce each other for stealing. *The Chronicle of the Lodz Ghetto* records that: 'Appearing at one of the precincts of the Order service [ghetto police], an 8-year-old boy filed a report against his own parents, whom he charged with not giving him the bread ration due to him.'[82]

In these circumstances, the traditional, conventional notion of the good mother came under intense strain. The 'natural' maternal impulse was compromised. Indeed, for some it might even be said that a dead child was of more value than a live one. Until the winter of 1941, all new-born babies were issued with a food card and children received special rations up to the age of three. Ringelblum noted that: 'At 7 Wołyńska Street a mother hid her dead child for a week in order to make use of the dead child's ration cards for that period.'[83] Czerniaków wrote that: 'In the public assistance shelters mothers are hiding dead children under the beds for eight days.'[84] Corpses were also abandoned—often hidden—in the streets. Adina Blady-Szwajger describes coming across something soft as she travelled through the ghetto: 'a baby's corpse, swollen, covered in newspaper'.[85] However, these desperate mothers were not trying to reap large profits from the deaths of their children, but were merely trying to ward off death by starvation a little longer either for themselves or for other children and family members.

Nor was it just women's roles that were severely challenged. As more and more people succumbed to death and disease, people's emotional

---

[80] Cited in Kassow, *Who Will Write Our History?*, 142.   [81] ibid.

[82] Dobroszycki (ed.), *The Chronicle of the Lodz Ghetto*, 6.

[83] Ringelblum, *Notes from the Warsaw Ghetto*, 325.

[84] Czerniaków, *The Warsaw Diary of Adam Czerniakow*, 300.

[85] Blady-Szwajger, *I Remember Nothing More*, 30.

responses became understandably muted. To respond emotionally, even
to the loss of a loved one, requires physical and mental strength. Ringelblum wrote: 'A very interesting question is that of the passivity of the
Jewish masses, who expire with no more than a slight sigh. Why are they
all so quiet? Why does the father die, and the mother, and each of the
children, without a single protest?'[86] In a sense, of course, they had been
forced to mourn the loss of their loved ones whilst they were still alive.

However, Ringelblum was careful to show that Jews were not an
undifferentiated mass and that gender shaped their responses. There was
certainly a crisis of masculinity. For example, Vladka Meed, who was a
teenager in the Warsaw ghetto, describes the collapse of her father:

> He was not only helpless but a broken, dejected man who could not take care
> of his family. He was undernourished, run down; he got pneumonia and
> died. In contrast, my mother was someone who did not give up. Internally
> she was a strong person. Somehow she had the strength to keep our home
> spotless without soap. By keeping the place clean, she was fighting diseases,
> especially typhus.[87]

Unable to fulfil their role of breadwinner, previously powerful men found
it particularly difficult to adapt to their bare-bones existence. Educator and
diarist Chaim Kaplan noted that formerly important and wealthy men
'now attend to their household's needs, returning home laden with
foodstuffs; in one pocket—a loaf of bread; in another pocket—an onion
[...] Authority has vanished; nobility has passed.'[88] 'Mrs. H', one of
Ślepak's interviewees, told her that she was forced to support the family as
her husband suffered from panic attacks as a result of being picked up for
forced labour.[89] Ultimately, despite their best efforts, men had to face the
hard fact that they could no longer protect their families. For example,
27-year-old Calel Perechodnik, in the ghetto of Otwock near Warsaw,
joined the ghetto police in the hope that his position would protect
his wife Anka and their 2-year-old daughter Alúska from deportation. In
a diary written whilst in hiding he stated: 'seeing that the war was not
coming to an end and in order to be free from the roundup for labour
camps, I entered the ranks of the Ghetto Polizei'.[90] It was, he soon

---

[86] Ringelblum, *Notes from the Warsaw Ghetto*, 206.

[87] Vladka Meed, *On Both Sides of the Wall: Memoirs from the Warsaw Ghetto*, trans.
Benjamin Meed (Tel Aviv: Hakibutz Hameuchad, 1973), 8.

[88] Cited in Raquel Hodara, 'The Polish Jewish Woman from the Beginning of the
Occupation to the Deportation to the Ghettos', *Yad Vashem Studies*, 32 (2004), 420–32.

[89] Ofer, 'Her View through My Lens'.

[90] Calel Perechodnik, *Am I a Murderer? Testament of a Warsaw Jewish Ghetto Policeman*,
ed. Frank Fox (New York: Westview, 1996), 9.

discovered, only a temporary stay of execution; he was later to find his own family amongst 8,000 other Jews being herded into cattle cars for deportation to Treblinka.

For many survivors of the Holocaust, disillusionment with their fathers and disappointment in their ability to protect them was to be a lasting legacy. Halina Birenbaum, who was a young girl in the Warsaw ghetto and would survive Auschwitz, remembers: 'Of the family, only my mother behaved courageously, without giving way to panic. She alone could control herself, comfort the rest of us and devise new ways of saving our lives.'[91]

Pre-war Europe was already experiencing an increase in the number of female-headed households. This was in part due to the deportations of the First World War and partly to the population migrations of the first part of the twentieth century.[92] Wartime conditions accelerated this demographic change as more and more women were left with the burden of providing for their families, and the adult population of the ghettos of eastern Europe became predominantly female. In the initial stages of the German invasion there was a widespread belief that it was only men who faced real danger. In 1939, Perechodnik wrote: 'I thought that nothing would happen to women and particularly to children, and, besides, the war was to end shortly.'[93] Many could not believe that the Germans would harm women and children—indeed, small children were actually given special food rations. Men were therefore encouraged to escape to Soviet-occupied eastern Poland and some Jewish men also responded to the plea made by the Polish government at the outbreak of the war for all young, able-bodied men to join the Polish army. These were either killed in battle or captured and interned in German prisoner-of-war camps. In contrast, few women fled, not only because they believed they were in no immediate danger but more often because there were seldom enough financial resources to allow whole families to escape, and women were more likely to take responsibility for elderly parents and small children.[94] By the end of October 1939 there were 164,307 men in Jewish Warsaw (46 per cent of the population) compared with 195,520 women (54 per cent). Women made up 65 per cent of the ghetto's population of 20- to 29-year-olds.[95]

[91] Halina Birenbaum, *Hope is the Last to Die: A Personal Documentation of Nazi Terror*, trans. David Welsh (New York: Twayne, 1967), 18.
[92] See Ofer, 'Motherhood under Siege', 42.
[93] Perechodnik, *Am I a Murderer?*, 7.
[94] See Renée Fodor, 'The Impact of the Nazi Occupation of Poland on the Jewish Mother–Child Relationship', *YIVO Annual of Jewish Social Science* 11 (1956/7), 270–2.
[95] Kassow, *Who Will Write Our History?*, 241.

Ślepak found that the women she interviewed experienced a strong degree of traditional gender role reversal as circumstances conspired to make them become the primary breadwinners and defenders of the family.[96] Because the men were forced to avoid being found outside during daylight hours, the tasks of standing for hours in dangerous food queues, as well as the procurement of employment and the ordeal of negotiating with both the Jewish and German authorities for the return of property or immunity from deportation, also fell to women. This was not, however, experienced as a liberation—and was, in truth, quite the reverse. Not only were they on occasion beaten for their efforts, but women were also to find out they were now not immune from the threat of forced labour. Indeed, this breakdown of the normal order actually exposed them to new threats. For although the men were missing or powerless, the power of gender had not gone away. If anything, in these reduced conditions, gender became more relevant and its implications—its power—more risky. Women were, for instance, increasingly at risk from sexualized humiliation, violence, and rape. On 10 January 1941, Mary Berg wrote in her diary that 'last night we went through several hours of terror . . . the Nazis searched the men . . . and then ordered the women to strip, hoping to find concealed diamonds . . . the women were kept naked for more than two hours while the Nazis put revolvers to their private parts and threatened to shoot them all'.[97]

Golda Wasserman describes the mass rape of women from the Tulchin ghetto (Ukraine):

> In the autumn of 1942, there were more than 3,000 Jewish families from the Ukraine, Bukovina, and Bessarabia resettled to the Tulchin ghetto . . . About fifteen kilometres from the ghetto, there were Italian and Hungarian reserve divisions. As demanded by the commissariat-officers of these divisions, the Romanian gendarme who was the Kommandant of Tulchin selected healthy young girls from the ghetto and sent them away, under the official pretence of working in the kitchen and bakery of those divisions. The girls returned from there having been raped, ill with venereal diseases. Many committed suicide back in the barracks, while some of them were killed when resisting or attempting to flee. Then the Kommandant selected new girls for 'work'. Selection was carried out every fifteen to twenty days. It is impossible to describe what was happening in the ghetto—the desperate screams of the girls, the pleas of their parents. Some girls tried to run along the road.

[96] Ślepak reported in Ofer, 'Her View through My Lens'. On the type of role reversal noted above, see Sara R. Horowitz, 'Memory and Testimony of Women Survivors of Nazi Genocide', in Judith R. Baskin (ed.), *Women of the Word: Jewish Women and Jewish Writing* (Detroit, MI: Wayne State University Press, 1994), 258–82; and Horowitz, 'Gender, Genocide and Jewish Memory', *Prooftexts*, 20/1&2 (Winter/Spring, 2000), 158–90.

[97] Berg, *Warsaw Ghetto: A Diary*, 37.

The Fascists shot them in the back. Only a few managed to hide in the villages, pretending to be locals, or were saved by partisans after long wanderings in the forests. I belong to the latter group. Among twenty-five other girls, I was picked to be sent to 'work'.[98]

In fact many contemporary witnesses testify to the rape of Jewish women and girls in occupied Europe. In Warsaw, a Jewish doctor stated that: 'One continually hears of the raping of Jewish girls in Warsaw. The Germans suddenly enter a house and rape 15- or 16-year-old girls in the presence of their parents and relatives.'[99] Another report states that on 18 February 1940 two teenage Jewish girls were raped in a Jewish cemetery in Warsaw by two German non-commissioned officers.[100] Even some Jewish commentators came to trivialize sexual assault, so ubiquitous had it become. In a shocking—and revealingly misogynist—diary entry Czerniaków remarked that: 'An old hag who had been raped appeared today, coiffure, with her lips painted, etc. Rejuvenated at least 20 years.'[101] Rape was also a crime committed by Jewish men. In Łódź, for example, a man named 'Ordinanz' was accused and convicted of rape in the ghetto's court.[102]

Increasingly, women were forced to adopt extreme measures in the struggle to keep themselves and their families from destitution. While prostitution was a fact of Jewish life before the war, dire necessity drove still more women to turn to sex as a means of supporting their families in the ghettos.[103] This was despite the fact that the Nazi authorities specifically prohibited Jewish prostitution.[104] Among Ślepak's respondents was 'C', a young woman of 23 who had married only a few days before the outbreak of war. After an abortive attempt to cross the Soviet border to join her husband who had escaped to Vilna at the beginning of the war, she returned to find her parents' home and restaurant had been looted by the Germans. What she described as an 'affair'—but which amounted to

---

[98] Cited in Anatoly Podolsky, 'The Tragic Fate of Ukrainian Jewish Women under Nazi Occupation, 1941–1944', in Sonja M. Hedgepeth and Rochelle G. Saidel (eds.), *Sexual Violence against Jewish Women during the Holocaust* (Waltham, MA: Brandeis University Press, 2010), 103.

[99] Cited in Helene J. Sinnreich, 'The Rape of Jewish Women during the Holocaust', in Hedgepeth and Saidel (eds.), *Sexual Violence Against Jewish Women during the Holocaust*, 110.

[100] David J. Hogan (ed.), *The Holocaust Chronicle* (Lincolnwood, IL: Publications International, 2007), 191.

[101] Czerniaków, *The Warsaw Diary of Adam Czerniakow*, 153.

[102] See Dobroszycki (ed.), *The Chronicle of the Lodz Ghetto*, 384.

[103] In 1940 Nazi health officials tried to establish the wearing of armbands by Jewish prostitutes to ensure that German soldiers could distinguish them from Polish prostitutes. See Roland, *Courage Under Siege*, 50.

[104] In inter-war Poland prostitution was legal for women over the age of 21. Between 1935 and 1936, of the 3,743 legally registered prostitutes working in Warsaw, more than one-third were Jewish. Person, 'Sexual Violence during the Holocaust', 107–19.

prostitution, however unwilling she was to call it that—with a Polish *Volksdeutscher* (a Polish citizen of German origin) who sublet a room in her parents' apartment allowed her to obtain the goods needed to reopen her parents' business. There is no reference to any condemnation from them.[105] In a similar manner, husbands at times benefited from their wives' associations with men who held positions of authority or who were economically powerful.

Both Šlepak's research and diaries written in the ghettos throughout eastern Europe reveal the establishment of sexual relationships in order to gain the protection of a powerful man and also the more ad hoc bartering of sex for food or coal. Feminist scholars such as Kirsty Chatwood have called this type of exchange 'a form of coercive prostitution' to be under-stood 'in terms of the victimization of women'.[106] Ringelblum noted in his diary that the Jewish police would sometimes delay sending people to the death camps in exchange for sex: 'There were cases in which these police, in addition to money, also demanded an insidious payment in kind—the women's bodies . . . for this purpose they had a special room in the hospital.'[107] The distinguished Holocaust scholar Raul Hilberg like-wise reports that on the eve of an *Aktion* (mass assembly, deportation, and murder of Jews) Jewish girls offered themselves to the ghetto policemen in a desperate attempt to save their lives. It was, however, to no avail, for the women were killed in the morning.[108]

Unsurprisingly, it is extremely difficult to gauge the extent of such activities, particularly as they have been largely strained out of the post-war historiography of the ghettos. In this respect, at least, it is worth admitting that much feminist scholarship has served to confuse matters rather than clarify them. This is partly the result of a reluctance to accept the concept of 'negotiated sex'. Many feminists argue that, given the context of oppres-sion and dire necessity that the women found themselves in, any notion of consensual sex is bogus. Yet this is a highly problematic assumption. It is certainly the case that the extreme power imbalances of life in the ghetto made the idea of consensual negotiated sex between free and equal indi-viduals questionable, to say the least. Refusing to acknowledge that even

---

[105] See Ofer, 'Her View through My Lens'.

[106] Kirsty Chatwood, 'Schillinger and the Dancer: Representing Agency and Sexual Violence in Holocaust Testimonies', in Hedgepeth and Saidel (eds.), *Sexual Violence against Jewish Women during the Holocaust*, 61.

[107] Cited in Nomi Levenkron, 'Death and the Maidens: "Prostitution", Rape, and Sexual Slavery during World War II', in Hedgepeth and Saidel (eds.), *Sexual Violence against Jewish Women during the Holocaust*, 20.

[108] Raul Hilberg, *Perpetrators, Victims, Bystanders: The Jewish Catastrophe, 1933–1945* (London: HarperCollins, 1993), 145.

women in extremity can be capable of making choices, however, renders the women involved faceless victims. It also silences those women who refused to see themselves as passive prisoners of circumstance. In fact, both contemporary witnesses and survivors testify to the existence of both prostitution and brothels in the ghettos. In Warsaw, evidence suggests that the restaurants, cafés, and nightclubs which operated in Warsaw up until July 1942 encouraged prostitution and that until the mass deportations of July 1942 brothels operated in the Warsaw ghetto. Władysław Szpilman, who worked as a pianist in a café in the Warsaw ghetto, writes scornfully in his memoir: 'To the sound of popping champagne corks, tarts with gaudy make-up offered their services to war profiteers seated at laden tables.'[109] And Janina Bauman observed a local prostitute who 'used to walk up and down Leszno Street at dusk wearing gaudy make-up. She was a prostitute... haggard and squalid. My heart contracted with compassion.'[110] In an early post-war interview a male survivor of the Łódź ghetto describes how women prostituted themselves for a piece of bread: 'For a slice of bread they would go into a yard or somewhere. Possibly the mother was working, so the daughter would use the opportunity.'[111]

As we have seen, for others, begging was their only means of survival. This was especially true for children. In many cases children were forced to take on adult responsibilities, particularly the procurement of food for their families. Often they went begging as their parents looked on, and sometimes children simply grabbed food from strangers in the street, eating it before the owner could grab it back.[112] Kaplan observed that:

> All along the sidewalks, on days of cold so fierce as to be unendurable, entire families bundled up in rags wander about, not begging but merely moaning with heartrending voices. A father and mother with their sick little children, crying and wailing, fill the street with the sound of their sobs. No one turns to them, no one offers them a penny, because the number of panhandlers has hardened our hearts.[113]

---

[109] Władysław Szpilman, *The Pianist: The Extraordinary Story of One Man's Survival in Warsaw, 1939–45*, trans. Anthea Bell (London: Victor Gollancz, 1999), 13.

[110] Janina Bauman, *Beyond these Walls: Escaping the Warsaw Ghetto—A Young Girl's Story* (London: Virago, 2006), 113. Janina and her family survived in hiding.

[111] Jacob M. Testimony in Donald L. Niewyk (ed.), *Fresh Wounds: Early Narratives of Holocaust Survival* (Chapel Hill, NC: University of North Carolina Press, 1998), 304–5. On the subject of 'hunger prostitution', see Elizabeth D. Heineman, 'Sexuality and Nazism: The Doubly Unspeakable?', *Journal of the History of Sexuality*, 11/1–2 (2002), 22–46.

[112] See Abram Lancman, Edmund Jonah, and Wladyslaw Bartoszewski, *Youth in the Time of the Holocaust* (Warsaw: Rytm, 2005), 44.

[113] Chaim A. Kaplan, *Scroll of Agony: The Warsaw Diary of Chaim A. Kaplan*, trans. and ed. Abraham I. Katsh (Bloomington, IN: Indiana University Press, 1999), 237.

Others were abandoned by parents who could no longer care for them. Still more were orphaned. Jack Klajman lost his father in the spring of 1941: 'they came with a wagon to take my father's body away as though he were a piece of trash'.[114]

The breakdown of the Jewish family produced many casualties. Ringelblum noted the huge increase in numbers at the children's shelter at 39 Dzielna Street in Warsaw. In January 1941, 480 children were housed there; in June the number had risen to 625 children.[115] Without their parents older children were often faced with caring for their younger siblings. This placed them in extremely vulnerable circumstances. After the death of their parents, 17-year-old Lucille Eichengreen was left to care for her 12-year-old sister, Karin, in the Łódź ghetto. When she tried to get a job at one of the ghetto's factories, the manager demanded payment. When Lucille explained that she was penniless 'he laughed and said that was not what he had in mind'.[116] The fact that Eichengreen turned down this proposition is made even more significant when we learn later in her testimony that Karin was deported in part because she lacked the protection of a valid work permit.[117]

Ringelblum made the important observation that many of those who risked their lives by crossing to the Aryan side to act as couriers—or *kashariyot*,[118] as they were called—for the resistance groups and to relay information, people, passports, and weapons in and out of the ghettos, or to sell belongings or purchase items to smuggle into the ghettos, were women. They usually ranged in age from 18 to 25, had blonde hair or hair dyed blonde, and blue eyes. Sexual attractiveness also proved an important asset to being able to successfully negotiate the various inspection and police patrols the women would necessarily encounter. The *kashariyot*, Ringelblum said,

---

[114] Jack Klajman, *Out of the Ghetto* (London: Vallentine Mitchell, 2000), 28.

[115] Cited in Ofer, 'Motherhood under Siege', 50. On the plight of children in the Warsaw ghetto, see Adolf Berman, 'The Fate of the Children in the Warsaw Ghetto', in Israel Gutman and Livia Rothkirchen (eds.), *The Catastrophe of European Jewry: Antecedents, History, Reflections* (Jerusalem: Yad Vashem, 1976), 400–21.

[116] Lucille Eichengreen, *From Ashes to Life: My Memories of the Holocaust* (San Francisco, CA: Mercury House, 1994), 48–9.

[117] For further discussion of Eichengreen's testimony, see Kirsty Chatwood, '(Re)-Interpreting Stories of Sexual Violence', in Esther Herzog (ed.), *Life, Death and Sacrifice: Women and the Family in the Holocaust* (Jerusalem: Gefen, 2008), 164–6.

[118] They were called *kashariyot* because they provided an important *kesher* (connection) with the world outside the ghetto. See Lenore J. Weitzman, 'Women of Courage: The *Kashariyot* (Couriers) in the Jewish Resistance during the Holocaust', in Jeffry M. Diefendorf (ed.), *Lessons and Legacies*, vol. 6: *New Currents in Holocaust Research* (Evanston, IL: Northwestern University Press, 2004), 112–52.

are venturesome courageous girls who travel here and there across Poland…
carrying Aryan papers which describe them as Polish or Ukrainian. One of
them even wears a cross, which she never leaves off and misses when she is in the
ghetto. Day by day they face the greatest dangers, relying completely on their
Aryan appearance and the kerchiefs they tie around their heads.[119]

Women were more able to do this than men, not least because Jewish men
were circumcised—and most Gentiles were not. There was, however, no such
difference between Jewish women and their non-Jewish counterparts—and
if they had blonde hair and blue eyes, then they were even more able to 'pass'
as Aryan.

Not all ghettos afforded the same opportunities for this clandestine
activity. In Łódź, where the ghetto was to all intents and purposes sealed
off from the outside world, it was particularly challenging. In Warsaw, by
contrast, smuggling provided employment for thousands of ghetto inhabitants. Despite the existence of the death penalty (decreed in October
1941) for smugglers, estimates at the time suggest that as much as 80 per
cent of food entering the ghetto was smuggled in.[120] Journalist Alexander
Donat describes the smugglers as 'the Ghetto's most important citizens, its
heroes'.[121] However, as with the other aspects of ghetto life, smuggling
was also subject to a strict hierarchy; middlemen, guards, and those who
risked their lives to purchase handfuls of goods to sell in the ghetto. At the
top were the professional smugglers, who wore smart clothes and ate in the
best restaurants, and appeared indifferent to the dangers they faced.
Women were not only less likely to reap the huge profits of the professional smugglers, but were altogether more vulnerable.[122]

Families headed by women were amongst the poorest in the ghettos.[123]
In Warsaw, around half of the ghetto's inhabitants were unemployed at
any one time and therefore lacked a regular income. Women, who had
constituted just 20 per cent of the Jewish workforce before the war, found
it particularly difficult to secure employment, and smuggling became a
primary means of survival—rather than a means of becoming rich. Among

---

[119] Ringelblum, 'The Girl Couriers of the Underground Movement' (19 May 1942),
Shoah Resource Center, <http://www.yadvashem.org/odot_pdf/Microsoft%20Word%20-%
202147.pdf>, site accessed 29 August 2016.
[120] See Israel Gutman, *The Jews of Warsaw, 1939–1943: Ghetto, Underground, Revolt*,
trans. Ina Friedman (Brighton: Harvester, 1982), 67. A clandestine economy started even
before the move to the ghettos with the issuing of the first ration cards.
[121] Alexander Donat, *The Holocaust Kingdom: A Memoir* (London: Corgi, 1967), 59.
[122] See Huberband, *Kiddush Hashem*, 34, 422.
[123] See Dalia Ofer, 'Cohesion and Rupture: The Jewish Family in East European
Ghettos during the Holocaust', in Peter Y. Medding (ed.), *Coping with Life and Death:
Jewish Families in the Twentieth Century* (Studies in Contemporary Jewry, 14) (New York:
Oxford University Press, 1998), 143–65.

the casualties were Feyge Margolies, a mother of two small children, who sneaked into Aryan Warsaw to buy goods to sell in the ghetto. She was caught and executed. Also murdered in this way was Dvoyre Rozenberg. Dvoyre's father had died, leaving her ill mother to care for several small children. As the eldest daughter, Dvoyre was forced to become the family's breadwinner. She fashioned a livelihood which consisted of smuggling a few kilograms of meat each day from nearby Otwock into the Warsaw ghetto. It was for this that she was killed.[124] Other women endured sexual assault. Avraham Tory, the secretary of the *Judenrat*, records that in the Kovno ghetto on 9 July 1943 a woman was forced to undress by a German officer. He commanded 'Spread your legs', and proceeded to examine her body orifices to check for hidden valuables.[125] Children too—some as young as 5 years old—sacrificed their lives squeezing through the ghetto walls or through the dark and dirty underground sewers to bring back food to feed their families, who were forced to wait anxiously at home. Others risked their lives to get to the other side of the wall only to return with nothing: the other side of the wall promised not salvation but all the miseries of life under the German occupation. Coupled with this was the ever-present fear of discovery.

This ubiquitous danger—of starvation, deportation, rape, and violence—made life for those on their own almost intolerable. Little wonder that many formed hasty partnerships. For example, Mary Berg made the observation that: 'One seldom meets a woman or a man alone. Men and women are attracted to each other even more than in normal times, as though thirsty for protection and tenderness.'[126] Although it is likely that the extreme deprivations of the ghetto had an anti-aphrodisiac effect for many, at least the better off among the ghetto population continued to crave sexual intimacy. There is also evidence to suggest that young people became increasingly unwilling to delay having sexual experiences.[127] It simply did not make sense for them to wait until marriage before consummating a relationship. Janina Bauman describes a friend being propositioned with the rationale 'with life as it is we shouldn't wait for our one true love before making love, because we might never live that long'.[128] It has also been suggested that many abandoned or orphaned children formed street gangs or makeshift families and became sexually

---

[124] Huberband, *Kiddush Hashem*, 158.
[125] Avraham Tory, *Surviving the Holocaust: The Kovno Ghetto Diary*, ed. Martin Gilbert (Cambridge, MA: Harvard University Press, 1991), 414.
[126] Berg, *Warsaw Ghetto: A Diary*, 111.
[127] See Roland, *Courage under Siege*, 48–50.
[128] Janina Bauman, *Winter in the Morning: A Young Girl's Life in the Warsaw Ghetto and Beyond 1939–1945* (London: Virago, 1991), 61.

active at a precocious age.[129] The lack of contraceptives made such encounters particularly risky as couples were forced to rely on coitus interruptus or condoms fashioned out of babies' pacifiers.[130]

At a time of such intense insecurity, intimate relationships became very important.[131] To put it simply, people didn't want to be alone and wanted to seek pleasure wherever they could. Marek Edelman, who was a commander in the Warsaw ghetto revolt, testifies to this:

> To be with someone was the only possible way to live in the ghetto. You would shut yourself up with another human being—in bed, in the cellar, anywhere—and then until the next round-up you were not alone ... People at that time wanted to form relationships more than ever before, more than ever in normal life. During the last deportations they ran to the *Judenrat*, looking for a rabbi, or anyone who would marry them, and they went to the *Umschlagplatz* [assembly point], as husband and wife.[132]

A sense of urgency and the belief that married men would not be deported for forced labour also led many young Jewish couples to get married in the ghettos despite the German decree forbidding them to do so.[133] Whilst they could not obtain official marriage licences, rabbis signed notes stating that the couples had married according to Jewish practice. Brides had to wear a Star of David on their wedding dress and wedding cakes were made out of potato peelings. However, once again, the elite were able to mark themselves out from the ghetto masses. A Warsaw diary entry cites the luxurious wedding of the daughter of Benjamin Zabludowski, a leading figure of the Jewish community: 'What is noticeable is that the champagne flowed like water.'[134] As Gustavo Corni rightly recognizes, what is important is not the accuracy of this description but the sense of indignity that the ghetto elites aroused.[135]

In 1942 there were mass deportations across all the ghettos of eastern Europe. Adam Czerniaków committed suicide during this time. He wrote in a suicide note to his wife: 'I am powerless. My heart trembles in sorrow

---

[129] See Roland, *Courage under Siege*, 177.

[130] Adam Czerniaków refers to such items: *The Warsaw Diary of Adam Czerniakow*, 330.

[131] For a discussion of oral testimony and sexuality in the ghettos, see Jonathan Friedman, 'Togetherness and Isolation: Holocaust Survivor Memories of Intimacy and Sexuality in the Ghettos', *Oral History Review*, 28/1 (Winter/Spring 2001), 1–16.

[132] Cited in Barbara Engelking, *Holocaust and Memory. The Experience of the Holocaust and its Consequences: An Investigation Based on Personal Narratives*, trans. Emma Harris, ed. Gunnar S. Paulsson (London: Leicester University Press, 2001), 127.

[133] Divorce, marriage, and funeral rites were all forbidden.

[134] Cited in Gustavo Corni, *Hitler's Ghettos: Voices from A Beleaguered Society 1939–1944* (London: Arnold, 2002), 175.

[135] Ibid.

and compassion. I can no longer bear all this.'[136] The daily deportations from Warsaw between 22 July and 21 September 1942 resulted in around 265,000 Jews being herded into sealed and overcrowded cattle trains and sent to the Treblinka death camp.

Each day thousands of Jews were forced to wait in the *Umschlagplatz*, without either food or water. Among the condemned were Cecilya Ślepak, her daughter, and the majority of her female subjects.[137] Her surviving notebooks, which she managed to pass to members of *Oneg Shabbat*, indicate that she was interviewing women as late as May 1942. Her subjects battled to survive until the very end. It is likely that even then many did not want to believe that they were going to their deaths. According to Marek Edelman, 'the Warsaw ghetto did not believe that their lives could be taken in such a manner'.[138] In response to the 'people, desperate and confused, delivered over to extinction', Rachel Auerbach wrote:

> My heart weeps even for the pettiest thief on Krochmalna Street; even for the worst of the knife wielders of narrow Mila, because even they were killed for being Jewish. Anointed and purified in the brotherhood of death. Ah, where are you, petty thieves of Warsaw; you illegal street vendors and sellers of rotten apples. And you, the more harmful folk—members of the great gangs who held their own courts; who supported their own synagogues in the Days of Awe; who conducted festive funerals and who gave alms like the most prosperous burghers.[139]

In August the ghetto's orphanages were liquidated. Before the war Dr Janusz Korczak (born Henryk Goldschmidt) had been the director of the largest Jewish orphanage in Warsaw. When the ghetto was established Korczak and the children were moved to a cramped building within the ghetto walls. On 5 August 1942 the Germans ordered that the 190 Jewish children be deported to Treblinka. Refusing offers from his Christian friends to take him into hiding Korczak accompanied the children to the *Umschlagplatz*, ultimately to go to the gas chambers with them.

Deportations continued until the ghetto was finally liquidated in May 1943. Faced with the inevitability of their destruction, and stripped of their families, the young people in the ghettos were both more able and more willing to engage in active resistance. While Jewish women were

---

[136] Joseph Kermish, 'Introduction', in Adam Czerniaków, *Yoman geto Varhsa* [Warsaw Ghetto Diary]: *6.9.1939–23.7.1942* (Jerusalem: Yad Vashem, 1968), xix.

[137] Rachel Auerbach reported that Ślepak's husband survived the war.

[138] Cited in Reuben Ainsztein, *Jewish Resistance in Nazi Occupied Eastern Europe* (London: Elek, 1974), 564.

[139] Cited in David G. Roskies, *The Jewish Search for a Useable Past* (Bloomington, IN: Indiana University Press, 1999), 38–9.

excluded from official leadership, they took on prominent roles in the underground resistance movement. The majority of the Jewish youth movements were socialist in origin, and therefore at least in principle granted equal rights to women. Prior to the war, in the expectation that it was men who were the first to be deported, several youth movements appointed female contingency leaderships.[140] Women such as Gisi (Gisela) Fleischmann, leader of the Slovakian Jewish community, have received a great deal of attention, but the women who participated in the forest partisan units or acted as couriers for the resistance, comparatively less so.[141] For those women who joined the Jewish or Soviet forest partisans, it was often necessary to secure the protection of a powerful man. While Nechama Tec states that 'if a woman did not like a man no one forced her',[142] it is likely that this was not true for all women. This sensitive issue of incidences of Jewish women being raped by Jewish men is only just beginning to be brought to light.

The resistance, however, attracted very few people of either gender. Far more significant in terms of numbers were those who simply escaped to the Aryan side, seeking salvation in hiding. Approximately 8,000 people managed to escape in this way from Warsaw alone, about two-thirds of whom were women. Of course, to escape many women were forced to abandon children or younger siblings, parents, and other family members. Whilst in hiding on the Aryan side, Warsaw ghetto fighter and activist Tuvia Borzykowski wrote: 'The streets look normal; nothing indicated that on the other side of the wall the greatest tragedy had taken place.'[143] Rachel Auerbach was among those who managed to escape to the Aryan side of Warsaw, where she was able to obtain Aryan documents and work as a courier for the Jewish underground and writer for the clandestine Jewish National Council.[144] Together with Hirsch Wasser she was responsible, in 1946, for digging up part of the *Oneg Shabbat* archives, which had been buried when the ghetto was liquidated. They, and

---

[140] Judith Tydor Baumel, *Double Jeopardy: Gender and the Holocaust* (London: Vallentine Mitchell, 1998), Chapter 4.

[141] See Yehuda Bauer, 'The Problem of Gender: The Case of Gisi Fleischmann', in *Rethinking the Holocaust* (New Haven, CT: Yale University Press, 2001), 167–85. For an excellent discussion of women's involvement in 'alternative leadership', see Judith Tydor Baumel, 'Women's Agency and Survival Strategies during the Holocaust', *Women's Studies International Forum*, 22/3 (1999), 337.

[142] Nechama Tec, 'Women among the Forest Partisans', in Ofer and Weitzman (eds.), *Women in the Holocaust*, 229.

[143] Tuvia Borzykowski, *Between Tumbling Walls*, trans. Mendel Kohansky (Tel Aviv: Hakkibutz Hameuchad, 1976), 123.

[144] For a description of her life on the Aryan side, see Rachel Auerbach, *Baym letstn veg: In Geto Varshe un oyf der arisher zayt* [At Road's End: In the Warsaw Ghetto and on the Aryan Side] (Tel Aviv: Am Oved, 1977).

Wasser's wife Bluma, were the sole survivors of *Oneg Shabbat*. While the extraordinary efforts of *Oneg Shabbat* undoubtedly provide a unique insight into life and death in the Warsaw ghetto, it is nevertheless little more than a glimpse. Whole families were murdered, leaving only the barest trace of their existence. The documents that remain from the *Oneg Shabbat* archives only serve to remind us of the vast chasm that the loss of Polish Jewry represents.

The voices of women from the ghettos thus reveal a variety of different experiences. There was no single ghetto experience. Gender, however, was both seen to be and was experienced as a critical force in shaping people's lives and deaths. The threat to the Jews was a threat to families—to family life and to the creation of new life—as well as a threat to individuals. Moreover, the victims of the Holocaust themselves acknowledged that this threat had different impacts on different genders. Importantly, too, we can see that what appeared to be the breakdown of patriarchal systems was not in fact a liberation for women. Quite the reverse proved to be the case, as the existential threat of the Holocaust left them more vulnerable, especially to sexualized attack. This was, as we shall see, only the beginning.

2

Hiding

It would be easy to follow those who were driven out of the ghettos straight to the concentration camps—and many histories do. But it is important, before we follow that path, not to forget those who had escaped into hiding. As we noted in the previous chapter, many ghettos proved to be porous—and, as the threat of deportation or liquidation grew ever greater, so the temptation of fleeing became harder to resist. Many of those who fled—at times, perhaps even a majority—were women. And, as we have seen, these women often possessed advantages that their menfolk did not. Some were better used to dealing with the Gentile world than their religious husbands. And they lacked the distinguishing feature—circumcision—which marked out most male Jews, religious or not.

But escape did not mean liberation, much less salvation. Women in hiding—especially Jewish women in hiding—were doubly vulnerable. They were vulnerable, of course, because they were Jews. They were subject to the Nazi racial laws; indeed, their very existence was an affront to the genocidal state. They were also victims of an anti-Semitic society. Although some non-Jews were sympathetic, many more were only too pleased to receive a reward for handing them over to the authorities, and others actively conspired in their extermination. These women were also, however, especially vulnerable, precisely because they were women. Those who were mothers, or had assumed a conventional caring role for families or friends, and who lacked the support of a male figure, had to assume intolerable burdens. All women—whether old or young, married or single—were also at the mercy of men. The sexual abuse and exploitation of women—by the invaders, the Aryan indigenous population, and by other Jews—was never systematic, but it was widespread. And the threat of rape was ever present. In that way, those who went into hiding—just as much as those who were deported to the camps—exhibit the continuing, deepening effects of gender on their experience of the Holocaust.

The issue of hiding also exposes the continuing effects of the Holocaust on the family. In a patriarchal society, children too are the victims of hierarchy—and their vulnerability was exacerbated, not dissipated, by the horrendous experiences through which they were living. Just like their mothers, boys and girls found themselves forced to cope without the familiar structures of an ordered life. Their fathers were often absent or unable to protect them. Their mothers, too, could not shield them—indeed, they sometimes needed their own children to protect them. It was an unsettling—a terrifying—world in which the old rules had been abandoned, without any new clarity about how to live in the present day. The threat of death, of abuse—sexual and otherwise—was omnipresent.

'Thousands of women were raped during the war, but no one hears about them ... The Anne Franks who survived rape don't write their stories', the Hungarian Holocaust survivor Judith Magyar Isaacson told her daughter.[1] And, indeed, this has—until comparatively recently—been the case. So much so, in fact, that when the Holocaust scholar Nechama Tec, a survivor of the Holocaust and sociologist who carried out one of the first major studies of hiding during the Holocaust, asked women about sexual abuse she found them reluctant to discuss the topic at all. This led her to conclude that 'Judging by the hesitation I encountered among interviewees to recount these coercive sexual experiences, I have to assume that most of these stories will die with the victims.'[2] Tec is correct in that, despite the work of three generations of scholars, it remains the case that rape during the Holocaust is both hard to find and hard to define. However, whilst rape does appear to play a limited role within the entirety of the Holocaust, a careful rereading of testimony—in particular, the silences within testimony—can reveal that women in hiding were extremely vulnerable to rape and sexual abuse.

It must be said that historians of the Holocaust have questioned whether it is useful—or even appropriate—to explore rape and sexual abuse in the context of the destruction of European Jewry. Rape, it is argued, is a universal fact of life in both war and civilian society, so its analysis adds little to the history of the specific events of the Holocaust. As a result even those who have specifically explored the experiences of women in hiding have tended to disregard the issue of rape and sexual abuse. As Joan Ringelheim has written: 'Some think it inappropriate to talk about these matters; discussions about sexuality desecrate the memories of the dead, or the living, or the Holocaust itself. For others, it is simply too difficult and painful. Still others think it may be a trivial issue.'[3]

---

[1] Judith Magyar Isaacson, *Seed of Sarah: Memoirs of a Survivor* (Chicago, IL: University of Illinois Press, 1991), 143–4.

[2] Nechama Tec, *When Light Pierced the Darkness: Christian Rescue of Jews in Nazi-Occupied Poland* (New York: Oxford University Press, 1986).

[3] See Joan Ringelheim, 'Women and the Holocaust: A Reconsideration of Research', in Carol Rittner and John K. Roth (eds.), *Different Voices: Women and the Holocaust* (New York: Paragon House, 1993), 377.

Moreover, it should be admitted that uncovering rape and sexual violence so many years after the event presents serious methodological challenges to the historian. To the most part we have to rely on the memories of survivors to uncover the existence of rape and sexual violence.[4] This is made more problematic still because accounts of experiences of rape and sexual abuse are mostly oblique or told through the lens of another person—a friend or a relative, for example. While these feints mirror the difficulties of talking or writing about rape in civilian society it nevertheless makes it difficult to undertake a serious, considered analysis of rape and sexual abuse during the Holocaust. In other words, although it is absolutely clear that large numbers of women were raped or sexually exploited we still struggle to distinguish between rape and sexual exploitation and ultimately we must accept that we will never know exactly how many women were raped or abused during the Holocaust.

The organized rape of Jewish women was certainly not part of the official German genocidal policy. 'The Law for the Protection of German Blood and German Honour' passed on 15 September 1935 applied both to marriage and extramarital affairs as well as forced intercourse. The fact that this legislation made any sexual contact—consensual or non-consensual—a criminal offence does not mean that Jewish women in the Reich were immune from sexual violence: far from it. We have already seen that Jewish women were raped in the ghettos. Moreover, the sexual exploitation and abuse of women—whether through violence or simple sexual humiliation—played a significant role in the Nazi attack on the Jewish family. It is noteworthy too that Jewish women were also vulnerable to sexual assault by other powerful men—whether they were allies of the Germans or even fellow Jews.

In fact, the prohibition on sex between Jews and Germans, far from prohibiting rape, actually made Jewish women more vulnerable. For the women, accusing a German of rape merely left them open to accusations of *Rassenschande* ('race defilement'). At best this would involve the woman's imprisonment. At worst this was a ticket to the camps. For the men, however, the situation was reversed. Precisely because all sexual contact was illegal, there was an inducement for Germans to silence their Jewish sexual partners. This was true for what might be described as consensual sex and still more necessary after rape. The price of rape for the woman therefore was very likely often to be death.

---

[4] See Annabelle Baldwin, 'Sexual Violence and the Holocaust: Reflections on Memory and Witness Testimony', *Holocaust Studies: A Journal of Culture and History*, 16/3 (2010), 112–34.

Furthermore, there is evidence to the effect that, in the German satellite countries of Croatia, Bulgaria, Hungary, Romania, Slovakia, and Lithuania—where it was the local authorities rather than the Germans who took responsibility for the persecution and murder of the Jews— Jewish women were subject to forced sex and to the sort of sexual violence that we might term rape.[5] Moreover, as the historian Wendy Lower has argued, actions on this, the periphery of the Nazi genocide, were less scrutinized and therefore potentially more brutal.[6] For women who were attempting to pass as Aryan the situation was particularly precarious.

Unlike Anne Frank and her family, hiding together in an attic with the help of Gentile friends, most Jewish women did not literally hide themselves away, but instead attempted to live the life of normal citizens by passing as 'Aryan', some alone and others with family members. Some acquired forged documents and moved from place to place, both in cities and small villages, hiding in convents and monasteries, in factories, and sometimes posing as non-Jews in forced labour or concentration camps. Others lived without documents and survived by concealing themselves in fields, forests, graveyards, attics, stables, cellars, and wardrobes, often moving constantly from one place to another. Physical hiding, Deborah Dwórk explains, 'meant that all or nearly all ties with society were severed'.[7] Whole families rarely went into hiding together as it was almost impossible to hide with very young children. The ability to be a parent to one's child had become impossible under Nazi rule. Children were not allowed to live and parents were unable to protect them. This constituted a very specific assault against women as they experienced the loss of their children as a physical blow. For the women forced to smother their babies, so hiding places would not be discovered, and for those who were compelled to leave them to survive alone, this meant an end to their biological and maternal roles as mothers and caregivers.

In Warsaw, where it is thought that more Jews went into hiding than in any other European city, it is estimated that about two-thirds of Jews in hiding on the so-called 'Aryan' side were women.[8] Writing on the

[5] Helen Fein, 'Genocide and Gender: The Uses of Women and Group Destiny', *Journal of Genocide Research*, 1/1 (1999), 53.

[6] Wendy Lower, '"Anticipatory Obedience" and the Nazi Implementation of the Holocaust in the Ukraine: A Case Study of Central and Peripheral Forces in the Generalbezirk Zhytomyr, 1941–1944', *Holocaust and Genocide Studies*, 16/1 (2002), 8.

[7] Deborah Dwórk, *Children with a Star: Jewish Youth in Nazi Europe* (New Haven, CT: Yale University Press, 1993), 68.

[8] Gunnar S. Paulsson, *Secret City: The Hidden Jews of Warsaw, 1940–1945* (New Haven, CT: Yale University Press, 2002). See also idem, 'The Demography of Jews in Hiding in Warsaw, 1943–1945,' in Antony Polonsky (ed.), *Polin: Studies in Polish Jewry*.

predominance of women among those who lived in open hiding in Poland, Lenore Weitzman notes that 'it may be explained, at least in part, by the fact that women were more likely to believe that they could pass initially and were more self-confident when they embarked on their new lives. Men, by contrast, were more reluctant to try.'[9] She compares being circumcised to 'other distinguishing physical or social characteristics, such as dark hair, or a prominent nose, or a distinctive accent'.[10] In addition to stereotypically Jewish features, the markings of emotional and physical suffering and a lack of financial resources limited men's and women's ability to pass as 'Aryan'.

Women's social and economic status, education, work experience, linguistic ability, and religious background also either facilitated or hindered the ability to hide. The country in which they were trying to hide or 'pass', however, was probably most important. In Poland—and particularly in Warsaw—women had achieved considerable cultural assimilation. Prior to the war religious Jewish families sent their sons to exclusively male Jewish schools. Following from this Weitzman makes the important argument that:

> Ironically, the 'inferior' non-Jewish education that Jewish girls were more likely to receive provided them with knowledge and contacts that helped them to pass—such as the ability to speak colloquial Polish, familiarity with Polish customs (and Catholic prayers and rituals), a sense of the patterns and nuances of social interaction, personal networks and contacts in the non-Jewish world of their Polish classmates, and sometimes a few friends to whom they might be able to turn for help.[11]

Paula Hyman supports this: '[T]he same families that chose for their sons various forms of private Jewish education, whether of traditional or modernized curriculum, often sent their daughters to public primary schools,

vol. 13: *Focusing on the Holocaust and its Aftermath* (London: The Littman Library of Jewish Civilization, 2000), 78–103.

[9] Lenore J. Weitzman, 'Living on the Aryan Side in Poland: Gender, Passing, and the Nature of Resistance', in Dalia Ofer and Lenore J. Weitzman (eds.), *Women in the Holocaust* (New Haven, CT: Yale University Press, 1998), 203.

[10] Ibid. For an excellent discussion of the myriad of ways in which women had to blend linguistically and culturally with the non-Jewish population, see Nechama Tec, 'Sex Distinctions and Passing as Christians during the Holocaust', *East European Quarterly*, 18/1 (March 1984), 113–23.

[11] Weitzman, 'Living on the Aryan Side in Poland', 204. On French Jews in hiding, see Susan Zuccotti, *The Holocaust, the French, and the Jews* (Lincoln, NE: University of Nebraska Press, 1993). On Dutch Jews who went into hiding, see Bob Moore, *Victims and Survivors: The Nazi Persecution of the Jews in the Netherlands 1940–1945* (London: Hodder, 1997).

where they were introduced to secular culture'[12]—which, unintentionally, better prepared them to survive. Prior contact with non-Jewish Poles meant less resistance when it came to trusting them later. In Poland there was a great deal of distrust of the Polish Gentile population amongst the Jews. This was significantly lessened when Jews were allowed to form meaningful relationships with people outside their own religious and cultural circles. Without these relationships it was also nearly impossible to escape the ghetto walls. To escape the Warsaw ghetto, for example, one needed money to bribe the German police and then friends willing to risk their lives on the other side. Acquiring false papers was also dependent on Polish cooperation. The best false papers consisted of a birth or baptism certificate of someone who had died, supplemented with a real photograph of the new owner which somehow managed to disguise any distinctive Jewish features, an authentic-sounding Aryan name, and a place of birth that the Germans could no longer verify.[13]

Vladka Meed was a young girl when the Germans occupied her native city of Warsaw. When her father's small haberdashery store was closed down, the family were left without an income. Her mother was terrified that her father and brother would be caught by the Germans and deported if they ventured outside, so, as the oldest girl, she was forced to adopt an Aryan identity and go out and sell clothes and other belongings to support her family. The family wrongly believed that the Germans would not hurt women. Having managed to escape the ghetto she survived on the Aryan side as a courier for the Jewish underground resistance movement. She remembers: 'During the murmured prayers my imagination would carry me back to a world now gone from me ... to my father, who had died of pneumonia in the ghetto. I saw him standing, his prayer shawl draped over his head.'[14] Meed was the only one of her family of five to survive. Her testimony, however, shows that it was not enough to speak perfect Polish; that Polish had to be completely idiomatically indistinguishable from that of non-Jewish Poles. It was also not enough to be familiar with local customs and cultures and comfortable with Christian prayers and practices; a Jew passing as Aryan needed to create an entire fictional history that was compatible with that of those around them. For some the strain, loneliness, and uncertainty of living under an assumed identity was so

---

[12] Paula E. Hyman, 'Gender and the Jewish Family in Modern Europe', in Ofer and Weitzman (eds.), *Women in the Holocaust*, 33.

[13] See Barbara Engelking, *Holocaust and Memory: The Experience of the Holocaust and its Consequences: An Investigation Based on Personal Narratives*, trans. Emma Harris, ed. Gunnar S. Paulsson (London: Leicester University Press, 2001), 46.

[14] Vladka Meed, *On Both Sides of the Wall: Memoirs from the Warsaw Ghetto*, trans. Benjamin Meed (Tel Aviv: Hakibutz Hameuchad, 1973), 216.

great that they decided to return to the ghettos and face an almost certain death with their fellow Jews.

In Germany, the situation was somewhat different. Although there were a substantial number of observant Jews, there were more Jews who were either partially or totally assimilated into the non-Jewish culture. These families were uninterested in following a traditionally Jewish way of life and instead engaged in the dominant cultural traditions, for example celebrating Christmas rather than observing Jewish holidays, and ignoring the Jewish dietary laws. In Germany men were more likely to hold prominent positions in banking and industry and children mostly attended non-Jewish schools. However, here too—perhaps on account of their greater involvement with their children—Jewish women seemed to have a better grasp of German society and culture than did the men. According to Marion Kaplan, some estimates suggest that between 10,000 and 12,000 German Jews went into hiding, and only about 25 per cent survived. 'Men in hiding were in greater danger of being caught than women', she wrote, explaining that most German men of military age had been drafted. She continues:

> Jewish women could blend in among German women more easily as servants or nannies. Indeed, one Jewish woman, introduced as the hider's aunt, had an ersatz coffee now and then with the Nazi block warden, while another, introduced as the hider's fiancée, had to accept the suspicious and dangerous friendship of a leader of the Nazi women's organization.[15]

Importantly, Kaplan also points to other perils of going into hiding in Germany: 'Some young women even resorted to exchanging sex for shelter, including working in brothels in Berlin.'[16] However, she also notes a *Rassenschande* court case involving Jewish women in hiding and reports that the women convicted of exchanging sex for shelter were then murdered.

It was not only in Germany that women were offered protection in exchange for sex. Janina Bauman, who escaped the Warsaw ghetto to go into hiding on the Aryan side with her mother and sister in January 1943, describes how she was propositioned by a Polish man who had discovered her hiding place. As he groped her—and clearly attempted to rape her—he stated: 'I have decided to help you. I'll take you with me to my own

---

[15] Marion Kaplan, *Between Dignity and Despair: Jewish Life in Nazi Germany* (New York: Oxford University Press, 1998), 203.

[16] Ibid., 209. In note 15 attached to the quoted material, Kaplan cites Holocaust scholar Konrad Kwiet, who told her that brothels in Berlin are mentioned in several memoirs deposited in the Wiener Library for the Study of the Holocaust and Genocide, London.

villa. You'll live safe with me there till the end of the war, or maybe forever.'[17] While she was able to evade her assailant it cannot be known how many other women succumbed to this type of pressure. They, of course, are less likely to write their testimony.

Other women who did indeed decide to seek protection have come to view it somewhat ambiguously. In her testimony published in 1993, Fanya Gottesfeld Heller describes what she classifies as a consensual sexual relationship between herself as a teenager and Jan, a Ukrainian militiaman who rescued and protected her family—from both the Nazis and the violently anti-Semitic Ukrainian villagers who hounded them. Her parents knew that it was the man's feelings for their teenage daughter that motivated him to hide them, feed them, and protect them. Gottesfeld Heller is clear that her parents did not verbally acknowledge the relationship, but they were well aware that their daughter was sexually involved with this non-Jewish, illiterate man from a lower social class. She has clearly had time to consider the relationship and ultimately must be allowed to interpret it in a way that makes sense to her. Indeed, she is very careful to emphasize the non-violent nature of their sexual relations: 'Jan was very gentle, careful not to rush me, passion so well-anointed with affection that during those first three days of our intimacy I could not say precisely when I stopped being a virgin.'[18] Nevertheless, whether a relationship based on such an extreme power imbalance can be understood in terms of consent is surely questionable, despite Gottesfeld Heller's insistence on its reciprocity. It is also not hard to imagine that if this is one of the 'better' relationships produced by this striking power imbalance, then the worst would surely amount to sexual exploitation—indeed, to rape.

The shame and guilt of having to resort to her sexuality in order to survive continued to haunt Gottesfeld Heller after her liberation even though the relationship without doubt saved her family. Trying to envisage a life married to Jan and as the mother of his children, she focused on the impossibility of finding a home as 'a lone Jew among Ukrainians, who hated and had murdered my people'.[19] She continues:

> How could I condemn my babies to grow up in Poland, or the Ukraine, the graveyard for millions of Jews? No, not a graveyard, for there were no graves. The Jews had been burned to ashes and the ashes had turned to dust which was in the air we breathed and the water we drank . . . I saw myself holding a

[17] Janina Bauman, *Beyond these Walls: Escaping the Warsaw Ghetto—A Young Girl's Story* (London: Virago, 2006), 166.

[18] Fanya Gottesfeld Heller, *Strange and Unexpected Love: A Teenage Girl's Holocaust Memoirs* (Hoboken, NJ: Ktav, 1993), 159.

[19] Ibid., 275.

baby to my breast, and my breast and the baby were black with the ashes of their murdered relatives. Black milk came out of my breast.[20]

To resolve this impossible conflict she decided instead to bury her experiences and enter into a hastily arranged marriage with a young Jewish man named Joseph:

> He was told that I was a very nice girl, intelligent, educated, and from a fine family, but that I'd had an affair with a *goy* [non-Jew]. 'You know', he said to me, 'if you tell me that you're a virgin, I'll buy you the nicest Persian lamb coat'. I told him, 'you can save yourself the coat'. He said nothing more and never asked me about Jan, not then and not ever, and I respected him for this.[21]

It appears from her testimony that Gottesfeld Heller interpreted her ability to build a new life for herself after the Holocaust as dependent on her ability to suppress her difficult and often ambiguous wartime experiences, and it was important for her to find a partner who could support her in this. The pejorative use of the term 'goy' clearly indicates the potential and ongoing stigma of a young Jewish woman who had entered into a sexual relationship with a non-Jewish man. By marrying a Jew, Gottesfeld Heller was able to avoid this fate by reabsorbing herself into a respectable Jewish community, thereby drawing a line between her present and her past. At the same time, however, it is equally obvious that Gottesfeld Heller was ultimately unable to bury the experience—not least because Jan, her wartime 'protector', was accused by her family of murdering her father upon liberation by the Soviet Army. She began therapy in 1969, and it was this process that very gradually led to her being able to write her memoir, in which the enduring silence of her family is a key theme.

In a similar vein, Joan Ringelheim presents the experience of a Jewish survivor whom she calls 'Pauline', who was molested by the male relatives of the people hiding her. Because Pauline was told that if she complained they would denounce her, she didn't tell her twin sister, who was hiding with her. Nor did she tell the young Jewish woman who checked on them from time to time.[22] In an interview in 1984, she confessed to Ringelheim that the effects of this on her life were enduring: 'I can still feel the fear . . . Sometimes I think it was equally as frightening as the

---

[20] Ibid.   [21] Ibid., 278.

[22] Joan Ringelheim, 'The Split between Gender and the Holocaust', in Ofer and Weitzman (eds.), *Women in the Holocaust*, 343. See also Myrna Goldenberg's excellent essay 'Rape during the Holocaust', in Zygmunt Mazur, Jay T. Lees, Arnold Krammer, and Władysław Witalisz (eds.), *The Legacy of the Holocaust: Women and the* Holocaust (Kraków: Jagiellonian University Press, 2007), 159–69.

Germans. It became with me a tremendous . . . I [didn't] know how [to deal with it] . . . what to do with it. I had nobody to talk [to] about it. Nobody to turn to.'[23] It was an experience that, as Pauline herself realizes, is not easily reconciled with traditional Holocaust narratives. She asks: 'In respect of what happened, [what we] suffered and saw—the humiliation in the ghetto, seeing people jumping out and burned—is this [molestation] important?'[24] After the war she didn't tell her husband or daughter what had happened. In the words of Ringelheim: 'Her memory was split between traditional versions of Holocaust history and her own experiences.'[25]

In the few testimonies that do manage to talk about rape and sexual abuse in hiding, the experiences are mostly hinted at or attributed to another person—a friend or aunt, for example. These feints, of course, mirror the difficulties of talking or writing about rape in civilian society and then being believed. For example, Fanya Gottesfeld Heller waited fifty years before writing about the rape of her aunt in front of her husband, after a Gestapo raid:

> Unable to find me, Gottschalk [an NCO who had developed a crush on her] and his henchmen left and went looking for me at the home of one of my aunts. When they didn't find me there, they raped her and forced her husband to watch. The rape had to be kept secret because if the Gestapo [presumably she is referring to the higher ranks] found out about it they would have killed her immediately, since Germans were forbidden to 'fraternize' with 'subhuman' Jews. My aunt told a few members of the family but they didn't believe her—they didn't want to hear or know about it. She never told her children, and for that reason, I have not disclosed her name.[26]

As perpetrators of rape know all too well, rape silences women in a way that deliberately alienates them from their families and communities.[27] Historically, a victorious army will rape the women of the conquered people as a permanent mark of their victory. By forcing Gottesfeld Heller's aunt's husband to watch the rape, the aggressors were reinforcing what they considered to be the passivity of their Jewish victims.

The situation of Jewish women in hiding or open hiding during the Holocaust was strikingly precarious—they were surviving on the margins of society, and this made them extremely vulnerable. These women were

[23] Ringelheim, 'The Split between Gender and the Holocaust'.   [24] Ibid.
[25] Ibid., 344.   [26] Gottesfeld Heller, *Strange and Unexpected Love*, 81.
[27] See Susan Brownmiller, *Against our Will: Men, Women, and Rape* (New York: Simon & Schuster, 1975), 35. See also Christoph Schiessl, 'An Element of Genocide: Rape, Total War, and International Law in the Twentieth Century', *Journal of Genocide Research*, 4/2 (2002), 198.

uniquely dependent on the support and 'sympathy' of the local popula-
tions to spare them from physical, emotional, and sexual vulnerability.
A young woman, 'A.G. (maiden name R.)', who escaped from the Warsaw
ghetto with her grandfather, describes seeking refuge in a flat belonging to
Roman, a Polish sailor, but, she says, she 'only stayed there a short while'
because 'Roman was always bothering me and we were afraid his jealous
wife would denounce us to the police.'[28] In other testimonies, we are told
that it was the fear of rape that prompted the decision to flee and hide. In
Tylicz, Poland, Rena Kornreich Gelissen was observed walking to work by
a German soldier who later that night, very drunk, decided to go looking
for her. Her parents covered her with straw and were forced to stand by
and watch as the soldier poked through the straw with his rifle threatening, 'Perhaps you want to tell me before I stab her through her pretty
eye!'[29] As a result of the encounter, her parents decided that it was too
dangerous for their daughter to remain at home and arranged for her to be
smuggled across the border into Slovakia.

Some women managed to outwit their attackers. For example, Lawrence
Langer cites a woman named 'Celia K.', who at 18 fled the ghetto and left
her mother, brothers, sister, nephews, and nieces to go into hiding with
one of her sisters. Her brother, a partisan, brought the two girls a gun,
warning them, '[T]his gun is more valuable than anything I have. I am
giving it to you and I want you to use it if the Germans ever capture you.
You must never, never under any circumstances get caught alive.' To
underscore this point he told them what the Germans were doing to the
Jewish women they caught, reminding them once more, 'If you know the
Germans are going to catch you, one of you must shoot the other and then
shoot yourself.'[30] In another memoir, a young woman named Ewa Safs-
zycka, at 17 years of age, escaped from the Siedlce ghetto (Poland) and hid
in an empty brick factory. There she encountered a watchman who, she
said, 'probably understood who I was'. She recounts: '[R]oughly he tried
to rape me, threatening that if I did not go along, he would denounce me.'
Ewa fought back, saying, 'Take me to the Germans,' and after that, she
said, 'he gave up and left'.[31]

---

[28] 'Eyewitness Testimony 26. On Both Sides of the Ghetto Wall', in Isaiah Trunk,
Jewish Responses to Nazi Persecution (New York: Stein & Day, 1982), 183.

[29] Rena Kornreich Gelissen (with Heather Dune Macadam), *Rena's Promise: A Story of
Sisters in Auschwitz* (London: Weidenfeld & Nicolson, 1996), 30–1.

[30] Lawrence Langer, *Holocaust Testimonies: The Ruins of Memory* (New Haven, CT: Yale
University Press, 1991), 10.

[31] Cited in Nechama Tec, *Resilience and Courage: Women, Men and the Holocaust* (New
Haven, CT: Yale University Press, 2003), 224.

Young girls trying to survive on their own often sought out—if they could—the protection of partisan groups. Helen Lewine was forced to hide in a hole in the ground for six months. Aged 13, she managed to seek out the protection of a partisan unit. She remembers:

> As a girl of 13, I had nobody and when I found out that there was a partisan unit, I felt yes, I want some protection. They will help me and I could help them—in any way they tell me. I think I looked more for myself. I did not want to be all by myself. I was still a child and I was looking for somebody, to belong someplace and to do whatever they wanted me to do.[32]

Lewine formed a relationship with the leader of the partisan group—a 21-year-old man—whom she went on to marry after the war. The experience of Lewine underscores the point that women—and in particular young women—were desperately trying to replace the families they had lost. Still very much a child, Lewine did not want to have to face survival on her own. Similarly, in Alicia Appelman-Jurman's testimony, her dread of being separated from her beloved mother in many ways overshadowed her fear of being caught by the Gestapo. Appelman-Jurman hid with her mother in Podole—a rural part of the Ukraine annexed by Poland after World War I. She writes:

> My mother and I decided on a plan that called for her to remain hidden in the ravine while I worked on building up a rapport with the local farmers. It was not enough just to work for them in the summer; I also had to earn their fondness and sympathy for the wintertime, when there would be no work and I would have to go begging. It was out of the question for my mother to try to work; she would be too easily recognized as a Jewess. The sadness and pain that had settled permanently in her eyes would betray her.
>
> We agreed that she would hide in the wheat fields or in the ravine during the day, and I would bring food for her after my work was through. When I thought of my mother hiding day in day out in the wheat—trembling at every sound, wondering if I would come back or if I had been found out and caught, and waiting, waiting all day with nothing to do, totally dependent on her child for survival—my heart ached for her. But that was how it had to be if we were to survive.[33]

Alicia had already lost her father and brothers when she and her mother went into hiding. Inevitably she also went on to experience the murder of

[32] 'Panel on Resistance and Non-Compliance', in Esther Katz and Joan Miriam Ringelheim (eds.), *Proceedings of the Conference: Women Surviving the Holocaust* (New York: Occasional Papers from The Institute for Research in History, 1983), 60.

[33] Alicia Appelman-Jurman, *Alicia: My Story* (New York: Bantam, 1990), 134.

her mother. Like the majority of those in hiding she was forced to try and survive alone.

Married couples in hiding were not only forced to separate but could very rarely keep children under the age of 16 with them. Janina David, an only child, was just 13 years old when she was forced to leave her parents in the Warsaw ghetto. Sheltered by a Polish woman and, ultimately, by a German-born husband on the Aryan side, she witnessed the destruction of the ghetto from her hiding place. She remembers:

> I sat in the back bedroom staring hypnotically at the column of smoke, trying to imagine what my parents were doing. It was easy to see Father with a gun, but what had happened to Mother? Was she crouching somewhere in a cellar as we did during those forty-eight hours before I left them? Was she trembling and crying alone, crowded among strangers, waiting for that final explosion? My heart turned over in misery. I had no right to leave her. My place was there. Even though I could not help or protect her at least there would have been the two of us together.[34]

While she longed to return to her mother, her own hiding place had become too dangerous and the family hiding her arranged for her to enter a Catholic convent under a false identity. She survived the war there, constantly terrified that her true identity would be discovered. Her parents did not survive.

The experience of hiding further contributed to the crisis of the Jewish family. Even more than in the ghetto, hiding made family life all but impossible; indeed, it made families more exposed to danger than individuals. Unable to protect their families, Jewish men experienced a powerful sense of impotence and failure to fulfil their gendered role as protectors and patriarchs. The diary of Aryeh (Leon) Klonicki-Klonymus, written in pencil in Hebrew and covering ninety small notebooks, describes this process in unremitting detail; he writes of his desperation to save his 3-month-old son, Adam, and keep his family together. Klonicki, a teacher, together with his wife Malwina née Hertzmann, also a teacher, and young baby fled Buczacz (Buchach) in eastern Galicia moving from one village to another in a futile attempt to find a safe hiding place. They lacked food, clothing, and money. The diary covers just a fortnight of this desperate plight. The first entry records:

> A new period has begun here since the end of June 1943: it is the era of 'liquidation'. A Jew is no longer allowed to remain alive. Whenever a Jew is met anywhere he is taken to be killed. They look for the Jews everywhere, in

---

[34] Janina David, *A Square of Sky: Memoirs of a Wartime Childhood* (London: Eland, 1992).

the hideouts, at the homes of Christian families and in the fields. If it weren't
for the hatred of local inhabitants one could still find a way of hiding. But, as
things are, it is difficult. Every shepherd or Christian child who sees a Jew
immediately reports him to the authorities who lose no time following up
these reports. There are some Christians who are ostensibly prepared to hide
Jews for full payment. But actually no sooner have they robbed their victims
of all their belongings, than they hand them over to the authorities. There are
some local Christians who have gained distinction in the discovery of Jewish
hideouts. There is an eight-year-old boy (a Christian one, of course) who
loiters all day long in Jewish houses and has uncovered many a hideout.[35]

In order to escape the Germans the Jews were forced to hide in increasingly desperate places—for example, cellars and underground sewers. At
one stage, hiding in a cellar with his son, Klonicki writes:

> I had some heated encounters with fellow Jews who were hiding. They
> demanded that I allow the strangling of my child. Among them were mothers
> whose children had already met this fate. Of course I replied to them that as
> long as I was alive such a thing would not come to pass.[36]

Women, often acting without their husbands, found their role as mother
just as hard to fulfil. Indeed, the very fact that they were mothers made
survival more difficult. Women with small children were often prevented
from accessing hiding places as children were such an obvious liability.
Edyta Klein-Smith, a child in the Warsaw ghetto, remembers hiding with
her stepfather together with a woman and her young baby. When the
Germans started banging on the door and shooting, the baby cried, so the
mother was forced to smother it.[37] The grim logic of survival left some
children witnesses to the murder of their siblings by their own parents.

Genia Weinberg actually gave birth to a baby boy in a sewer in the
Polish city of Lvov (Lwów). All she had at her disposal was a pair of rusty
scissors and a towel. Although he was born alive the mother knew that it
would be almost impossible to care for a baby under such dire conditions.
She was therefore faced with the dilemma of whether to attempt to keep
the child at all costs or to sacrifice its life for the sake of her fellow Jews in
hiding, for its cries would certainly attract attention from the streets above.

---

[35] Aryeh Klonicki and Malwina Klonicki, *The Diary of Aryeh Klonicki (Klonymus) and his Wife Malwina, with Letters Concerning the Fate of their Child Adam*, trans. Avner Tomaschaff (Tel Aviv: Ghetto Fighters House, 1973), 25.

[36] Cited in David Patterson, *Along the Edge of Annihilation: The Collapse and Recovery of Life in the Holocaust Diary* (Seattle, WA: Washington University Press, 1999), 194–5.

[37] Lynn Smith, *Remembering: Voices of the Holocaust. A New History in the Words of the Men and Women Who Survived* (New York: Carroll & Graf, 2006), 121.

It is difficult to know exactly what happened but it appears that the baby's life was sacrificed to the safety of the group.[38]

Klonicki and his wife, however, left their hiding place. Desperately trying to find more help, Klonicki describes how one of the few 'Christians' willing to assist the family, their former maid Franka, was prevented from doing so by fear. '[S]he is afraid. Posters have been placed throughout town announcing the death penalty for anyone hiding Jews. This is the reason for our being out in the field rather than at her home.'[39] Klonicki bemoaned the fact that they had had Adam circumcised:

> What a pity that I gave in to my zealously devout father-in-law and allowed my son to undergo circumcision. Now vengeance is being taken upon us in an awful way. Had he remained uncircumcised, there would have been no difficulty in finding a peasant to look after him till the war's end, but now they are afraid to do so.[40]

Instead, the fate of Adam seemed sealed: 'How many times', wrote Klonicki, 'would I look at my little child, so handsome and full of life, and it would seem to me that it is not a child I am looking at but a box filled with ashes'.[41] However, they were finally able to find a convent that agreed to take in their son:

> On a dark night as the rain was coming down in torrents my wife and I took our boy with a sack full of belongings . . . We left him together with the sack in the corridor of the convent and hurriedly ran off. The nuns had advised us to keep the whole thing secret. We are overjoyed at having succeeded in arranging for our child's keep under such favourable conditions. I was not bothered by the fact that they would baptize the child.[42]

It is thought that Aryeh and Malwina were murdered by the Germans in a forest near Buczacz sometime in January 1944. Aryeh's notebooks were found buried in the ground together with a letter Malwina had written to her relatives in America but never got to send. She wrote to them: 'I want so much to bring up my adored son, to get pleasure from him, is it possible? It is even difficult to dream about.'[43] It is not known what happened to Adam. After the war family members in the USA and Israel, as well as the Joint Distribution Committee (a Jewish humanitarian assistance organization), carried out extensive searches for the child. Like many such investigations, they proved futile. For adult survivors trying to find their children after the war, it has not been easy. Particularly when

---

[38] The story is told by Robert Marshall, *In the Sewers of Lvov: The Last Sanctuary from the Holocaust* (London: Fontana, 1991).
[39] Klonicki and Klonicki, *The Diary of Aryeh Klonicki (Klonymus) and his Wife Malwina*, 31.
[40] Ibid., 21–2.   [41] Ibid., 24.   [42] Ibid., 33–4.   [43] Ibid., 46.

children were baptized and had their names changed, they were often destined never to be found.

The fate of many Jewish children remains unknown. Approximately 10,000 mostly Jewish children aged between 5 and 16 years from Germany and German-annexed territories were sent on the *Kindertransport* to England prior to the outbreak of war in 1939.[44] Most would never see their parents again. A further 6,000 children were sent to Palestine by the Youth Aliyah Jewish child rescue organization. In France, the 5,000 inhabitants of the isolated village of Le Chambon-sur-Lignon (Auvergne region) volunteered to hide a group of Jewish children who had managed to escape from their children's home just before the Nazis arrived to deport them.[45] Other families, in both western and eastern Europe, were forced to leave their children in Catholic orphanages, nurseries, convents, monasteries, and boarding schools. On occasion, the Gentile nannies, servants, and other domestic workers employed by Jewish families before the war risked their lives to shelter Jewish children.

For all parents, regardless of individual circumstances, these forcible separations were agonizing. For many women, in particular, who had given birth to the children and for the most part had been their primary carers, the pain must have been unbearable. Many of the resistance organizations who found hiding places for Jewish children refused to reveal their whereabouts even to the children's parents for fear that if caught and interrogated they might under duress reveal names and addresses. In Poland, the Governor-General Hans Frank issued a decree on 15 October 1941 to the effect that anyone—including the clergy—found harbouring a Jewish adult or child was sentenced to death. In November 1941, Ernst Kundt, the governor of Radom district (Poland), ordered the death penalty for any Jew who left the ghetto and any Gentiles who supplied them with food or shelter. Posters were put up around Poland informing people of this fate. A further directive was issued by the SS on 28 October 1942, extending the death penalty to anyone *knowing* of a Jew in hiding and failing to report it. If this were not enough, the existence of concentration and death camps on Polish soil was an additional reminder of the punishments that could be meted out to anyone who

[44] For the stories of some of these children, see Karen Gershon (ed.), *We Came as Children: A Collective Autobiography of Refugees* (London: Macmillan, 1996), and Bertha Leverton and Shmuel Lowensohn (eds.), *I Came Alone: The Stories of the Kindertransport* (Lewes: Book Guild Publishing, 1990).

[45] See Patrick Henry, 'Banishing the Coercion of Despair: Le Chambon-sur-Lignon and the Holocaust Today', *Shofar: An Interdisciplinary Journal of Jewish Studies*, 20/2 (2001), 69–84.

opposed the German occupation. It was at this time that the Germans also began liquidating Jewish orphanages.

Nevertheless, the Council for Aid to Jews, *Żegota*,[46] established in December 1942 and operating under the control of the Polish underground, continued to provide false papers to Jews in hiding. Individual Gentiles unconnected with the organization also continued to risk their own and their family's lives without any thought of reward.[47] At a time when the Polish population were also experiencing extreme financial hardship they provided clothing and food without knowing how long they would be needed. Many of these Poles were unable to confide in even their closest family members.[48] Fearful not just of the German authorities but also of the disapproval of their anti-Semitic neighbours, they also experienced psychological isolation. Emanuel Ringelblum, his wife Judyta, and 14-year-old son Uriel were rescued by *Żegota*. In March 1944, the family were discovered with sixty other people, including the Christian Poles who were hiding them, in an underground bunker in a suburb of Warsaw. They were all shot amongst the ruins of the Warsaw ghetto.

Some children were just a few hours old when their parents gave them to strangers in the vain hope that they might be spared, or even left them outside non-Jewish homes or institutions. Very young children were sometimes smuggled out in suitcases and given sleeping medicine to ensure their compliance. Older children—prematurely matured by their wartime experiences—were all too aware that they were soon to be separated from their parents. Ewa Bergstein was 5 years old when her father led her out of the Staszów ghetto (Poland). She recalls:

> In looking back over the 44 years of my life, that day, when I let go of my father's hand, was the most difficult and traumatic day of my life. I was only 5 years old but I knew that I was letting go of my whole life; my family, my world. A metamorphosis took place within me. I ceased being a child and became an introspective and shrewd observer of life with an innate skill for survival.[49]

[46] See Joseph Kermish, 'The Activities of the Council for Aid to Jews (Żegota) in Occupied Poland', in Israel Gutman and Efraim Zuroff (eds.), *Rescue Attempts during the Holocaust: Proceedings of the Second Yad Vashem Conference* (Jerusalem: Yad Vashem, 1977), 367–98.

[47] Many such Gentiles would be honoured after the war by Israel as 'Righteous Gentiles'—the official term given by Yad Vashem to describe Christian Europeans who had helped to save the Jews and risked their own and their families' lives. See Władysław Bartoszewski and Zofia Lewin, *Righteous among Nations. How Poles Helped the Jews. 1939–1945* (London: Earls Court Publications, 1969).

[48] See Carol Rittner and Sandra Myers (ed.), *The Courage to Care: Rescuers of Jews during the Holocaust* (New York: New York University Press, 1989), and Tec, *When Light Pierced the Darkness*.

[49] Mordecai Paldiel, 'Fear and Comfort: The Plight of Hidden Jewish Children in Wartime-Poland', *Holocaust and Genocide Studies*, 6/4 (1992), 397–8.

Parents could not know when—if ever—they would be reunited and could only too easily imagine the myriad sufferings their child might be forced to endure. Orthodox—and particularly Haredi Jews—not only had to suppress the potential disapproval of their fellow Jews at entrusting their children to outsiders, but they also feared that their children might be christened and forever be separated from their faith. More than this, Jewish children represented the 'biological continuity of the Jewish people'.[50] Chana Marcus Banet who, on account of her 'unimpeachable Aryan appearance' and false identification papers, was able to survive in hiding with her two children describes how, 'As a pious Jew my heart was filled with sorrow as I watched my children being turned into Catholics before my eyes.'[51]

Others hoped—perhaps out of desperation—that by staying within the ghetto walls and obeying all the German regulations they would be allowed to survive the war. Many parents did not anticipate that the war would last for so long. Children who looked more obviously 'Jewish'— with dark skin, dark eyes, curly hair, a long nose—were more likely to be hidden from the public gaze, as were children who came from Yiddish-speaking families. Once children were able to talk, their chances of survival diminished significantly as their very speech might reveal something of their familial background. During the round-ups women had to ensure that their children remained absolutely silent. Children were trained not to laugh, cry, or express their needs in any voluble way. They were forced to hide in tiny spaces such as wardrobes, ovens, and under beds for hours on end. Ephraim Shtenkler was hidden by a Polish woman and forced to live in a cupboard or under a bed from the age of 2 until he was 7. When the war ended his feet were so twisted that he was unable even to stand up.[52] Others had to dye their dark hair blonde and pretend to be Christian.[53] Adam Pruszkowski was hidden in an orphanage after escaping from the Warsaw ghetto. He writes:

> I had never been parted from my parents...I was afraid of everybody and everything...they knew that I was different, a Jew...I knew that I was not allowed to say anything about myself just as I knew I mustn't get undressed

[50] Sharon Kangisser Cohen, *Child Survivors of the Holocaust in Israel: 'Finding their voice': Social Dynamics and Post-War Experiences* (Brighton: Sussex Academic Press, 2005), 66.

[51] Chana Marcus Banet, *They Called Me Frau Anna* (New York: CIS, 1990), 145–6.

[52] For Ephraim Shtenkler's testimony, see Laurel Holliday (ed.), *Children's Wartime Diaries: Secret Writings from the Holocaust and World War II* (London: Piatkus, 1995), 21–32.

[53] See Diane L. Wolf, *Beyond Anne Frank: Hidden Children and Postwar Families in Holland* (Los Angeles, CA: University of California Press, 2007).

in front of anyone . . . paralysed with fear and timidity I didn't make friends with anyone.[54]

Most of these experiences have been recounted only retrospectively. It was extremely dangerous for any child to write a diary whilst in hiding.

Whilst some children managed to escape from the ghettos, they were separated from their parents and unable to find anyone to take them in. They were therefore inevitably caught by the Germans and left to face their deaths alone. Others who had initially been given shelter by sympathetic Gentiles were cast out to fend for themselves as pressures and stress increased and people became increasingly fearful. Whole families were murdered for concealing Jews and it was a rare individual who was willing to risk not only their own but their family's safety for the sake of a Jewish child. Joanna Beata Michlic has drawn attention to the Warsaw Ghetto uprising of 1 August 1944 as instrumental to many Christian Poles casting out the children in their care to fend for themselves. In the middle of October, following the uprising, the Germans forced the civilian population of Warsaw to leave the capital city. Frightened of attracting attention, they left their charges behind.[55] Christian Poles who decided to stay together with the Jewish children they were hiding were forced to live like Jewish fugitives in the cellars and dug-outs in the devastated city.[56]

Clearly, Jews were sometimes exploited by those who purported to help them. Blackmailers—*schmaltzowniks*—extorted money from Jews desperate to evade the Nazi authorities. Ringelblum recorded that:

> Extortion by *schmaltzowniks* begins the moment the Jew crosses through the gates of the Ghetto, or rather while he is still inside the Ghetto gates, which are watched by swarms of *schmaltzowniks*. Every Jew who leaves the Ghetto is prey for a *schmaltzownik* . . . The *schmaltzowniks* operate in every place where Jews have some contact with the Aryan side—at all the posts near the walls, at the exit gates, along the routes to the work posts, at the work posts, etc., in short, wherever Jews try to 'break loose', to detach themselves from the work post and go to a flat on the Aryan side. The *schmaltzowniks* walk around in the streets stopping anyone who looks Semitic. They frequent public squares, especially the square near the Central Railway Station, cafes,

[54] Child Survivors' Association of Great Britain, *Zachor* [Remembrance]: *Child Survivors Speak* (London: Elliot & Thompson, 2005), 102–3.

[55] Joanna Beata Michlic, *Jewish Children in Nazi-Occupied Poland: Survival and Polish–Jewish Relations during the Holocaust as Reflected in Early Postwar Recollections* (Search and Research: Lectures and Papers) (Jerusalem: Yad Vashem, 2008), 60. Cf. Joanna K. M. Hanson, *The Civilian Population in the Warsaw Uprising of 1944* (Cambridge: Cambridge University Press, 1982).

[56] Michlic, *Jewish Children in Nazi-Occupied Poland*, 61.

and restaurants, and the hotels where Jews who were foreign citizens used to be interned. The *schmaltzowniks* operate in organized bands... They are a real plague of locusts, descending in their hundreds and maybe even thousands on the Jews on the Aryan side and stripping them of their money and valuables and often of their clothing as well.[57]

Some of these blackmailers were children, who approached anyone they suspected of being Jewish in the street, in streetcars, and all manner of other public places. Others were professionals, including civil servants and teachers.[58] If caught, resistance organizations would punish the blackmailers—often by death. Other Gentiles, whilst not engaging directly in blackmail, found sheltering Jews to be a lucrative source of revenue. For example, subletting rooms to Jews in hiding was extremely profitable as the Jews were hardly in a position to negotiate their rents.[59]

Of the very young children who survived the war, some grew up with no knowledge of their Jewish identity. Nor did they know their real name, or that of their parents, or even their place of birth. Their formative years were spent in exile with a day-to-day existence very different from the one their parents had intended. Ultimately, we cannot know how many children were ever reunited with their parents or other family members, how many were taken in by Jewish homes and orphanages after the war, and how many others remained with the people who had rescued them, in some cases adopted by them. Jewish organizations such as the Jewish Agency were committed to finding Jewish children after the war and either reuniting them with their families or taking them to Jewish orphanages. Every Jewish child represented a victory over the Nazis and it was felt essential that their Jewishness be restored.

Even those few children who were reunited with their parents no longer recognized them. A few did not want to be reunited with them. This was especially true of children who had not been close to their families prior to the war.[60] In Alexander Donat's *The Holocaust Kingdom*, his wife Lena speaks of the problems in having to get to know her son Włodek again. Although Lena was one of the few lucky enough to survive Majdanek and

[57] Cited in Jan Tomasz Gross with Irena Grudzińska, *Golden Harvest: Events at the Periphery of the Holocaust* (Oxford: Oxford University Press, 2012), 93.

[58] Ibid., 94–5.

[59] Ibid., 96–104. On this subject see also Jan Gradowski, *Rescue for Money. Paid Helpers in Poland, 1939–1945* (Search and Research Series 13) (Jerusalem: Yad Vashem, 2008), and Tec, *When Light Pierced the Darkness*, 87–98.

[60] For more on this subject see the excellent work by Emunah Nachmany Gafny, *Dividing Hearts: The Removal of Jewish Children from Gentile Families in Poland in the Immediate Post-Holocaust Years* (Jerusalem: Yad Vashem, 2009).

Auschwitz and also find her son again, the reunion was not easy. Parted from his mother as a very young child, Włodek had been raised as a Catholic in a climate of anti-Semitism where children had been taught that the Jews killed Jesus. Not only was Lena herself traumatized by her concentration camp experiences but she was confronted with a child she found it hard to bond with. Włodek too could not accept his mother or his new Jewish life.[61]

The historian Saul Friedländer, like Włodek, was also given a new identity. Born into a bourgeois Jewish family in Prague, he was placed in a Catholic boarding school in Vichy France in 1939 when he was 9 years old. His name was changed from Pavel in Prague to Paul in France and then to Paul-Henri Ferland: 'an unequivocally Catholic name...so as to make it even more authentic'.[62] He experienced a 'real and profound confusion' over a name he could not as yet get used to.[63] Friedländer's parents knew when they sent him into hiding that he was most likely lost to them forever, but also realized that this was their son's only real chance of survival. His desperate mother Elli wrote in a letter to her non-Jewish acquaintance:

> I beg you, dear madame, to agree to look after our child and assure him your protection until the end of this terrible war. I don't know yet how he could be safeguarded, but I have complete confidence in your goodness and your understanding...If we must disappear, we will at least have the happiness of knowing that our beloved child has been saved...We can no longer exist legally...I beg you to excuse the appearance of this letter. My hands no longer obey me.[64]

Although the decision to be parted from their only child must have been intolerable for both Friedländer's parents, for his mother the forced separation from her child was especially terrible. For the little boy too the loss of maternal love and protection was appalling. On a train he experienced a moment of profound trauma: 'I screamed in terror...But suddenly, by a miracle, my mother, who had set out to search for me, appeared. I ran to her, threw myself into her arms sobbing...I opened my eyes: it was Madame Chancel stroking my forehead to calm me.'[65] Indeed, neither Elli nor her husband survived the war. For Friedländer the loss of his parents was compounded by the sense that he had survived on 'the edge of the catastrophe' and had been spared the suffering of his

---

[61] Alexander Donat, *The Holocaust Kingdom: A Memoir* (London: Corgi, 1967), Chapter 9.
[62] Saul Friedländer, *When Memory Comes*, trans. Helen R. Lane (New York: Noonday, 1991), 79.
[63] Ibid., 94.   [64] Ibid., 78.   [65] Ibid., 101–2.

parents and fellow Jews. He writes, 'I remained, in my own eyes, not so much a victim as—a spectator.'[66] So complete was the obliteration of his Jewish heritage that he had decided to become a priest. Christianity and its protective figures of God the Father, Mary, and Jesus provided him with a sense of the family he lacked. He writes that, in the image of the Holy Virgin, he 'rediscovered something of the presence of the mother'.[67] The rituals of Christianity and the experience of going to church itself provided him with a further sense of security. He writes, 'I was intoxicated by the splendour of the Chasubles and the Ciboria, the heady odour of the incense and the softness of the majesty of the music.'[68] He was stopped from joining the priesthood in June 1946 when a Jesuit described to him the terrible events that had taken place in Auschwitz.[69] He writes: 'I felt myself to be Jewish . . . It is true that I knew nothing of Judaism and was still a Catholic. But something had changed . . . an identity was emerging . . . from that day on in some manners or others I felt Jewish.'[70]

Friedländer, however, like many other children who survived the war in hiding, felt that he had to remain silent about his experiences even after the war had ended. What right did he have to complain when he had not suffered the concentration camps? It was only when he went to Israel that he felt able to reclaim his Jewish identity and changed his name yet again, this time to 'Shaul' ('Saul' in English). However, even in Israel things were not easy. Children such as Friedländer were told what they already believed, that they were not true Holocaust survivors—they had not survived the concentration and death camps—and therefore had no right to suffer. Many waited several decades before finally talking about what they had endured. Lili Silberman, hidden by her family in a convent, recalled that even her parents were subsequently unwilling to listen to her:

> I was encouraged to believe that I was too young to understand, and that the only thing that mattered was that we were all very lucky to be alive and together again. While I grew up waiting for my parents to ask about that once-orphaned child, I was to remain secretly tormented by my painful memories.[71]

Friedländer, who has become one of the most eminent historians of the Holocaust, has clearly dedicated his life to understanding not only the

---

[66] Cited in Ellen S. Fine, 'Intergenerational Memories: Hidden Children and the Second Generation', in John K. Roth and Elizabeth Maxwell (eds.), *Remembering for the Future: The Holocaust in an Age of Genocide*, vol. 3 (New York: Palgrave, 2001), 81.

[67] Friedländer, *When Memory Comes*, 122.   [68] Ibid., 119.

[69] Ibid., 137–8.   [70] Ibid., 138.

[71] <http://archive.adl.org/children_holocaust/story_beyond_tears2.html> (accessed 31 August 2016).

events of the Holocaust but also by definition his own fragmented personal history. He asks: 'Isn't the way out for me to attach myself to the necessary order, the inescapable simplification forced upon one by the passage of time and one's vision of history, to adopt the gaze of the historian?'[72] Clearly, too, other hidden children have also tried to piece together their difficult histories. For many, who like Friedländer were never to be reunited with their parents, finding out about their places of origin, circumstances of hiding, or the exact fate of their families has proved difficult. In 1991 in New York City, 1,600 Jewish Holocaust survivors met to talk—some for the first time—about their experiences in hiding during the Holocaust.[73] Since then the World Federation of Jewish Child Survivors of the Holocaust holds an annual conference with special attention paid to the experiences of children who survived the war in hiding. Over the following years support groups have arisen specifically to meet the needs of child survivors, and psychiatrists— many former hidden children themselves—have undertaken extensive research in this area.[74]

For those who survived the war by passing as Aryan, feelings of isolation, of being able to trust no one—not even other Jews in hiding—greatly defined their experiences. The fear of potential abuse or discovery was always present. Ida Fink's semi-autobiographical novel *The Journey* describes such feelings. Fink and her sister were able to start their particular journey of survival because their father, a doctor, was affluent enough to purchase Aryan birth certificates for his daughters. The two sisters, assuming their false identities, stayed for a while in a German work camp. Fink describes her meeting with a fellow Jew:

> Nothing about the way she looked would arouse the slightest suspicion. She was absolutely perfect, and in the best sense of the word, completely natural, not at all flashy. She had delicate features, thick, lustrous, chestnut-coloured hair; her eyes were chestnut-coloured, too. What was striking was the winsome, simple beauty of her round, slightly childish face. But I recognized her immediately, and she recognized me too. She tossed her head and turned away. I could tell she was angry. I watched her sulking; I looked at her delicate profile, her ski boots, her elegant, bell-shaped, light blue coat.[75]

[72] Friedländer, *When Memory Comes*, 144.
[73] See Jane Marks, *The Hidden Children: The Secret Survivors of the Holocaust* (London: Piatkus, 1993).
[74] See Robert Krell, 'Therapeutic Value of Documenting Child Survivors', *Journal of the American Academy of Child Psychiatry*, 24/4 (1985), 397–400.
[75] Ida Fink, *The Journey*, trans. Johanna Weschler and Francine Prose (London: Hamish Hamilton, 1992), 77.

Passing as Aryan or living life as a Gentile meant a complete withdrawal from the past. Jews passing as Aryan both lived outside the law and were fugitives from it. They were dependent on others for their very survival, yet at the same time able to trust no one. As this chapter has shown, these circumstances provided openings for encounters leading to rape and sexual abuse.

The steady refusal to pursue gender as a line of inquiry has meant ignoring the often gendered nature of lived experience. This avoidance of gender analysis is particularly evident when exploring the question of hiding during the Holocaust. A study of women's testimonies reveals different types of experiences. However, rather than calling attention to sexual violence to retrieve women's Holocaust experiences from oblivion, researchers have instead been eager to emphasize the myriad ways in which women attempted to resist their fate and hold onto their dignity by exhibiting moral, heroic, or noble behaviour.[76] For example, Lenore Weitzman, who has carried out pioneering research on women in hiding during the Holocaust, argues that passing as 'Aryan' should be understood as a form of resistance and that many of the Jewish women living under false identities 'were consciously defying Nazi orders and deliberately trying to subvert the murderous intentions of the Nazis'.[77] The problem with this approach is not only that it is likely that the majority of women were solely intent on trying to save themselves from an increasingly frightening fate, but also that survivors may feel pressure to present their experiences of hiding through the lens of heroism. Ironically, then, even some attempts to recapture experiences of women in hiding have tended to silence those who were raped.

As Gottesfeld Heller's testimony shows, experiences of sexual exploitation—or negotiated sex—are a particularly vulnerable area of women's experiences. For survivors and their families there is an understandable reluctance to confront the fact that a family member or friend might have been raped or, perhaps more uncomfortable still, engaged in sexual activity for the procurement of food or protection.[78] That Jewish women were sometimes forced to succumb to the sexual demands of Jewish men to survive has unsurprisingly remained a largely silent chapter of Holocaust history. This discussion is not intended to expose survivors'

---

[76] See, for example, Judith Tydor Baumel, *Double Jeopardy: Gender and the Holocaust* (London: Vallentine Mitchell, 1998); and Brana Gurewitsch (ed.), *Mothers, Sisters, Resisters: Oral Histories of Women Who Survived the Holocaust* (Tuscaloosa, AL: University of Alabama Press, 1998), xii.

[77] Weitzman, 'Living on the Aryan Side in Poland', 217.

[78] See Joan Ringelheim, 'Gender and Genocide: A Split Memory', in Ronit Lentin (ed.), *Gender and Catastrophe* (London: Zed Books, 1997), 25.

most personal or humiliating moments or to suggest that survivors of the Holocaust are concealing aspects of their survival. Rather, it points to the possible implications of 'the unsaid' and 'the unspeakable'[79] in making sense of narratives of lived experience. Arguably, rape and sexual abuse— the violation of one's body at the hands of someone seeking to cause both physical and mental suffering—is one of the loneliest and most alienating things that can happen to a person. As the perpetrator is usually all too aware, it silences the victims and leaves them alone in a world they can no longer recognize. The experience of rape in particular shows the victim that the world is not as it seems. Sex is transformed from an act of intimacy into a tool of violence or coercion and even language is destroyed as 'no' becomes 'yes', and 'stop' gives rise to further pain.[80]

In this way, rape is synonymous with torture and, as Jean Améry has famously argued, 'Whoever has succumbed to torture can no longer feel at home in the world . . . That one's fellow man was experienced as the antiman remains in the tortured person as accumulated horror.'[81] To feel excruciating pain meted out at the hands of another is to lose control over one's body, mind, and ultimately one's life. In her study of torture, which is clearly informed by her reading of Améry, Elaine Scarry explains: 'Physical pain does not simply resist language but actively destroys it, bringing about an immediate reversion to a state anterior to language, to the sounds and cries a human being makes before language is learned.'[82] Such a vocabulary does not speak of shared experiences, of being part of history, but of agony and humiliation. And as Lawrence Langer goes even further to argue, victims of the Holocaust who experienced physical torture have often felt shame at their inability to prevent that torture. He cites one survivor who explains, 'I was ashamed . . . and when I'm ashamed, I don't like to talk about it.'[83] If the torture involves sexual violence, then it becomes even harder to discuss.

[79] See Annie G. Rogers, Mary E. Casey, Jennifer Ekert, James Holland, Victoria Nakkula, and Nurit Sheinberg, 'An Interpretive Poetics of Languages of the Unsayable', in Ruthellen Josselson and Amia Lieblich (eds.), *Making Meaning of Narratives in the Narrative Study of Lives* (London: Sage, 1997), 77–106. For Rogers et al., 'What is unspeakable exists as a deep and haunting sense of something that begs for words but is also forbidden to be spoken', 86.

[80] On the debate over rape as an act of violence or a sexual act (or both), see Christine M. Chinkin, 'Rape and Sexual Abuse of Women in International Law', *European Journal of International Law*, 5 (1994), 50–74.

[81] Jean Améry, *At the Mind's Limits: Contemplations by a Survivor on Auschwitz and its Realities*, trans. Sidney Rosenfeld and Stella P. Rosenfeld (Bloomington, IN: Indiana University Press, 1980), 40.

[82] Elaine Scarry, *The Body in Pain: The Making and Unmaking of the World* (Oxford: Oxford University Press, 1985), 4.

[83] Langer, *Holocaust Testimonies*, 88.

Writing about rape should have the potential to write the victim back into the world.[84] This has proved to be difficult in the case of the Holocaust, where rape and sexual abuse have tended to be written out of its history. Survivors of rape have been ignored. The role of gender in mediating the experiences of the Holocaust has been overlooked—or even denied. The result has been that rape during the Holocaust—and particularly the rape of women in hiding during the Holocaust—remains underexplored and increasingly hard to uncover. What is more, this silence is fuelled by the emergence of an unintended hierarchy of suffering during the Holocaust—structured by possible factors such as time spent in particular ghettos and concentration camps, or survival in hiding—and this has inevitably affected how survivors have interpreted the Holocaust in their post-war lives.

The fact that Anne Frank's story has become the paradigm of hiding has meant it is widely assumed that the only danger faced by people in hiding was being caught and deported.[85] However, women in hiding also faced other dangers, including threats or acts of sexual assault against them. Indeed, it is here that we are most likely to uncover experiences of rape and sexual abuse. Not only women, but also their children, were sexually abused by those purporting to shelter them both during and after the Holocaust, in both Jewish and non-Jewish households. Furthermore, the majority were captured in the end. Most of the men and women who somehow managed to survive the war were forcibly separated from their children. Very few were ever reunited. Instead they had to accept that they were unable to fulfil their parental roles as protectors of their children. Many were left never knowing the exact hardships and sufferings their children had had to endure.

---

[84] See Roberta Culbertson, 'Embodied Memory, Transcendence, and Telling: Recounting Trauma, Re-establishing the Self', *New Literary History*, 26/1 (1995), 169–95.

[85] This point is also made by Joan Ringelheim, 'The Split between Gender and the Holocaust', 345.

3

Concentration Camps

On 7 March 1944, on the eve of the Jewish festival of Purim—the festival celebrating the deliverance of the Jewish people from a genocide thousands of years before, and ending only a few months later—3,800 Czech Jews were murdered in the gas chambers of Auschwitz-Birkenau.[1] Before they were killed they were made to send postcards home informing friends and family that they were alive and well. They knew not to ask why. These Jews had been deported from the Theresienstadt ghetto-camp, where they had been mostly able to stay together as families. In contrast to other concentration camps, Jewish women who entered Theresienstadt already pregnant were not prevented from giving birth. It was only prohibited if women became pregnant whilst incarcerated in the camp. Then, following the order for compulsory abortion in July 1943,[2] a woman was either forced to have an abortion or deported to a death camp in the East together with the child's father. For children who were orphans or who had been separated from their parents Theresienstadt had a home for babies and infants.

On arrival at Auschwitz, the Czech Jews were sent straight to the *Familienlager* (family camp) BIIb—a 'showpiece' built at Birkenau in September 1943 for the purpose of a visit by the International Committee of the Red Cross to refute accusations of the mass murder of the Jews.[3] After the initial September transport was gassed, other transports arrived from Theresienstadt in May 1944. During the ten months of the camp's existence approximately 18,000 prisoners were held there. They were able to keep most of their belongings—including toys—and wear their civilian clothes. Their heads were not shaved, and although they did have numbers tattooed upon their arms, they were not subjected to hard labour. They

---

[1] Photocopies of the lists of these Jewish victims exist in the archives of the Auschwitz-Birkenau State Museum.

[2] Dalia Ofer and Lenore J. Weitzman (eds.), *Women in the Holocaust* (New Haven, CT: Yale University Press, 1998), 7.

[3] In fact the Red Cross were so satisfied by their visit to Theresienstadt that they decided not to proceed with their scheduled visit to Birkenau.

were occasionally able to receive letters and parcels. Children were given slightly better rations.[4] There was even a kindergarten for children aged 3 to 6 years of age and a school for older children up to 14.[5] Fredy Hirsch, a 28-year-old German Jewish *Kapo* (leader of a work commando), headed the school, somehow organizing writing equipment and textbooks. One of the teachers—Ota Kraus—recorded in his diary a Passover Seder (ritual feast) organized for the children on 31 April 1944. He wrote:

> As long as they believed in miracles, not everything had yet been lost. Afterward, an improvised children's choir sang the song about happiness and freedom from the Ninth Symphony of Beethoven. All the block's residents joined the song. Over three hundred children and adults sang together 'All men are brothers.'[6]

The older children were also allowed to organize a puppet theatre to entertain the younger ones with puppets fashioned from rags. Occasionally members of the SS watched the shows and played with the children. The children studied German and even produced their own newspaper. They were also allowed to paint the walls of their barracks. Although conditions were more favourable than in the rest of Auschwitz-Birkenau, men were nevertheless separated from women and small children, and families were only able to see each other during the hour before evening roll call. Most importantly, there was also a high mortality rate. It is estimated that 20 per cent died of starvation and disease. Furthermore, despite the fondness that some of the SS had developed towards the children, after the children had served their purpose—to dispel rumours about the mass extermination of the Jews—most were dispatched to their deaths in the nearby gas chambers. Fredy Hirsch himself committed suicide when he realized the fate that awaited him. A former prisoner remembers:

> Through openings that we had drilled in the wooden walls, we observed in mute terror and dread what was happening next door in the camp. We saw with horror how hordes of mercenary brutes under the supervision of the SS were using clubs to load men and women, elderly people, and at the end, those lovely little children, children who had no idea of how perilous the

[4] Aleksander Lasik, Franciszek Piper, Piotr Setkiewicz, and Irena Strzelecka (eds.), *Auschwitz 1940–1945: Central Issues in the History of the Camp*, vol. 1 (Oświęcim: Auschwitz-Birkenau State Museum, 2000), 96.

[5] See Helen Kubica, 'Children', in Israel Gutman and Michael Berenbaum (eds.), *Anatomy of the Auschwitz Death Camp* (Bloomington, IN: Indiana University Press, 1994), 415.

[6] Cited in Nili Keren, 'The Family Camp', in ibid., 437.

situation was, clutching primitive toys, shivering with cold and hunger, clinging desperately to their mothers.[7]

Zalman Gradowski, an Orthodox Jewish *Sonderkommando* (special detachment) prisoner, was forced to work in the gas chambers of Auschwitz-Birkenau where his entire family had been murdered on arrival at the camp—his mother, wife, two sisters, brother-in-law, and father-in-law. He documented the extermination of the first transport of Czech Jews; how he witnessed mothers walking in naked procession to their deaths with their babies in their arms. They gave their children any remaining food, kissed them, and stroked their hair to calm them. These women had lived in Auschwitz long enough to know their fate. In an essay entitled 'The Czech Transport' he describes how 'The victims walked proudly, boldly, with firm steps.'[8] They sang the Czechoslovak national anthem, '*Kde domnov můj?*' ('Where is my homeland?') and the *Hatikvah* ('Hope'), the Jewish anthem, as they walked. 'All glanced scornfully at the line of officers, not wishing to grace them with direct gazes. No one pleaded, no one sought mercy... They didn't want to give them the pleasure of watching them beg for their lives in despair.'[9] Nevertheless he was disappointed by their apathy. At no time did they rebel against their fate. They were, he claimed, obedient to the end. Gradowski tried to record everything he heard in the last moments of death and buried his diary, written in Russian, Polish, German, and French, and dedicated 'to the memory of my family burnt alive at Birkenau', in a glass bottle in a pit with the ashes of the victims.[10] It was found in 1962. Knowing that there was no way he would be allowed to survive, Gradowski wrote: 'Dear discoverer of these writings! I have a request of you: this is the real reason I write, that my doomed life may attain some meaning, that my hellish

---

[7] Cited in Tadeusz Iwaszko, Helena Kubica, Franciszek Piper, Irena Strzelecka, and Andrzej Strzelecki, *Auschwitz 1940–1945: Central Issues in the History of the Camp*, vol. 2 (Oświęcim: Auschwitz-Birkenau State Museum, 2000), 228–9.

[8] Cited in David G. Roskies (ed.), *The Literature of Destruction: Jewish Responses to Catastrophe* (Philadelphia, PA: Jewish Publications Society, 1989), 557. Cf. Nathan Cohen, 'Diaries of the Sonderkommando', in Gutman and Berenbaum (eds.), *Anatomy of the Auschwitz Death Camp*, 523.

[9] Cited in Roskies (ed.), *Literature of Destruction*, 558.

[10] For a history of the manuscripts and their discovery, see Ber Mark (ed.), *The Scrolls of Auschwitz* (Tel Aviv: Am Oved, 1985). For the Yiddish edition, see idem, *Megiles Oyshvits* (Tel Aviv: Am Oved, 1977). Cf. Jadwiga Bezwinska and Danuta Czech (eds.), *Amidst a Nightmare of Crime: Manuscripts of Members of* Sonderkommando (New York: Howard Fertig, 1992). Photographs taken by members of the *Sonderkommando* have also survived the war. For a discussion of the photographs, see Dan Stone, 'The *Sonderkommando* Photographs', *Jewish Social Studies: History, Culture, and Society*, 7/3 (2001), 131–48.

days and hopeless tomorrows may find a purpose in the future.'[11] The
pages contain the words spoken to SS officers by a woman with her 9-year-
old daughter, a beautiful little girl with plaited hair:

> 'Murderers, thieves, shameless criminals! Yes, now you kill innocent women
> and children. You blame us, helpless as we are, for the war. As if my child and
> I could have brought this war upon you. You think, murderers, that with our
> blood you can hide your losses on the front. But the war is already lost...
> You will be carved up alive. Our brothers all over the world will not rest until
> they have avenged our blood... You will pay for everything—the whole
> world will take revenge on you.' Then she spat in their faces and ran into the
> bunker with her child.[12]

Gradowski, a devout Jew, continued to recite the *Kaddish*—the prayer for
the dead—after each of the gassings.

From across Europe Jews were transported to the death camps of
Poland via *Sonderzüge* (special trains). All of the death camps were con-
veniently situated along major rail routes. Up to seventy-five people were
locked into each windowless cattle truck without access to fresh air, food,
water, or toilet facilities. They were stifling hot in summer and freezing
cold in winter. Among the passengers were women with babies only a few
days old. A bucket would serve as a latrine and, as journeys would last
around six days, they quickly overfilled. As people became increasingly
desperate, fights broke out. Children cried incessantly or not at all as
they became too listless. When they reached their final destination, the
dead often outnumbered the living. Olga Lengyel, a Jewish physician
imprisoned in Auschwitz, describes how 'the corpses that had been with
us for days were bloated hideously and in various stages of decomposition.
The odours were so nauseating that thousands of flies had been attracted.
They fed on the dead and attacked the living, tormenting us incessantly.'[13]
On arrival at Auschwitz, under glaring searchlights, *Kapos* and SS guards
accompanied by fierce dogs shouted at the new arrivals through loud-
speakers to disembark the train leaving their belongings behind them.
Men were forcibly separated from women and shoved into rows of five.
Those judged unfit to work—the elderly (people over the age of 50), the
weak, and children under the age of 15—were never registered but were
immediately sent to their deaths in the gas chambers. The underground
gas chambers were designed to resemble showers complete with imitation
shower heads. Signs in the entranceway said, 'To the baths and disinfecting

---

[11] Cited in Roskies, *Literature of Destruction*, 548.   [12] Ibid., 558.
[13] Olga Lengyel, *Five Chimneys Chimneys: The Story of Auschwitz*, trans. Clifford Coch
and Paul P. Weiss (Chicago, IL: Ziff-Davis, 1947), 14.

rooms'. Notices announced 'Cleanliness brings freedom.' The Jews were told to hang up their clothes on numbered hooks, tie their shoes together, and remember where they left them.

Leib Langfus, another Jewish *Sonderkommando* prisoner, also buried documents near the crematoria in the hope that they would be found one day. Like Gradowski he wrote in his wooden bed in his barracks in Birkenau, secretly recording the atrocities he was forced to witness.[14] For example, that a certain SS officer 'had the custom of standing at the doorway...and feeling the private parts of the young women entering the gas bunker'. He continues: 'There were also instances of SS men of all ranks pushing their fingers into the sexual organs of pretty young women.'[15] For the Jewish members of the *Sonderkommando*, many of whom came from observant backgrounds, the experience of the naked women was especially terrible.

Up to 2,000 people were murdered in a single gas chamber at any one time by mass asphyxiation with lethal chemicals released from prussic acid derived from *Zyklon-Blausäure*, or Zyklon B, pellets. After the gassings, which took about fifteen to twenty minutes, doors were unlocked and crews of prisoners arrived to strip the swollen and entangled bodies of artificial limbs, glasses, gold teeth, hair, and jewellery. Earrings were removed and pliers pulled rings from the women's fingers. The bodies were then thrown into the crematory ovens. The ashes were used for fertilizer in the nearby fields or dumped in the local forests and river.[16] Dr Miklós Nyiszli, a Hungarian Jewish doctor who worked as a physician to the *Sonderkommando*, provides an important eyewitness account:

The doors opened, the trucks arrived, and a Sonderkommando squad loaded the clothing and the shoes separately. They were going to disinfect them...The bodies were not lying here and there throughout the room, but piled in a mass to the ceiling. The reason for this was that the gas first inundated the lower layers of air and rose but slowly toward the ceiling. This forced the victims to trample one another in a frantic effort to escape the gas. Yet a few feet higher up the gas reached them. What a struggle for life there must have been! Nevertheless it was merely a matter of two or three minutes' respite. If they had been able to think about what they were doing, they would have realized they were trampling their own children, their wives, their relatives. But they couldn't think. Their gestures were no more than the reflexes of the instinct of self-preservation. I noticed that the bodies of the

[14] Gideon Greif, *We Wept without Tears: Testimonies of the Jewish* Sonderkommando *from Auschwitz* (New Haven, CT: Yale University Press, 2005), 46.
[15] Mark (ed.), *The Scrolls of Auschwitz*, 200.
[16] Saul Friedländer, *Nazi Germany and the Jews 1939–1945*, vol. 2: *The Years of Extermination* (London: Weidenfeld & Nicolson, 2007), 503.

women, the children, and the aged were at the bottom of the pile; at the top, the strongest. Their bodies, which were covered with scratches and bruises from the struggle which had set them against each other, were often interlaced. Blood oozed from their noses and mouths; their faces, bloated and blue, were so deformed as to be almost unrecognizable. Nevertheless some of the Sonderkommando did recognize their kin... The Sonderkommando squad, outfitted with large rubber boots, lined up around the hill of the bodies and flooded it with powerful jets of water. This was necessary because the final acts of those who die by drowning or by gas is an involuntary defecation. Each body was befouled, and had to be washed. Once the 'bathing' of the dead was finished—a job the Sonderkommando carried out by a voluntary act of impersonalization and in a state of profound distress—the separation of the welter of bodies began. It was a difficult job. They knotted thongs around the wrists, which were clenched in a vise-like grip, and with these thongs they dragged the slippery bodies to the elevators in the next room... The bodies lay in close ranks: the old, the young, the children. Blood oozed from their noses and mouths, as well as from their skin—abraded by the rubbing—and mixed with the water running in the gutters set in the concrete floor.[17]

More people were murdered at Auschwitz than at any other camp— almost one million men, women, and children died there, 90 per cent of them Jews deported from Hungary, Poland, France, the Netherlands, Greece, Czechoslovakia, Belgium, Germany, Austria, Croatia, Italy, and Norway.[18] Not all of them died in the gas chambers. Many were shot or beaten to death. At the same time, we know more about Auschwitz than about the other death camps at Bełżec, Sobibór, Chełmno, and Treblinka. Not only did much of the camp remain intact after its liberation by the Soviet army, but we have more testimony than from any other concentration camp.[19] In that way, although its sheer scale made it untypical, it is not unrepresentative. Auschwitz thus forms a useful—if horrific—test-case for exploring gender in the Holocaust.

In November 1943 Langfus witnessed the gassing of 600 Jewish boys aged between 12 and 18 years who met their deaths alone: 'A transport was brought, consisting entirely of children. They came from Shaulen in the Lithuanian region of Kovno (now known as Kaunas), where they were seized from their mothers' homes and were put into lorries during their fathers' absence when they were working.'[20] A further *Sonderkommando*

[17] Miklos Nyiszli, *Auschwitz: A Doctor's Eyewitness Account*, trans. Tibère Kremer and Richard Seaver (New York: Arcade, 1993), 51–3.

[18] Nikolaus Wachsmann, *KL: A History of the Nazi Concentration Camps* (London: Little, Brown, 2015), 291.

[19] Ibid., 292.

[20] Leib Langfus, 'Manuscripts of *Sonderkommando* Member', in Mark (ed.), *The Scrolls of Auschwitz*, 197–202.

member, Zalman Lewenthal, describes what happened when the children realized they were going to die:

> When the children saw the clouds of thick smoke, they realized at once that they were being taken to their death. They began to run in all directions within the courtyard, mad with fear, pulling out their hair, and not knowing how to save themselves. The Kommandoführer and his assistants beat the children savagely in order to force them to undress. They beat them until the club broke, whereupon it was replaced with another, and the man continued to beat the children on the head. The strong men won. The children undressed, instinctively frightened to death. Naked and barefoot, they clung to each other to protect each other from the blows.[21]

The fact that many young women came with children also condemned them to certain death. The commandant of Auschwitz, Rudolf Höss, wanted to avoid the commotion that would have resulted from children being separated from their mothers. In his memoir he recalls that children often entered the gas chambers with a toy in their hands and writes that 'I noticed that women who had either guessed or knew what awaited them nevertheless found the courage to joke with their children to encourage them, despite the mortal terror visible in their own eyes.'[22] He recalls the different responses of the mothers. One woman with four children asks him 'How can you bring yourself to kill such beautiful, darling children? Have you no heart at all?'[23] Another woman who, he notes, 'did not look in the least like a Jewess',

> Waited until the end, helping the women who were not undressed and who had several children with them, encouraging them and calming the children. She went with the very last ones into the gas chamber. Standing in the doorway, she said: 'I knew all the time that we were being brought to Auschwitz to be gassed. When the selection took place I avoided being put with the able-bodied ones, as I wished to look after the children. I wanted to go through it all, fully conscious of what was happening. I hope that it will be quick. Goodbye!'[24]

Höss also describes how 'On one occasion two small children were so absorbed in some game that they quite refused to let their mother tear them away from it.' He continues:

> The imploring look in the eyes of the mother, who certainly knew what was happening, is something I shall never forget . . . I nodded to the junior

---

[21] Cited in Greif, *We Wept without Tears*, 14.
[22] Rudolf Höss, *Commandant of Auschwitz: The Autobiography of Rudolf Hoess*, trans. Constantine FitzGibbon and Joachim Neugroschel (London: Phoenix, 2001), 149.
[23] Ibid., 150. [24] Ibid., 131.

non-commissioned officer on duty and he picked up the screaming, struggling children in his arms and carried them into the gas-chamber, accompanied by their mother who was weeping in the most heart-rending fashion. My pity was so great that I longed to vanish from the scene: yet I might not show the slightest trace of emotion.[25]

Any woman who was visibly pregnant would also be sent straight to the gas chambers. Thus the fate of women was inextricably bound to that of their children. As Gerda Weissmann Klein writes, 'I had learned to associate children with death.'[26]

The only children who were spared were those who looked older than their age. Ruth Klüger and her mother were amongst the few transferred out of the family camp to the main camp at Auschwitz. Although only 12 years old her mother urged her to say she was 15. In that way, her life was spared.[27] Olga Lengyel, however, had not had time to become adjusted to the brutish world of Auschwitz and initially believed the promises of the SS that children would be looked after in a special children's camp. She asked the SS officer on the disembarking platform of Birkenau whether her 11-year-old son could join his little brother in the children's camp to shelter him from the hardships of an adult camp. Thinking—or allowing herself to think in the absence of other options—that the Germans would not harm children, she was comforted when her mother was also allowed to join her sons. The flames coming from the chimneys of the crematoria and the smell of burning flesh that dominated the camp soon told her that both her mother and sons had been sent to the gas chamber.[28] Other women refused to believe that their children were not safe in a children's camp. The physical connection to their children remained so strong that 'Young mothers, who had lost their children, continued to sing lullabies.'[29] To accept the death of their children would be to accept their own death. Lengyel survived the war consumed by feelings of guilt. She writes at the start of her testimony: '*Mea culpa*, my fault, *mea maxima culpa*! The world understands that I could not have known, but in my heart the terrible feeling persists that I could have, I might have, saved them.'[30]

---

[25] Ibid., 154.
[26] Gerda Weissmann Klein, *All But My Life* (New York: Hill & Wang, 1975), 227. Polish-born, Weissmann Klein was to survive labour camps and a death march and become a well-known writer and human rights activist in the USA.
[27] Ruth Klüger, *Landscapes of Memory: A Holocaust Girlhood Remembered* (London: Bloomsbury, 2003).
[28] See Lengyel, *Five Chimneys*.
[29] Bertha Ferderber-Salz, *And the Sun Kept Shining* (New York: Holocaust Library, 1980), 117.
[30] Ibid., 11.

The enormity of it all placed untold pressure on individuals and also subverted normal understandings of gender. Husbands and fathers, separated from and unable to protect their families, soon learnt the fate of their wives and children. Forced to choose between survival and their role as mothers, some women abandoned maternal responsibilities. A few—we do not know how many—distanced themselves or even denied their own children. One survivor tells of a 10-year-old girl who refused to go to the 'left'—'to death'—so was held down by three SS men as she kicked and thrashed about. She screamed at her mother to help her. One of the SS men approached the young mother to ask if she wanted to go with her daughter. The mother refused.[31]

Those spared an immediate death in the gas chambers of Auschwitz-Birkenau were led into a low, narrow building and made to discard their clothes and hand over any last possessions such as family photographs, jewellery, prayer books, letters, medicines, and tooth brushes. The loss of these final objects meant that they were now bereft of everything that had been part of them—that had mattered to them. They quite literally had nothing to shelter and protect them from what lay ahead. And, in case anyone had been foolish enough to try to hide anything about their person, oral, rectal, and vaginal cavities were also searched. Suitably vulnerable, they proceeded to have their heads, underarms, and pubic areas shaved before receiving an ice-cold shower. Young girls witnessed their mothers' shame as they saw them naked for the first time: an irrevocable breach of familial propriety.

They were then given either blue-and-white striped prison dresses or the clothes of murdered Soviet prisoners and ill-fitting wooden clogs. The primitive clogs quickly caused foot sores, which in the insanitary conditions of the camp quickly became infected. A prisoner with infected feet would not be able to work and would therefore be put to death. Although the clothing often reeked of disinfectant, it was usually filthy, stained with blood and faeces, and infested with vermin. To complete this violent process of assault and denudation their names were replaced by numbers tattooed painfully upon their left forearms. Jewish prisoners also had a triangle tattooed underneath their numbers. The new arrivals were no longer individuals but *Zugänge* (new prisoners) soon to die of thirst, starvation, forced labour, shooting, or gas. Few prisoners lived beyond six months. Prisoners from the warmer climates of southern Europe who had not been conditioned by imprisonment in the ghettos of eastern Europe were among the first to perish. Not being able to

---

[31] Cited in Lawrence Langer, *Holocaust Testimonies: The Ruins of Memory* (New Haven, CT: Yale University Press, 1991), 12.

understand the rapidly delivered German orders of the SS or the Polish of the *Kapos* also condemned them to an early death.

Although it would have been unbearable for anyone, for women the process of introduction into the world of the concentration camps was perhaps especially traumatic. Most female survivors, regardless of their particular background, remember with remarkable detail the trauma of their initiation into the camps. Olga Lengyel writes: '[W]e were compelled to undergo a thorough examination in the Nazi manner, oral, rectal, vaginal . . . We had to lie across a table, stark naked while they probed. All that in the presence of drunken soldiers who sat around the table, chuckling obscenely.'[32] And Judith Magyar Isaacson remembers:

> A woman in a striped dress grabbed me by the hair and attacked me with scissors. Another drove a razor around my crown . . . A shove in the buttocks propelled me along the assembly line. 'Raise your arms!' came the command in German. Two females shaved my armpits in unison . . . A voice barked: 'Spread your legs!' A razor moved into my crotch. A shower of disinfectant hit my armpits and scalp. A sudden spray scorched my vulva. An attendant shoved me from behind. I landed outdoors.[33]

This process was understandably horrific for religious Jews. Jewish law dictates that women, once married, refrain from displaying their hair in public. Depending on their level of orthodoxy, most religious women conceal all or part of their hair under wigs, scarves, or hats. Hair is akin to physical nudity and expresses a woman's sexuality. It also represents spiritual nakedness. Furthermore, many east European Jews, whilst not Orthodox, nevertheless came from homes where nudity was kept private, and they felt just as much shame and anger at their predicament. For many women the forcible and violent removal of their hair—often resulting in damage to the scalp—was an act of mutilation and humiliation: a sexual assault, second only to rape. Rena Kornreich Gelissen remembers: 'I try to prevent tears from falling down my disinfected cheeks. Only married women shave their heads. Our traditions, our beliefs, are scorned and ridiculed by the act they commit.'[34] Sara Nomberg-Przytyk, who was from a Hasidic background in Poland, recalls:

> 'Spread your legs', yelled the *blokowa* [block senior]. And the body hair was shorn too . . . We ceased to exist as thinking, nonsentient things that they

[32] Lengyel, *Five Chimneys*, 83.

[33] Judith Magyar Isaacson, *Seed of Sarah: Memoirs of a Survivor* (Chicago, IL: University of Illinois Press, 1991), 66–7.

[34] Rena Kornreich Gelissen (with Heather Dune Macadam), *Rena's Promise: A Story of Sisters in Auschwitz* (London: Weidenfeld and Nicolson, 1996), 63.

could examine from all angles... It did not bother them that we were women and without our hair we felt totally humiliated.[35]

The savagery of the act—of forcibly shaving a woman's head—is made all the more apparent when one remembers that this was the punishment that would subsequently be meted out to women deemed to have collaborated with the Germans in occupied France, Belgium, Italy, Norway, and the Netherlands. Women suspected of fraternizing with the enemy—by having sexual relations with them, by bearing their children, or even those suspected of having abortions—would go on to be publicly sheared and in some cases daubed with tar and paraded half naked so that their countrymen could enjoy their distress. For them, as for the women brutalized in the Nazi concentration camps, the removal of their hair was a consciously humiliating—degrading—process of dehumanization. Today reports of rape continue to include episodes of forcible hair removal as perpetrators attempt to desexualize their victims. And in prisons across the world ranging from North America to the Arab countries hair removal is still used to control and shame both male and female prisoners.

At Auschwitz-Birkenau female survivors say that, robbed of their hair, they felt like they were 'animals' or 'sub-human'. Livia Bitton-Jackson (born Elli L. Friedmann in Samorin, Czechoslovakia) writes:

> The haircut has a startling effect on every woman's appearance. Individuals become a mass of bodies. Height, stoutness or slimness: There is no distinguishing factor—it is the absence of hair which transformed individual women into like bodies. Age and other personal differences melt away. Facial expressions disappear. Instead, a blank, senseless stare emerges on a thousand faces of one naked, unappealing body. In a matter of minutes even the physical aspect of our numbers seems reduced—there is less of a substance to our dimension. We become a monolithic mass. Inconsequential.[36]

Whether the Nazis specifically intended the forcible removal of hair as a means of humiliation is somewhat ambiguous. As Kirsty Chatwood points out, hair was collected for exportation to Germany (for use in mattresses, for example), and its removal could also have been a way of controlling the spread of lice, which were endemic in the camps.[37] However, what is clear

---

[35] Sara Nomberg-Przytyk, *Auschwitz: True Tales from a Grotesque Land*, trans. Roslyn Hirsch, eds. Eli Pfefferkorn and David H. Hirsch (Chapel Hill, NC: University of North Carolina Press, 1985), 14.

[36] Livia E. Bitton-Jackson, *Elli: Coming of Age in the Holocaust* (London: Grafton, 1984), 79.

[37] Kirsty Chatwood, '(Re)-Interpreting Stories of Sexual Violence', in Esther Hertzog (ed.), *Life, Death and Sacrifice: Women and Family in the Holocaust* (Jerusalem: Gefen, 2008), 163.

is that without hair many of the women felt so degraded that they could not even feel normal human emotions:

> The shaving had a curious effect. A burden was lifted. The burden of individuality. Of associations. Of identity. Of the recent past. Girls who have continually wept at separation from their parents, sisters and brothers now begin to giggle at the strange appearance of their friends... When response to names comes forth from completely transformed bodies, recognition is loud, hysterical. Wild, noisy embraces. Shrieking, screaming disbelief.[38]

Another woman remembers that when she entered the camp, 'One [of the guards] pointed at me and said to his cohort, "Look at those beautiful breasts."' She continues, '[this] was the last remark about my physical appearance that I would hear for a long time to come. At the precise time my head was shaved, I ceased to exist as a human being.'[39]

Given these assaults on the self, it is unsurprising that some women—particularly young girls—succumbed to hopelessness. Many threw themselves on the electrified fences, knowing—hoping—that this would kill them. David Patterson argues that the cumulative experience of the initiation into the concentration camps amounted to the obliteration of one's personhood. He cites Polish writer and Auschwitz survivor Seweryna Szmaglewska:

> You lost the capacity of proving to yourself, in a moment of doubt, that you are still the same human being you were when you came here. That being is gone, and only a miserably wretched creature remains in her place. A naked creature deprived of everything and avidly covering her body with someone else's sweat-saturated garments in spite of keen disgust.[40]

As Patterson explains, 'the self here is invaded by the other, both in the form of blows received and in the form of the very skin and sweat of the other, resulting not only in disgust but in *disjuncture*'.[41]

Conditions after this horrific initiation were unspeakable. Everyday life was a struggle for survival in the most barbarous environment. Contagious diseases, starvation, and overwork were combined with grossly insanitary

---

[38] Bitton-Jackson, *Elli*, 67.

[39] Cited in Monika J. Flaschka, '"Only Pretty Women Were Raped": The Effect of Sexual Violence on Gender Identities in the Concentration Camps', in Sonja M. Hedgepeth and Rochelle G. Saidel (eds.), *Sexual Violence against Jewish Women during the Holocaust* (Waltham, MA: Brandeis University Press, 2010), 81.

[40] Seweryna Szmaglewska, *Smoke over Birkenau*, trans. Jadwiga Rynas (New York: Henry Holt, 1947). Cited in David Patterson, *Sun Turned to Darkness: Memory and Recovery in the Holocaust Memoir* (New York: Syracuse University Press, 1998).

[41] Ibid., 161.

living quarters. Lice were endemic in Auschwitz and women soon became covered in boils and pus-oozing scabs. Without water to wash in, soap, or toilet paper, women soon became infested by fleas and caked in filth; without toothbrushes or even rags to wipe their teeth their mouths became fetid. Dehumanized by their admission and by day-to-day existence, it is unsurprising that Olga Lengyel writes that it became 'a struggle to overcome the disgust we felt for our companions, and for ourselves'.[42]

They were dehumanized—but not, paradoxically, even in the most extreme conditions—desexualized. From the very beginning until the very end, women remained women: both in their sense of self and in the way they were treated by camp guards. Gender, in that sense, was the last thing to survive the camps.

Women were thus singled out for sexual humiliation under the gaze of men. The very jeers they were met with during the initiation process—'Jewish sluts', 'Jewish bitches', 'Jewish whores'—set the tone for what was to follow as women fell victim to sexualized violence at the hands of both male and female concentration camp guards and medical personnel. Furthermore, the violation of women entering the concentration camps—the tattooing, the removal of their hair, the invasion of their body cavities—was not ad hoc but part of a systematic process of degradation, humiliation, and commodification fine-tuned until it caught all women in its wake, from the mature to the barely pubescent; from the Haredi to the secular; the rich to the poor. Eva Schloss was 15 years old when she arrived in Auschwitz. She writes:

> From time to time SS men came in and strolled around to look and leer at our bodies. It was a sport for them to pinch the bottoms of younger, attractive women and I felt really degraded when one of the men walked near to me and then pinched my bottom.[43]

Czech political prisoner Vera Laska elaborates:

> On the rare occasions that the women were marched to the real showers, the grapevine somehow reached the lewdest of the SS, who came to jeer, tease and taunt the defenceless women. Stripping the women naked was also practised at times of camp selections or on long and boring afternoons. When the SS had nothing better to do than to order a roll call and expose the powerless women to a cruel parade . . . They were pushed and shoved into the shower rooms, ordered to strip naked and line up to have all their hair shaved from their heads, underarms and pubic regions. In this pandemonium, as

[42] Lengyel, *Five Chimneys*, 22.
[43] Eva Schloss (with Evelyn Julia Kent), *Eva's Story: A Survivor's Tale by the Step-Sister of Anne Frank* (London: W.H. Allen, 1988), 77.

they stood quivering and huddling to hide their nakedness, their modesty
was further violated by the SS men . . . They made lewd remarks, pointed at
them, commented on their shapes, made obscene suggestions, poked into
their breasts with their riding crops and [set] their dogs onto them. It was the
most shocking of all shocks, a deep blow to their very womanhood . . . The
depravity of the men, indulging themselves in this cheapest, basest and most
disgusting of games, as much for the pleasure of seeing naked females as for
the sport of frightening them out of their minds, was one of the cruellest
tortures to which women were subjected in the concentration camps. Those
newly arrived in the jaws of hell were crushed under the deluge of foul
language, obscene gestures and the fact that they were paraded like cattle on
the market in front of men. To many women it meant an unforgiveable and
never to be forgotten humiliation.[44]

The conditions of the camps most definitely exposed women to the risk
of rape by SS men *and* women, the German civilians who ran the factories
in which the prisoners worked, and also by other prisoners, in particular
by low-level prisoner functionaries such as the *Kapos*. While the SS
were responsible for the overall running of the camps, everything else
but the direct administration of the concentration camps was in the
hands of prisoners of authority—*Lagerältesters* (camp elders), *Blockältesters*
(block elders), and *Kapos*. They were responsible for enforcing discipline,
meting out punishments, supervising work, and so on. Many of these
prisoners used extreme violence—and sometimes sexual violence—to
ensure obedience.

The brutality of the concentration camps diminished sensitivity to
human suffering and intensified the sense of entitlement and superiority
necessary to rape. Chatwood describes it well when she writes that rape
during the Holocaust was a 'by-product of the dehumanization process of
genocide.'[45] The large number of testimonies to rape recorded by the
University of Southern California Shoah Foundation's Visual History
Archive bear witness to this. A Jewish woman from Rhodes describes
how she and her friends were raped by SS guards in Auschwitz: 'And all of
a sudden, the door opened, and three Nazis came and they dragged us on
the floor, they violated us, sexually violated us. They smelled like beer, you
know. They raped us . . . '[46] Testimonies also describe how Irma Grese, a

[44] Vera Laska, 'Women in the Resistance and in the Holocaust', in Carol Rittner and
John K. Roth (eds.), *Different Voices: Women and the Holocaust* (New York: Paragon House,
1993), 264.
[45] Kirsty Chatwood, '(Re)-Interpreting Stories of Sexual Violence', 162.
[46] Cited in Helene J. Sinnreich, 'The Rape of Jewish Women during the Holocaust', in
Hedgepeth and Saidel (eds.), *Sexual Violence against Jewish Women during the Holocaust*,
111.

high-ranking SS woman, delighted in the sexual torture of her victims. And Ruth Elias writes that:

> Drunken SS men sometimes made unexpected appearances in our blocks; the door would suddenly be flung open, and they would roar in on their motorcycles. Then the orchestra was ordered to play, and the SS men would sing along while they continued to drink, their mood getting ever more boisterous. Young Jewish women would be pulled from their bunks, taken away somewhere, and raped. Raping Jewish women wasn't considered Rassenschande (race defilement) therefore it was allowed... I cannot describe the pitiable state of these poor women when they came back to the barracks.[47]

It is also highly unlikely that these women survived. If he was caught having sexual relations with a Jewish woman an SS man would most likely be stripped of his much-coveted position in a concentration camp and sent to the Russian front.[48]

Even those women who had continued to menstruate in the ghettos experienced amenorrhea within the camps. For many women the loss of the menstrual cycle which they experienced was deeply traumatic and a further blow to their psyches as they worried about their potential to be mothers and wives. Livia Bitton-Jackson writes: 'Married women keep wondering about the bromide in their food again and again. Will they bear children again? What will their husbands say when they find out?'[49] Gerda Weissmann Klein was terrified that she would never be able to menstruate again. She wanted a baby so badly that she felt that she 'would endure anything willingly so long as that hope was not extinguished'.[50] In a patriarchal society, this threat was not merely emotional; it was, in a very real sense, existential. Women's central, primary role as mothers and care-givers was assumed; indeed, it was integral to their sense of self, their place in the community, and the condition for the continuation of their existence.[51]

---

[47] Ruth Elias, *Triumph of Hope: From Theresienstadt and Auschwitz to Israel*, trans. Margot Bettauer Dembo (New York: John Wiley, 1998), 120.

[48] See Zoë Waxman, 'Testimony and Silence: Sexual Violence and the Holocaust', in Zoë Brigley Thompson and Sorcha Gunne (eds.), *Feminism, Literature and Rape Narratives: Violence and Violation* (New York: Routledge, 2010), 117–30. Cf. Hedgepeth and Saidel (eds.), *Sexual Violence against Women during the Holocaust*.

[49] Bitton-Jackson, *Elli*, 103–4. Rumours circulated to the effect that bromide was being used experimentally to cause mass sterilization.

[50] Weissmann Klein, *All But My Life*, 155–6.

[51] Nancy Chodorow, *The Reproduction of Mothering: Psychoanalysis and the Sociology of Gender* (Berkeley, CA: University of California Press, 1978).

Menstruation itself was never free from fear. If women did menstruate in the camps they were told that they would be shot. In this climate of anxiety—generated both by threats from the Nazis and the envy of other women—few were willing to admit their position, and those who did have a normal menstrual cycle had to suffer the additional indignity of having no access to sanitary protection. Rena Kornreich Gelissen writes that when she had a period in Auschwitz, 'I scour the ground for anything that might help me hinder the flow. There is nothing.'[52] In the frequent selections they were forced to stand naked with blood running down their legs. As Trudi Levi, a Jewish Hungarian woman, remembers: 'We had no under-pants, nothing to keep the blood from dripping on to our legs or on to the ground. That was the ultimate degradation and it was the last menstrual period many of us had in camp. The body does not waste reproductive energy on starving humanity in severe shock.'[53]

In Auschwitz fears surrounding reproduction were compounded by the women's knowledge of the pseudo-scientific experiments on women's reproductive organs and forced sterilization which took place in the infamous Block 10 via radiation, injections, and surgery.[54] Block 10 was a grim two-storey barracks in the main camp of Auschwitz. It was identical to the other blocks, except that its windows were kept closed and were boarded up to ensure there was no contact with other prisoners. Inside, it housed a special room containing two gynaecological tables and an X-ray room. On 1 April 1943 Rudolf Höss ordered that part of the block be given to Professor Carl Clauberg and his assistant Dr Johannes Göbel for their special experimentation on female prisoners. Assisting them were twenty-two female prisoners working as nurses, aides, and secretaries. Here, we see that, even amidst the degradation of Auschwitz, gender was inescapable.

Reichsführer Heinrich Himmler was interested in finding the most effective means to sterilize people on a mass level and without their knowledge whilst leaving them still able to engage in slave labour.[55] At Nuremberg in 1947 Karl Brandt, Karl Gebhardt, Rudolf Brandt, Joachim Mrugowsky, Helmut Poppendick, Viktor Brack, Adolf Pokorny, and Herta Oberheuser were charged, along with other crimes, for their participation

---

[52] Kornreich Gelissen, *Rena's Promise*, 81.

[53] Trudi Levi, *A Cat Called Adolf* (London: Vallentine Mitchell, 1995), 12.

[54] On the subject of women's reproduction during the Holocaust, see Ellen Ben-Sefer, 'Sex and the City: Women, Sexuality, and Reproduction', in Zygmunt Mazur, Jay T. Lees, Arnold Krammer, and Władysław Witalisz (eds.), *The Legacy of the Holocaust: Women and the Holocaust* (Kraków: Jagiellonian University Press, 2005), 57–72.

[55] Peter Longerich, *Heinrich Himmler* (Oxford: Oxford University Press, 2002).

in these atrocities.[56] In Auschwitz two German physicians, Dr Carl Clauberg and Dr Horst Schumann, headed the sterilization experiments. Clauberg, who joined the Nazi party in 1933, was committed to curing infertility in Aryan women whilst at the same time sterilizing non-Aryan women. He had impressed Himmler by curing the infertility of the wife of a high-ranking SS officer. Whilst he boasted that he was able to sterilize several hundred or possibly several hundred thousand women in a single day at minimum cost, it is not clear how many women suffered at his hands.[57] His method was to inject women with an irritant directly into their uteruses and fallopian tubes without anaesthetic.[58] Afterwards the women were unable to urinate for several days and were left with hard distended abdomens and high fevers. Many developed complications such as peritonitis and septicaemia. One Czech survivor remembers:

> Dr. Clauberg ordered me to lie down on the gynaecological table. I was able to observe Sylvia Friedmann [a prisoner orderly] preparing an injection syringe with a long needle. Dr. Clauberg used the needle to give me an injection in my womb. I felt that my belly would burst with pain, I began to scream so that I could be heard throughout the entire block. Dr. Clauberg told me roughly to stop screaming immediately, otherwise I'd be returned at once to the camp, to Birkenau [i.e., the gas chamber] ... After this experiment I had inflammation of the ovaries.[59]

Schumann, a major in the SS and lieutenant in the Luftwaffe, started his experiments with X-rays. He selected his victims himself; mostly healthy men and women. Most of the victims suffered severe burns. Following the X-rays men would often undergo castration and women the removal of their ovaries.

The prisoner-patients were mostly Jewish and selected directly on arrival at Auschwitz—some married women and some girls as young as 14, although women who had worked as prostitutes were also taken there to be screened for sexually transmitted diseases. From September 1943, the head doctor, Dr Alina Brewda, was a Jewish gynaecologist from Poland. Many of the nurses were also Jewish. They tried to tell the bewildered new arrivals that they were in fact fortunate as they were

---

[56] See Robert J. Lifton, *The Nazi Doctors: Medical Killing and the Psychology of Genocide* (London: Macmillan, 1986).

[57] Cited in Susan Benedict and Jane M. George, 'Nurses and the Sterilization Experiments of Auschwitz: A Postmodernist Perspective', *Nursing Inquiry*, 13/4 (2006), 279.

[58] See Ellen Ben-Sefer, 'Forced Sterilization and Abortion as Sexual Abuse', in Hedgepeth and Saidel (eds.), *Sexual Violence against Jewish Women during the Holocaust*, 160–2.

[59] Cited in Danuta Czech, *Auschwitz Chronicle, 1939–1945: From the Archives of the Auschwitz Memorial and the German Federal Archives*, trans. Barbara Harshav, Martha Humphreys, and Stephen Shearier (New York: Henry Holt, 1990), 810.

escaping the gas chambers. They also held the women down during the excruciatingly painful injections they were forced to endure. After the women were sterilized they had to undergo artificial inseminations with sperm taken from Jewish male prisoners forced to masturbate for this purpose. The women who were of course kept ignorant as to the purpose of the experiments were terrified that they might become impregnated with deformed children. X-rays then determined if the sterilizations had been successful. The X-rays were often done so badly that the women suffered serious burns. Following this most of the women were either murdered by lethal injection or sent to the gas chambers.[60] In January 1944, Clauberg left Auschwitz to escape the advancing Russian army and continue his experiments at Ravensbrück on both Jewish and Roma and Sinti women. Women there, deformed by repeated experiments, were nicknamed 'rabbits'.[61]

It was not only in Auschwitz that gender played out. Indeed, this was a universal experience—and even led to the creation of a separate, large-scale camp for women. Ravensbrück, the largest women's concentration camp, was opened in the Lake District of Mecklenburg on 15 May 1939 for 'deviant' women such as communists, socialists, Jehovah's witnesses, prostitutes, criminals, and so on.[62] Then on 26 March 1942 a specific women's camp was established at Auschwitz-Birkenau, separated from the men's camps by electrically charged barbed wire. The motivation for the camp was in part connected to the development of the Nazi policy of the exploitation of slave labour to a policy of annihilation through labour, and in part an attempt to ease the overcrowding at Ravensbrück. It was clearly understood that imprisoning women was different to imprisoning men, and officials from Ravensbrück travelled to Auschwitz to oversee the development of the new camp. Between the inception of the camp until mid-August 1942, approximately 17,000 women—mostly Jewish—were brought to Auschwitz.[63] There were thirty barracks in the women's camp, with five more quickly added in 1943.[64]

---

[60] Ibid., 284.
[61] See Rochelle G. Saidel, 'Integrating Ravensbrück Women's Concentration Camp into Holocaust Memorialization in the US', in Marcia Sachs Littell (ed.), *Women in the Holocaust: Responses, Insights and Perspectives (Selected Papers from the Annual Scholars' Conference on the Holocaust and the Churches 1990–2000)* (Merion Station, PA: Merion Westfield, 2001), 67.
[62] See Sarah Helm's recent book, *If This Is a Woman: Inside Ravensbrück, Hitler's Concentration Camp for Women* (London: Little, Brown, 2015).
[63] Iwaszko et al., *Auschwitz 1940–1945*, 172.
[64] Irena Strzelecka, 'Women', in Gutman and Berenbaum (eds.), *Anatomy of the Auschwitz Death Camp*, 394.

Conditions were far worse in the women's camp, as women were not considered to be capable of hard labour for any sustained period. The SS women and the female *Kapos* who controlled the women prisoners ruled with a brutality that matched their male counterparts. Höss himself stated that:

> [E]verything was much more difficult, harsher and more depressing for the women, since general living conditions in the women's camp were incomparably worse. They were far more tightly packed in, and the sanitary and hygienic conditions were notably inferior. Furthermore the disastrous overcrowding and its consequences, which existed from the very beginning, prevented any proper order being established in the women's camp. The general congestion was far greater than in the men's camp. When the women had reached the bottom, they would let themselves go completely. They would then stumble about like ghosts, without any will of their own, and had to be pushed everywhere by the others, until the day came when they quietly passed away. These stumbling corpses were a terrible sight.[65]

It was sometimes the case that pregnant women were admitted into the camp, either because they were married to Gentile husbands, or because their pregnancy was not yet noticeable.[66] However, they were encouraged to come forward with promises of better living conditions and additional food. Gisella Perl, a Romanian Jewish gynaecologist deported to Auschwitz in 1944, describes the scene:

> One of the SS chiefs would address the women, encouraging the pregnant ones to step forward, because they would be taken to another camp where living conditions were better. He also promised them double bread rations so as to be strong and healthy when the hour of delivery came. Group after group of pregnant women left Camp C. Even I was naïve enough, at that time, to believe the Germans, until one day I happened to have an errand near the crematories and saw with my own eyes what was being done to these women.

> They were surrounded by a group of SS men and women who amused themselves by giving these helpless creatures a taste of hell, after which death was a welcome friend. They were beaten with clubs and whips, savaged by dogs, dragged around by the hair, and kicked in the stomach with heavy German boots. Then, when they collapsed, they were thrown into the crematory—alive.[67]

---

[65] Höss, *Commandant of Auschwitz*, 134–5.

[66] On 6 May 1943 a German decree enacted '[das] Verbot der Einweisung schwangerer Häftlinge in die Frauenkonzentrationslager Ravensbrück bzw. in die Frauenbteilungen der Konzentrationslager Auschwitz' (Prohibition of the admission of pregnant inmates into the women's concentration camp of Ravensbrück or the women's section of Auschwitz).

[67] Gisella Perl, *I Was a Doctor in Auschwitz* (New York: International Universities Press, 1948), 80–2.

Liana Millu describes what happened when a fellow prisoner's pregnancy continued undetected. The woman somehow managed to conceal
her condition by bandaging her stomach with torn-up rags. She gave birth
to a live baby but bled profusely. Both died shortly after. It is unclear from
Millu's account whether the mother and baby were left to die alone or
were murdered when an SS man discovered them.[68]

Pregnant women were specifically targeted for medical experimentation. The infamous German physician, Dr Josef Mengele, was particularly
interested in how women suffering from typhus might pass the disease on
to their children. He therefore infected women in the final stages of their
pregnancies to see whether or not the placenta might serve as a barrier to
infection. Then blood samples were drawn from the arteries of the babies
immediately after birth. This frequently resulted in their deaths.[69] On
other occasions he would carefully supervise a pregnancy and birth and
then send both mother and baby straight to the gas chambers.

Knowing that new-borns would not on any account be allowed to
survive, many inmate doctors made the decision that the children must
die so that their mothers might live. They saved poison for this purpose,
but in its absence were forced to smother the babies or drown them in
buckets of water. At times they managed to kill the baby without the
mother's knowledge in an attempt to spare her at least some measure of
pain, but many mothers were only too aware of the situation. Judith
Sternberg Newman, a nurse at Auschwitz, describes the drowning of a
new-born baby:

> Two days after Christmas, a Jewish child was born on our block. How happy
> I was when I saw this tiny baby... Three hours later, I saw a small package
> wrapped in cheese cloth lying on a wooden bench. Suddenly it moved.
> A Jewish girl employed as a clerk came over, carrying a pan of cold water... She
> picked up the little package—it was the baby, of course—and it started to cry
> with a thin little voice. She took the infant and submerged its little body in the
> cold water... After about eight minutes the breathing stopped.[70]

Lucie Adelsberger, a German-Jewish doctor who worked in the makeshift
hospital barracks at Birkenau, performed many secret abortions in Auschwitz.
These abortions—sometimes on foetuses as old as six months—were mostly
done without anaesthesia. Labour was induced and if still alive the babies
would be strangled or drowned. Adelsberger remembers: 'We stockpiled

[68] Liana Millu, *Smoke over Birkenau*, trans. Lynne Sharon Schwartz (Philadelphia, PA:
Jewish Publications Society, 1991), 55–6.

[69] Iwaszko et al., *Auschwitz 1940–1945*, 266.

[70] Judith Sternberg Newman, *In the Hell of Auschwitz: The Wartime Memoirs of
J.S. Newman* (New York: Exposition, 1963), 42–3.

all the poison in the camp for this purpose, and it was not sufficient. One time there was no poison available, and so the mother strangled the child she had just delivered...She was a Pole, a good mother who loved her children more than anything else. But she had hidden three small children back home and wanted to live for them.'[71] Gisella Perl decided that she must participate in the clandestine abortions after witnessing pregnant Jewish women being thrown into the crematoria ovens still alive. She states:

> No one will ever know what it meant to me to destroy these babies. After years and years of medical practice, childbirth was still to me the most beautiful, the greatest miracle of nature. I loved those newborn babies not as a doctor but as a mother and it was again and again my own child whom I killed to save the life of a woman...And if I had not done it, both mother and child would have been cruelly murdered...[72]

Mengele himself once tried to explain the perverse logic that governed his actions:

> When a Jewish child is born, or a woman comes to camp with a child already...I don't know what to do with the child. I can't set the child free because there are no longer any Jews who live in freedom. I can't let the child stay in the camp because there are no facilities in the camp that would enable a child to develop normally. It would not be humanitarian to send a child to the ovens without permitting the mother to be there to witness the child's death. That is why I send the mother and the child to the gas ovens together.[73]

Mengele, of course, was no humanitarian. He delighted not only in the suffering of female prisoners but also in their humiliation. To him pregnancy was an opportunity for sexual taunting. Olga Lengyel remembers:

> Whenever there was an opportunity, Dr. Mengele never neglected asking women embarrassing and offensive questions. When he learned one day that a pregnant prisoner had not seen her husband, a soldier, for many months, he could not hide his amusement. Another time he discovered a fifteen-year-old girl who had evidently been impregnated in the camp. He subjected her to a long interrogation and wanted to learn even the most intimate details of her affair. When this curiosity was satisfied, he did not hesitate to earmark his victim for the next selection.[74]

---

[71] Lucie Adelsberger, *Auschwitz: A Doctor's Story*, trans. Susan Ray (London: Robson, 1996), 255.

[72] Perl, *I Was a Doctor in Auschwitz*, 22.

[73] Cited in Nomberg-Przytyk, *Auschwitz*, 69.

[74] Cited in Hermann Langbein, *People in Auschwitz*, trans. Harry Zohn (Chapel Hill, NC: University of North Carolina Press, 2004), 337.

How women were able to partake in the physically and emotionally demanding act of giving birth in such physically and emotionally weakened states is hard to imagine. What is more, women who did manage to successfully conceal their pregnancies and give birth undiscovered were of course denied both prenatal and postnatal care. In many cases they were forced to engage in backbreaking hard physical labour both up to the moment of birth and immediately after. Babies were delivered with unsterilized instruments and nothing to cut the umbilical cord. New mothers were unable to feed their babies as malnutrition meant that they had little or no milk. In desperation some women tried to feed their babies the camp bread, soup, or ersatz coffee, which inevitably speeded their deaths. The babies were also particularly vulnerable to the rats and diseases which plagued the camp.[75] Stanisława Leszczyńska, a Polish woman who worked as a midwife at Auschwitz, writes that they 'died a slow hungry death. Their skin turned thin, like parchment, transparent, so that one could see the tendons, veins and bones.'[76]

It is not known how many babies were born in the camp as there were no separate registers for children.[77] If a baby was deemed to be suitable for Germanization—for example, if they were blonde-haired and blue-eyed—they were quickly separated from their mother for resettlement under the *Lebensborn* programme (kidnapping children of 'Aryan' appearance for relocation to the *Reich*). Any children that survived received their concentration camp numbers usually on their thighs or buttocks but sometimes on their arms.[78] 'Auschwitz Kasernenstrasse' was entered as the place of birth.[79] It also appears that by 1944 Jewish babies were not murdered immediately after birth as the birth and serial numbers of eight Jewish babies were recorded in that year.[80] However, it is most likely that they ended up being gassed along with their mothers or burned alive in the crematoria. If a child was allowed to survive it was likely to be for a specific purpose and for a specific time.

Ruth Elias is one of the very few women who survived to testify to her own experience of giving birth in Auschwitz. She was deported to Auschwitz from Theresienstadt in the very early stages of pregnancy but

[75] On this subject, see Beverley Chalmers, *Birth, Sex and Abuse: Women's Voices under Nazi Rule* (Guildford: Grosvenor House, 2015).

[76] Cited in Karl A. Plank, *Mother of the Wire Fence: Inside and Outside the Holocaust* (Louisville, KY: Westminster John Knox, 1994), 27–8. See also Stanisława Leszczyńska, 'Raport położnej z Oświęcimia' [Report of a Midwife from Auschwitz], in *Przegląd Lekarski* [Overview of Medicine], 1 (1965) (available at <http://www.wmpp.org.pl/pl/pielegniarki-na-frontach/ii-wojna-%C5%9Bwiatowa/stanis%C5%82awa-leszczy%C5%84ska.html>, site accessed 2 September 2016).

[77] Kubica, 'Children', 421.   [78] Ibid.

[79] Iwaszko et al., *Auschwitz 1940–1945*, 268.   [80] Ibid., 240.

had been unable to find a prisoner willing to perform a termination. After the birth Mengele ordered that Elias' breasts be tightly bandaged in order to see how long a new-born baby could survive without food. For six days Mengele came to check her breasts and examine her new-born daughter. Each day 'He asked me politely how I felt and whether the baby was crying.'[81] Elias felt the bandage getting damp and her breasts filling with milk but was unable to feed her howling child. Told that she was to go with her child to the gas chamber she was forced to kill the little girl, whom she called only 'my child', by injecting her with morphine obtained from a fellow prisoner working as a dentist. She was only 22 years old and not yet ready to die herself. Years later she tried to recall her feelings at the time:

My child, you were born with such a lovely little body. Your legs are soft and pudgy, and they have tiny creases. What beautiful clear features you have. Dark hair and little fingers with such small fingernails. When you first saw the light of day you were a pretty baby. Now, for three days, your crying has not stopped. Your pale skin turns red when you scream, and your lovely little face is distorted. Am I imagining it or is your face getting smaller? Your legs thinner? Oh why, my child, are you not allowed to drink your mother's milk? If you could, you would fill out and not wither so quickly. Is your voice getting weaker, your crying and screaming gradually turning into a whimper? My child, how can I help you in your suffering? How can I keep you alive? Please don't leave me.

... How can we put an end to this misery? Is there anything that I as your mother can do? Do I have the right to even think about ending both our lives? How can you and I live through this? When will the pain end?

Here, my child, take this pacifier made of bread soaked in coffee; maybe it will alleviate your hunger. You have scarcely any strength left to suck on it. You're already six days old, and still I see no way out of this terrible plight. Oh God, please let us both die.

My child, you've turned ashen-grey, just a tiny skeleton covered with skin. You can't even whimper anymore. And all those bedsores. Are you still breathing? Come, Mengele, examine my child. Feast your eyes on her! Is your medical curiosity finally satisfied? Now do you know how long a newborn child can live without food, you devil in human form![82]

Other babies were kept alive for Mengele's pseudo-scientific research projects if they were twins (Mengele also kept alive adult twins), or if they showed signs of dwarfism, gigantism, or other irregularities such as non-matching eye colour (heterochromia).[83] The very few babies who survived

---

[81] Elias, *Triumph of Hope*, 148.   [82] Ibid., 143–53.   [83] Ibid., 261.

the camps did so mainly because they were born in the last few weeks before liberation.[84]

If gender remained resilient—indeed, inescapable—then very few of the other structures and assumptions that had underpinned life before the camps survived Auschwitz. This was true for men, who now lived beyond and outside the family. It was equally, perhaps especially, poignant for women, denied family life, excluded from their domestic sphere, and living in conditions worse than those of their male counterparts. The barracks, which were built on swampland, without any insulation, were freezing in winter and oppressively hot in summer. As well as lice and fleas, women were plagued by the rats which attacked their ailing bodies. A couple of buckets served as sanitary facilities for an entire barracks.[85] Gisella Perl writes that:

> There was one latrine for thirty to thirty-two thousand women and we were permitted to use it only at certain hours of the day. We stood in line to get into this tiny building, knee-deep in human excrement. As we all suffered from dysentery, we could rarely wait until our turn came, and soiled our ragged clothes, which never came off our bodies, thus adding to the horror of our existence by the terrible smell which surrounded us like a cloud. The latrine consisted of a deep ditch with planks thrown across it at certain intervals. We squatted on these planks like birds perched on a telegraph wire, so close together that we could not help soiling each other.[86]

Women had to be prepared to fight for everything from access to the latrine, to space on a bunk, to a place on a supposedly easier work crew, to the revolting and pitiful food rations. The prisoners were constantly hungry. Olga Lengyel writes that the soup the prisoners were so desperate to get hold of contained such ingredients as buttons, keys, tufts of hair, dead mice, and, on one occasion, a small metal sewing kit complete with needles and thread.[87]

In this brutal environment, everything had to be 'organized'—from a piece of bread, to a bowl to hold the soup in, to a better place to sleep, to a scrap of paper for a diarrhoea-ridden inmate. Unsurprisingly Olga Lengyel states that 'some inmates pressed by hunger stole the miserable rations of their neighbours. Many who were inadequately clothed snatched the poor rags of others in the washroom.'[88] It was imperative that prisoners adapt to their new existence if they were not to succumb to the fate of the hopeless

---

[84] See Wendy Holden, *Born Survivors* (London: Little, Brown, 2015).
[85] Strzelecka, 'Women', 401.   [86] Perl, *I Was a Doctor in Auschwitz*, 33.
[87] Lengyel, *Five Chimneys*, 37.   [88] Ibid., 110.

'*Muselmann*' (Muslim)[89] and seek death on the electric wired fences. However, if caught in the act of organizing, women were subjected to violent beatings or specifically timed public floggings. They were also punished for working too slowly, for soiling themselves if unable to access the latrine in the unlit barracks, and for any number of minor misdemeanours. As well as beatings they were made to kneel on sharp gravel for hours whilst holding bricks in their upraised hands, strung up by chains, or confined to the 'standing cells' in the main camp for as long as a month. Just outside the cells was the 'Death Wall', where whole families could be shot. Also to be dreaded were the collective punishments whereby entire blocks could be made to kneel with bricks for hours on end. Any prisoner deemed to have instigated such an event would find their life very difficult.

The twice-daily roll calls added to the women's suffering. The counting of prisoners could take several hours and many of the exhausted women would collapse. If lucky they would escape with a beating. If not, they could expect to be dispatched to the gas chambers. In addition to the roll calls, random selections were carried out and sick and ailing prisoners would either be sent straight to the gas chambers or to Barrack 25 to await their deaths. Women held in this building were given no food or water as it didn't make sense to waste resources on the condemned. Zalman Lewenthal recounts their final moments:

It was early in 1944. A cold, dry, lashing wind was blowing. The ground was frozen solid. The first truck, loaded to capacity with naked women and young girls, pulled up at crematorium III. They did not stand pressed tightly against one another, as usual; they had been so emaciated that they just lay inertly one on top of another, in a state of extreme exhaustion. They moaned and groaned. The truck stopped, the canvas was lifted, and the human mass was thrown out, the way one dumps gravel on the ground. Those lying at the edge fell onto the hard surface, hitting their heads, which drained them of whatever strength they had left in their bodies, so that they just lay there, motionless. The remaining [women] kept falling on top, pressing them with their weight. Groans were . . . heard. Those thrown out of the trucks last tried to extricate themselves from the pile of bodies, stood shakily, trying to walk . . . Trucks kept pulling up, the human load was thrown out, and when everyone had finally arrived, all of them were driven like cattle in the direction of the gas bunker. One heard frightful screams of despair and loud sobbing . . . terrible . . . they expressed immense pain . . . different muffled voices merged into one . . . and kept rising up from underground so long

---

[89] This was the slang used in Auschwitz for prisoners who had abandoned the will to live and who were on the verge of death. In the women's camp at Ravensbrück the term was *Muselweib* (a feminine version). See Wolfgang Sofsky, *The Order of Terror: The Concentration Camp* (Princeton, NJ: Princeton University Press, 1997), 152–68, n. 5.

that finally a 'Red Cross' automobile [a truck for gassing Jews] pulled up...and put an end to their pain and despair.[90]

Prisoners were surrounded by other people every second of every minute of every day. Around 1,000 women lived in each block. They also worked closely together either in the camp's agricultural industries—for example, growing vegetables and raising poultry—or building roads, digging ditches, and so on.[91]

Other women worked in the camp's kitchens and factories, or if fortunate—and fluent in many languages—as messengers and clerics. Some worked in *Canada* (so named by Polish prisoners after a country thought to hold untold riches), where the belongings of the thousands of murdered men, women, and children were warehoused and sorted. The women who worked in the six barracks that made up *Canada* were fortunate in so far as they could exchange their ragged garments for the clothes of the dead and gorge themselves on the food they found among their belongings. Kitty Hart (born Kitty Felix), a Polish Jew who survived the war because she was to be one of the very few women removed from the camps to work in a factory, writes that she was able to:

> [P]ut on fresh underwear and new clothes and shoes every day. We slept in nightshirts of pure silk and even smuggled bedsheets, the most striking luxury in Auschwitz, into our block. When our underwear and dresses got dirty, we simply threw them on the big pile from which we had picked them out.[92]

Although they were searched before they returned to their barracks, this did not stop them stealing as many items as they could. A stolen watch, for example, could be used to bribe a *Kapo*. However, while the lives of women detailed to *Canada* were certainly materially better than those of the others, working as they did near the arrival ramp they also became witnesses to the procession of men, women, and children as they walked to the gas chambers. Hart continues:

> Women passed us, tired from the journey, clutching their babies. Sometimes a small child wheeled a doll in a little pram or jumped over a skipping rope. A mother would change a nappy or put a bonnet over a child's head if the sun was too hot. We lay on the lawn and watched. Or looked away. One of our group might get up to look behind the block to see what was happening at another of the crematoria. No need...The wind would blow the smoke our way, making us cough and choke, darkening the sun. That lovely baby

---

[90] Cited in Strzelecka, *Women*, 405.
[91] Iwaszko et al., *Auschwitz 1940–1945*, 193.
[92] Cited in Langbein, *People in Auschwitz*, 139.

we had seen not so long ago, the little boy playfully running backwards and forwards, were now gone.[93]

Having seen this, the women knew the price they would have to pay: the SS would ensure that no one who had witnessed the killing would survive to tell the story.

It was sensible to form alliances with other prisoners, and efforts were made to recreate something of the life they had left behind. The memoirs of female survivors suggest that women responded to the suffering they were forced to endure by trying to maintain familial or emotional bonds.[94] Some women survived the camps with close relatives—daughters, mothers, sisters, cousins—while others formed such close friendships with other prisoners that they became surrogate families. Women even 'adopted' children to look after. Giuliana Tedeschi, an Italian Jewish woman and mother of two children who found herself alone in Birkenau, describes the comfort this gave her: 'Zilly's hand, a small, warm hand, modest and patient, which held mine in the evening, which pulled up the blankets around my shoulders, while a calm, motherly voice whispered in my ear, "Good night, dear—I have a daughter of your age!" '[95]At Majdanek, Halina Birenbaum describes how her sister-in-law helped her to survive:

> The shock that followed the unexpected loss of my mother, my frantic terror at the sight of the watchtowers, the machine-guns, the green uniforms of the SS…drove me almost to the point of insanity…and at a time when I should have forced myself to be as resistant as possible, I broke down completely…Meanwhile Hela fought with redoubled strength—for herself and for me. She shared every bite she acquired with me…Had it not been for Hela's efforts, I would not have roused myself from apathy and despair.[96]

When Hela died, however, Halina was forced to survive on her own.

Women from religious Jewish families were particularly keen to recreate the closely- knit nature of family life. Even in Auschwitz some of these women tried to observe the Jewish festivals; fasting on Yom Kippur, for example. These relationships allowed women both to care for each other and also to pool scant resources such as food and clothing. However, in the brutal world of the concentration camps, families—real or not—were

---

[93] Kitty Hart[-Moxon], *Return to Auschwitz: The Remarkable Story of a Girl who Survived the Holocaust* (London: Grafton, 1983), 155.

[94] Nomberg-Przytyk, *Auschwitz*, 35.

[95] Giuliana Tedeschi, *There Is a Place on Earth: A Woman in Birkenau*, trans. Tim Parks (London: Lime Tree, 1993), 9–10.

[96] Halina Birenbaum, *Hope is the Last to Die: A Personal Documentation of Nazi Terror*, trans. David Welsh (New York: Twayne, 1967), 94–6.

unable to protect each other. Sara Nomberg-Przytyk remembers that: 'A young girl whose mother was assigned to the gas did not want to be separated from her. She wanted to die with her mother. They tore her from her mother by force.'[97] The brutality and deprivations of the concentration camps also invariably meant that caring for someone meant doing so at somebody else's expense. When Rena Kornreich Gelissen managed to get her younger sister a place on her bunk, she acknowledges: 'I do not ask what will happen to the girl who was sleeping next to me . . . This is a selfish act, perhaps, but I have a sister who I have to keep alive and she is all that matters.'[98]

There were networks of support based on factors such as shared places of origin, political affiliation, and religiosity. At the same time, many testimonies document the fierce and often violent divisions among prisoners based on factors such as position within the camp hierarchy, political affiliation, religious observance, or geographical origin. Helen Lewis (born Helena Katz in Bohemia) describes the deep sense of division in Auschwitz between the Yiddish-speaking *Ostjuden* (east European Jews) and the more assimilated west European Jews:

> There were three hundred of us newcomers who had previously been in Terezin [Theresienstadt] and in the family camp at Birkenau. We came from Czechoslovakia, Germany and Austria and we shared a fairly similar background and outlook . . . The five hundred prisoners who had arrived some weeks earlier came from Poland and the Baltics, as well as Hungary and Romania. Most of them had had a strict religious upbringing, which gave them a strong sense of identity, but sadly manifested itself in their hostility towards us and their rejection of our group. They could speak the languages of their home countries, but preferred to talk to each other in Yiddish, a language which I and the rest of my group didn't understand. They bitterly resented our lack of religious ardour; we thought them uneducated, uncivilised even.[99]

As Lewis' testimony indicates, Orthodox Jewish women—like their male counterparts—continued to find ways to observe religious traditions. Women would go to great lengths to obtain *siddurim* (prayer books) and observe the Sabbath, lighting candles made from bits of grease and oil saved from the factories where some prisoners worked.[100] In ways such as this women were able to resist the efforts of the SS to eradicate not only their religious identities but the very core of their beings. Other women

---

[97] Nomberg-Przytyk, *Auschwitz*, 35.   [98] Kornreich Gelissen, *Rena's Promise*, 72.
[99] Helen Lewis, *A Time to Speak* (Belfast: Blackstaff, 1992), 75.
[100] See, for example, Bitton-Jackson, *Elli*, 166. Bitton-Jackson also describes the lighting of the Hanukkah candles.

tried to retain something of their pre-war lives by remembering poetry and songs. Ruth Elias writes that in Auschwitz, remembering the lyrics of songs acted as 'spiritual and mental nourishment', since she and her friends 'knew intuitively that if we gave up spiritually and intellectually, we would be giving up all hope of survival'.[101] And other women found a degree of solace in the careful remembering of the meals they had made for family and friends. Exchanging recipes with the women around them also allowed them to dream of being free again.[102]

Very few women had the mental or physical energy to imagine escape. Those who did attempt flight were met with severe punishment. The most famous escape attempt is by Mala Zimetbaum, a 19-year-old Jewish girl from Belgium. On 24 June 1944, she actually managed to escape from Birkenau with her Polish boyfriend Edek Galiński. Zimetbaum's position as a *Läuferin* (runner)—she was fluent in Flemish, French, German, Polish, and Yiddish—gave her access to important information in the camp, and she was often able to remove names from selection lists. The couple managed to escape using stolen SS uniforms and identity documents. Although there is little conclusive information about their escape, prisoner rumours suggest that Zimetbaum managed to steal documents giving details about the gassings, which she intended to smuggle to the outside world. Accounts vary as to how they were captured, but it is thought that approximately two weeks after their escape, Zimetbaum and Galiński were arrested and publicly executed in Auschwitz.[103] It is still possible to see Galiński's scribbles on the walls of the bunker he was imprisoned in prior to his execution. The archives at Yad Vashem contain many testimonies recalling Zimetbaum slapping the face of the SS man who was about to hang her, before slashing her wrists with a razor blade that she had somehow managed to conceal. The story of Mala Zimetbaum is significant for it allows survivors of Auschwitz to stress that humanity and bravery existed even in hell.

Women were especially vulnerable to the manipulations of the prisoner-functionaries who came to work in the women's camp. In the perverted logic of the concentration camps it was often those with a

[101] Elias, *Triumph of Hope*, 123. For a discussion of the role of music in Auschwitz, see Shirli Gilbert, *Music in the Holocaust: Confronting Life in the Nazi Ghettos and Camps* (Oxford: Oxford University Press, 1995), Chapter 4.

[102] See Myrna Goldenberg, 'Food Talk: Gendered Responses to Hunger in Concentration Camps', in John K. Roth and Elizabeth Maxwell (eds.), *Remembering for the Future: The Holocaust in an Age of Genocide* (Basingstoke: Palgrave, 2001), 248–57.

[103] See Martin Gilbert, *The Holocaust: The Jewish Tragedy* (London: Fontana, 1987), 695. Cf. Giza Weisblum, 'The Escape and Death of the "Runner" Mala Zimetbaum', in Yuri Suhl (ed.), *They Fought Back: The Story of the Jewish Resistance in Nazi Europe* (New York: Crown, 1967), 182–281.

criminal background who were promoted to positions of power over the other inmates. These prisoners, who had access to better food and more comfortable living quarters, were able to distance themselves from the misery of the masses. They identified more with their German overseers and recognized the sufferings of their fellow prisoners only to the extent that they could exploit them. Seweryna Szmaglewska reported that 'Everyone who is weak, helpless, and sick is persecuted, punished, trampled.'[104] And it was hunger that dictated their every action. As Lucie Adelsberger writes:

> Anyone acquainted with hunger knows that it is not just a vegetative, animal sensation in the stomach, but a nerve-shattering agony, an attack on the entire personality. Hunger makes a person vicious and corrupts his character. Many things about the inmates that rightly appear monstrous to an outsider become comprehensible and partly excusable from the perspective of hunger.[105]

Polish writer and journalist Tadeusz Borowski, imprisoned at Auschwitz, described hunger powerfully: 'One isn't really hungry until one regards another human being as something edible.'[106]

Sexual relationships provided an important means for women to resist starvation. In the words of Lengyel, 'food was the coin that paid for sexual privileges'.[107] Gisella Perl, desperate for something that she would be able to use as shoelaces, describes what happened when she attempted to exchange her bread for a piece of string from a male Polish prisoner:

> I stopped beside him, held out my bread and asked him, begged him to give me a piece of string in exchange for it. He looked me over from head to foot, carefully, then grabbed me by the shoulder and hissed in my ear: 'I don't want your bread...You can keep your bread...I will give you a piece of string but first I want you...you...' For a second I didn't understand what he meant...His hand, filthy with the human excrement he was working in, reached out for my womanhood, rudely, insistently. The next moment I was running, running away from that man, away from the indignity that had been inflicted on me, forgetting about the string, about the shoes, about everything but the sudden realization of how deeply I had sunk.[108]

With nothing else at their disposal, dire necessity drove some women to exchange sex for better food, clothing, or anything that might increase

---

[104] Cited in Langbein, *People in Auschwitz*, 95–6.   [105] Ibid., 95.
[106] Ibid., 98.   [107] Lengyel, *Five Chimneys*, 182.
[108] Cited in Lisa Pine, 'Gender and the Holocaust: Male and Female Experiences of Auschwitz', in Amy E. Randall (ed.), *Genocide and Gender in the Twentieth Century: A Comparative Survey* (London: Bloomsbury, 2015), 47.

their chances of survival. Myrna Goldenberg calls this 'sex for survival'.[109] This is a difficult area to write about. The legal scholar Catherine MacKinnon powerfully argues that the extreme power imbalances generating this type of relationship mean that the sex could never be described as consensual.[110] However, I would suggest that women nevertheless did consent to sex in Auschwitz and even on occasion initiated it. To deny this is to deny women's ability to make strategic choices even in extremity— for example, to employ sex as another commodity to be bartered. If we are to see women in history as active agents—rather than as one-dimensional victims—then we need to take seriously the choices they make, even if they do not accord with our own moral values. Furthermore, there are differences between rape, coerced sex, prostitution, and abuse, not least in the ways in which women interpret their experiences. Whilst there are often very fine lines between these experiences we do have to acknowledge ambiguities. Gisella Perl writes that her initial moral aversion to the brutal exchange of sex for food slowly gave way to a grudging understanding. Here she describes one such encounter.

> Detachments of male workers came into Camp C almost daily, to clean the latrines, build streets, and patch up leaking roofs. These men were trusted old prisoners who knew everything there was to know about camp life, had connections in the crematories and were masters at 'organizing'. Their full pockets made them the Don Juans of Camp C. They chose their women among the youngest, the prettiest, the least emaciated prisoners and in a few seconds the deal was closed. Openly, shamelessly, the dirty, diseased bodies clung together for a minute or two in the fetid atmosphere of the latrine— and the piece of bread, the comb, the little knife wandered from the pocket of the man into the greedy hands of the woman. At first I was deeply shocked at these practices. My pride, my integrity as a woman revolted against the very idea. I begged and preached and, when I had my first cases of venereal disease, I even threatened to refuse treatment if they didn't stop prostitution. But later, when I saw that the pieces of bread thus earned saved lives, when I met a young girl whom a pair of shoes, earned in a week of prostitution, saved from being thrown into the crematory, I began to understand and forgive.[111]

[109] Myrna Goldenberg, 'Rape during the Holocaust', in Zygmunt Mazur, Jay T. Lees, Arnold Krammer, and Władysław Witalisz (eds.), *The Legacy of the Holocaust: Women and the Holocaust* (Kraków: Jagiellonian University Press, 2007), 159–69.

[110] See Catherine A. MacKinnon, 'Rape, Genocide, and Women's Human Rights', *Harvard Women's Law Journal*, 17/5 (1994), 5–16. Cf. idem, *Are Women Human? And Other Dialogues* (Cambridge, MA: Harvard University Press, 2006).

[111] Perl, *I Was a Doctor in Auschwitz*, 78–9.

What is more, not all these relationships were mercenary. Men and women still sought love and affection even in Auschwitz. Ruth Elias also writes of the couplings that happened in the washrooms. However, for her, they signalled 'the desperate drive to get as close as possible to a loved one and to give each other a sense of security and belonging, a desperate desire to fill our hopeless lives with love'.[112] For people robbed of all those they had loved the desire for some connection—intellectual, emotional, physical, sexual—could be overwhelming.

Joan Ringelheim interviewed a woman named 'Susan', who was imprisoned in Auschwitz when she was 21 years old and quickly became a 'privileged prisoner'. A Polish male prisoner came to Susan one day and offered her some sardines. He told her when and where to meet him, and, not apparently realizing what his motives were, she did. She then told Ringelheim, 'he grabbed and raped me'.[113] This is an important story for it demonstrates the fact that although some of the women who were raped in the camps might have been given food afterwards it was nevertheless, irrefutably still rape. It is also interesting to note that Susan is careful to convey that it was not a Jewish prisoner, but a Polish prisoner, who raped her. Not only does this connect the story to classic narratives of Polish anti-Semitism, but it avoids encroaching on one of the ultimate taboos: the possibility that Jewish men might have raped Jewish women. Of course, the sharp separation of inmates into male and female camps to a degree forestalled such a possibility. But it is noteworthy that, whereas records were kept of Jewish men raping Jewish women in the ghettos, the aura of sanctity which now surrounds the experience of the camps has prevented even survivors from articulating this possibility.[114]

Every Jew, male or female, young or old, religious or secular, was ultimately condemned to death. However, the hellish world of Auschwitz proves beyond all doubt that for Jewish women the racism and sexism of the Nazis cast them in a particularly vulnerable position. Because it was a crime for Jewish women to be pregnant, and because Jewish children were seen to represent a future threat to the purity and safety of the Aryan race, women who entered the camp either pregnant or with young children were condemned to a certain death. Those women

---

[112] Elias, *Triumph of Hope*, 114.

[113] Joan Ringelheim, 'The Split between Gender and the Holocaust', in Ofer and Weitzman (eds.), *Women in the Holocaust*, 341.

[114] The taboo surrounding the subject is exemplified in the story of male rape—of child sexual abuse—by a Jewish man outlined in Roman Frister's *The Cap: The Price of a Life* (New York: Continuum, 1999). Strikingly, most reviews ignore this incident and none, to my knowledge, explore the ethnicity or religion of the rapist.

whose pregnancy was not yet noticeable or who became pregnant after entering the camp would have to choose between their own and their children's lives. As part of the genocidal intent to destroy their reproductive capacity, racially inferior Jewish and Roma and Sinti women and men were also subjected to Nazi medical experiments in mass sterilization. Not deemed to be human, these women and men became experimental subjects—or even objects, nothing more than living specimens on which to work.

Whilst the racial laws made rape by the SS rare, Jewish women were subjected to sexual intimidation and sexual abuse from their first moments in the camps. Women who survived the initiation process were also subject to exploitation by the *Kapos* and other prisoner functionaries, both Jewish and non-Jewish. Beginning with a painful search of the most vulnerable parts of their bodies and followed by the brutal removal of their hair, women experienced a violent assault that robbed them of their identity and sense of agency. For religious Jewish women this sense of loss was particularly acute. Finally, the replacement of their names by tattooed serial numbers told them that there could be no return to their pre-war lives. They were now subject to the dictates of anyone who had more power than them—from the SS guards to the miserable prisoners in charge of the soup cauldrons. This made women—and in particular young women—particularly vulnerable to rape and sexual abuse. Most women carried with them this awareness even if they did not experience it themselves. For other women sex became a necessary commodity for survival.

4

After the War

The Holocaust, as we have seen repeatedly, was a gendered process. It specifically targeted women. It targeted them as sexual beings. It targeted them as caregivers. And it targeted them as mothers and child bearers. The collapse of the political and social structures that the Holocaust engendered did not, remarkably enough, undermine the structures and importance of gender itself. This was even true—in fact, it was most starkly expressed—in the camps, where gender dictated the location, treatment, and fate of victims. Liberation changed much. But it did not change the importance of gender.

This truth can be illustrated in many different ways, but it is best captured by an examination of life, love, sex, and parenthood in the Displaced Persons (DPs) camps set up in the aftermath of the Holocaust. In the concentration and death camps pregnant women and mothers of small children had been sentenced to an immediate death. Jewish children represented a Jewish future, a continuation of Jewish existence, and therefore could not be allowed to survive. In the wake of the Nazi defeat, the birth of Jewish children consequently seemed to represent a triumph over Nazism. Jewish babies born to women who had been destined for murder were literally termed *Maschiachskinder* (children of the Messiah).[1] The Nazis had sentenced the Jews to death just for being Jewish—for having one or more Jewish grandparent. As a result, each Jewish child born after the Holocaust represented hope from a place of total despair and a tangible investment in Jewish survival. Jewish children were seen not only as a new beginning but also helped immortalize the dead through the commitment to Jewish continuity.

However, this focus on reproduction meant, as the historian Atina Grossmann has written, that Jewish men and women needed to conform

[1] Atina Grossmann, 'Victims, Villains, and Survivors: Gendered Perceptions and Self-Perceptions of Jewish Displaced Persons in Occupied Postwar Germany', *The Journal of the History of Sexuality*, 11/1–2, Special Issue: Sexuality and German Fascisms (January/April 2002), 309.

to specifically gendered roles.[2] She argues, 'Just as the persecution and murder of all Jews had been differentiated by age and gender, so too was their return to life.'[3] This chapter will look at some of the ways in which gender continued to structure the lives of men and women after the war had ended, in particular the ways in which the extreme focus on women's sexuality and their reproductive function ironically reinforced the Nazi obsession with women's reproductive roles. The Nazis had divided women into those deemed worthy to bear pure Aryan children and those 'non-women' who must be prevented from having children by whatever means necessary. In the aftermath of the Holocaust, Jewish women were told that the roles had been reversed and it was now *their* duty to bear healthy Jewish children. This reversal, of course, only had the effect of reinforcing distinctions and hierarchies of gender. In that respect, at least, liberation was far from liberating, as an exploration of gender in the Allied zone of occupied Germany shows all too clearly.

Most of the survivors were aged between 16 and 40 and had few remaining family members still alive. Very few children and almost no old people survived the war. Estimates have proved extremely difficult—and any figures are only approximate—but, at the end of the war on 8 May 1945, it is thought that around 200,000 Jews had survived the forced-labour camps, concentration camps, death camps, and death marches. Thousands more survived in hiding, in Soviet exile, or in partisan groups. The majority had not grasped the full extent of the catastrophe. Livia Bitton-Jackson writes: 'I had known about the gas chambers all along. Its shadow followed us even when we left Auschwitz driven by its fear. But I had stubbornly clung to the myth of the camp for elderly and children',[4] continuing to hope, for example, that rumours of special accommodation for the needy—for the elderly and children—were true. For many survivors, all they had left was the memory of those whom they had lost. The survivors were also penniless and homeless and facing still dangerous and uncertain futures. Nearly all the concentration camps had been liberated prior to the end of the war and the prisoners freed with only limited rations to find their own ways home.[5] Released from Auschwitz, Sara Nomberg-Przytyk remembers: 'I was alone, no one was

---

[2] See Atina Grossmann, *Jews, Germans, and Allies: Close Encounters in Occupied Germany* (Princeton, NJ: Princeton University Press 2007).

[3] Ibid., 204.

[4] Livia E. Bitton-Jackson, *Elli: Coming of Age in the Holocaust* (London: Grafton, 1984), 191.

[5] See Dan Stone's excellent study, *The Liberation of the Camps: The End of the Holocaust and its Aftermath* (New Haven, CT: Yale University Press, 2015).

waiting for me, there was no one to return to.'[6] And Primo Levi wrote, 'In the majority of cases, the hour of liberation was neither joyful, nor lighthearted.'[7] Samuel Pisar, one of the youngest Holocaust survivors, who was 16 at liberation, echoes this, stating: 'No, for us this was not the happy ending. It was the beginning of something unknown, disturbing, painful.'[8] Dr Hadassah Bimko Rosensaft, a young Jewish doctor who survived Auschwitz-Birkenau and Bergen-Belsen, explains further:

> For years, I have seen a film on television showing the world's reaction to the end of the war. In Times Square in New York, in the streets of London and Paris, people were dancing, singing, crying, embracing each other. They were filled with joy that their dear ones would soon come home. Whenever I see that film, I cry. We in Belsen did not dance on that day. We had nothing to be hopeful for. Nobody was waiting for us anywhere. We were alone and abandoned.[9]

In the months after the war tens of thousands continued to die of starvation, disease, and the after-effects of malnutrition.[10] Allied soldiers, appalled at what they were witnessing and desperate to reach out to the emaciated survivors, gave them their rations of chocolate, cheese, and calorific tinned food. However, it was too much for their shrunken stomachs and many survivors, who were unable to stop eating after dreaming of such riches for so long, succumbed to diarrhoea and other gastrointestinal illnesses, which in their weakened states proved fatal. According to some estimates, approximately 2,000 prisoners died from being given the wrong food after liberation.[11] At the same time the liberating troops did manage to save thousands of dying survivors. In Bergen-Belsen, British military medical personnel, together with the stronger of the survivors and volunteer medical students, treated many of the typhus-ridden Jews. Dr Bimko Rosensaft was appointed to organize the medical efforts. She worked round the clock to save as many of the survivors as possible.[12]

---

[6] Sara Nomberg-Przytyk, *Auschwitz: True Tales from a Grotesque Land*, trans. Roslyn Hirsch, eds. Eli Pfefferkorn and David H. Hirsch (Chapel Hill, NC: University of North Carolina Press, 1985), 154.

[7] Primo Levi, *The Drowned and the Saved*, trans. Raymond Rosenthal (London: Abacus, 1988), 70.

[8] Samuel Pisar, *Of Blood and Hope* (London: Cassell, 1979), 98.

[9] Hadassah Rosensaft, *Yesterday: My Story* (Jerusalem: Yad Vashem, 2004), 55.

[10] Michael R. Marrus, *The Holocaust in History* (Harmondsworth: Penguin, 1993), 195.

[11] Ben Shepard, *After Daybreak: The Liberation of Belsen, 1945* (London: Jonathan Cape, 2005), 42.

[12] Hadassah (also known as Ada) Bimko Rosensaft was deported to Auschwitz-Birkenau from the ghetto of Sosnowiec (Poland) in August 1943. As she had medical experience (she had qualified as a dental surgeon) she was assigned by Josef Mengele to work in the

The British military rabbi Leslie Hardman was part of the British Army who liberated Bergen-Belsen on 17 April 1945. The camp had originally been set up in 1943 by Heinrich Himmler as an internment camp for Jews who were to be held as hostages to be exchanged for German nationals in Britain and America. Only a handful, however, benefitted from this exchange, and by 1945 Jews from all over eastern Europe had been deported there. Although it was a concentration camp and not a death camp (which meant it lacked gas chambers and the means systematically to murder its victims), conditions quickly become so awful that a major typhus epidemic had broken out. In a women's typhus barracks Hardman and his colleagues found conditions to be so overcrowded that more than a thousand seriously ill women lay naked or semi-naked on the bare floor. He describes one of his first encounters with a young girl, an inmate, who later became his guide:

> I shall always remember the first person I met. It was a girl, and I thought she was a negress. Her face was dark brown, and I afterwards learnt that this was because her skin was in the process of healing, after being burnt. When she saw me she made as though to throw her arms around me; but with the instinct of self-preservation, I jumped back. Instantly I felt ashamed; but she understood, and stood away from me.

> I looked at her; fear, compassion, and shame were struggling for mastery within me; but she was the more composed of the two. We walked into the compound, keeping our voluntary 'no-man's-land' between us. Suddenly my body stiffened, and I stood still in my tracks. Before and around me were lying dozens of emaciated bodies, naked, semi-naked, huddled together.

> 'Are they all asleep?' I asked.

> 'No, they're dead; they've been there for days', the girl replied unemotionally, stating the simple fact.

> I tried to look at them again. I had to look in order to know, to learn, and if possible to help, but these were beyond help: these, my people. The foul stench which polluted the air sickened me, and only the girl's presence enabled me to overcome my nausea.

> As we walked on, towards us came what seemed to me to be the remnants of a holocaust—a tottering mass of blackened skin and bones, held together somehow with filthy rags.

infirmary at Birkenau in October 1943. A year later Mengele sent her as a member of a 'medical team' to Bergen-Belsen. Here, in December 1944–January 1945, she was entrusted with the care of 150 Jewish children. Dr Bimko Rosensaft later became a member of the Central Committee of Liberated Jews in the British Zone of Germany, and head of its health department. In 1947, she became vice-chairman of the Central Committee's Council, responsible for Jewish survivors throughout the British zone.

'My God, the dead are walking!' I cried aloud, but I did not recognise my voice.

'They are not dead', said the girl. 'But they will soon be.'[13]

Gerald Raperport was one of ninety-six medical students brought from London in May 1945. In an article published in a hospital journal in 1945, he wrote:

> Men and women would walk around the camp stark naked, cold as it was, and think nothing of it; they would sit side by side on the latrines and gaze on passers-by unblushingly, expressionlessly. Before long we ceased to marvel at the sight of emaciated figures crawling out of their huts with eating bowls in their hands which they had first used as bedpans, emptying them down the nearest latrine, wiping them on the filthy rags that served as clothing, and then returning to the huts to take their meals from these self-same bowls. And when the food was brought, those that were strong enough would fall upon it and fight for every morsel they could obtain, thinking only of themselves and caring nothing for those who could not move and who consequently went without, all gibbering unintelligently in high-pitched tones the while like a swarm of angry monkeys. Death was meaningless for them and corpses reviled them not a bit: we would do 'corpse-rounds' each morning to pick out the dead in much the same way as a nurse would do a [ward] round here in England and with the identical atmosphere of routine normality.[14]

Around 10,000 unburied corpses were found lying on the ground, among them the emaciated, typhus-ridden bodies of Anne Frank and her sister Margot.[15] As the task of burying so many bodies on the sandy Belsen soil was onerous, the British Army used bulldozers to shovel them into the graves, often splitting the bodies as they did so.

Survivors continued to die from the after-effects of starvation and disease for months following liberation.[16] The British journalist Richard Dimbleby was among the first to report the horror. He described how a female survivor screamed at a soldier for milk to feed her baby before thrusting it into his arms and running off. 'When he opened the bundle, he found that the baby had been dead for days. This day at Belsen was the

---

[13] Cited in L.H. Hardman and Cecily Goodman, *The Survivors: The Story of the Belsen Remnant* (London: Vallentine Mitchell, 1958), 2–3.

[14] Gerald Raperport, 'Expedition to Belsen', *The Middlesex Hospital Journal*, 45 (1945), 21–4. Cited in Suzanne Bardgett and David Cesarani (eds.), *Belsen 1945: New Historical Perspectives* (London: Vallentine Mitchell, 2006), 58–9.

[15] See Zoë Waxman, *Anne Frank* (Gloucestershire: The History Press, 2015), Chapter 3.

[16] Robert H. Abzug, *Inside the Vicious Heart: Americans and the Liberation of Nazi Concentration Camps* (New York: Oxford University Press, 1985), 151.

most horrible of my life.'[17] The experience was so distressing that Dimbleby was unable to complete the radio report and his eyewitness testimony was not broadcast until several days later. The staff at the BBC found the report almost impossible to believe. By the middle of May the concentration camp barracks at Belsen had been burnt down to prevent further disease and the remaining survivors transferred to a nearby military camp. It became the DP camp of Bergen-Belsen and the largest of its kind in Germany.

While the survivors continued to die in the newly evacuated camps, General Dwight Eisenhower, Commander of the Allied Forces in Europe, implemented a formal policy of repatriation for DPs—the term used by the Allies to describe foreign nationals unable to return to their countries of origin. This was possible for non-Jews and also—though often difficult—for Jews from western, northern, and southern Europe. But it proved to be almost impossible for east European Jews from Communist-occupied countries. Jews trying to return to homes in Poland, Hungary, Romania, Czechoslovakia, and Bulgaria faced much heartache. Most desperately wanted to find the husbands, wives, fiancées, children, parents, brothers, and sisters they had long fantasized about being reunited with, but rarely did this happen. Some survivors discovered that every single Jewish person they had known before the war was now dead.[18]

Parents were particularly desperate to find out if their children had managed to survive. They begged the people whom they had entrusted with hiding them for information on their fate. Yehuda Bauer has estimated that in France alone up to 7,000 Jewish children were hidden.[19] In cases where children had been hidden secretly and moved from place to place they often could not be found. In extremis, as we have seen, parents had been forced to abandon their children on the doors of non-Jewish homes and institutions. It was almost impossible to piece together what had happened to the children. Parents were also often no longer able to recognize the children they had left behind and the children, if very young when left, did not remember them either.[20] Frequently the children had

[17] Reported in John J. Michalczyk, *Filming the End of the Holocaust: Allied Documentaries, Nuremberg and the Liberation of the Concentration Camps* (London: Bloomsbury, 2014), 32.

[18] Yael Danieli, 'The Impact of the Holocaust Experience on Survivors in the U.S.', in Israel Gutman and Avital Saf (eds.), *The Nazi Concentration Camps: Structure and Aim, The Image of the Prisoner, The Jews in the Camps: Proceedings of the Fourth Yad Vashem International Historical Conference—January 1980* (Jerusalem: Yad Vashem, 1984), 605.

[19] Yehuda Bauer, *A History of the Holocaust* (London: Franklin Watts, 2002), 305.

[20] See Joanna Beata Michlic, 'Rebuilding Shattered Lives: Some Vignettes of Jewish Children's Lives in Early Postwar Poland', in Dalia Ofer, Françoise S. Ouzan, and Judy Baumel Schwartz (eds.), *Holocaust Survivors: Resettlement, Memories, Identities* (New York: Berghahn, 2011), 46–87, and idem, 'The War Began for Me after the War', in Jonathan Friedman (ed.), *The Routledge History of the Holocaust* (London: Routledge, 2011), 482–97.

been told that their parents had died. Some children who had forgotten or who had never been taught Yiddish were unable even to converse with their parents. Other children were so emotionally scarred by their wartime experiences that they found it difficult to express or even receive affection. Robert Krell survived in hiding in Holland for three years. He was 5 years old when his parents came to find him. He recalls that:

> Liberation was not particularly liberating, for within a few days I was 'liberated' from those I loved ... to rejoin my father and mother who had emerged from their respective hiding places. I cried in protest, and they had to prove I was theirs with photos taken when I was aged about one and a half. Of course, I was actually the luckiest of all children in having my parents survive. Try telling that to a 5 year old with no memory of them, after nearly three years with another family.[21]

On occasion desperate parents tried to claim a child that was not theirs, so badly did they want to believe that their son or daughter had survived. Sometimes the children—especially if they had been baptized, given new names, and raised as Christian—were rehidden in their Christian communities so that they could not be returned to the strange, emaciated Jews who had somehow come back from the dead. Some of these children continued to deny their Jewish heritage throughout their adult lives. In Poland, hostility towards the Jewish survivors was so intense that many rescuers feared persecution from their neighbours. Therefore they did not want to draw attention to the fact that they had saved Jewish children. They also did not want to put the children—whom in some cases they had grown to love—in jeopardy. On other occasions rescuers asked for remuneration in order to surrender their charges. The local police were rarely sympathetic to the Jewish survivors and there were many lawsuits as families sought to keep children who were not their own.[22]

In other cases, the children found themselves alone. Janina David, who was smuggled out of the Warsaw ghetto, did not know the exact fate of her parents. All she knew was that they had died:

> My parents are dead. They died in concentration camps, or betrayed by their fellow citizens, on a city street. I shall never know how, or when, or exactly where it happened and where they were buried. There will be no tomb, the whole country is a tomb, the whole earth a vast grave and, somewhere, they are a part of it.[23]

[21] Cited in Martin Gilbert, *The Day the War Ended: VE-Day 1945 in Europe and around the World* (London: HarperCollins, 1995), 73–5.

[22] On the enormous challenges of finding Jewish children after the war, see Emunah Nachmany Gafny, *Dividing Hearts: The Removal of Jewish Children from Gentile Families in Poland in the Immediate Post-Holocaust Years* (Jerusalem: Yad Vashem, 2009).

[23] Janina David, *A Square of Sky: Memoirs of a Wartime Childhood* (London: Eland, 1992), 429–30.

Livia Bitton-Jackson survived together with her mother and brother, and returned to her home in Czechoslovakia to discover that her much-loved father had died in Bergen-Belsen just two weeks before liberation. Engulfed by grief she asked, 'How are we going to face the future without Daddy?'[24] Indeed, many survivors felt unable to face the future. Particularly when they were the sole survivors of previously large families they were plagued by the question of why they survived when so many others had not.

Survivors also experienced further violence. Jews were killed in pogroms throughout Poland. They were beaten and murdered in the streets and also lost their lives when Jewish buildings were bombed. In Kraków, for example, in August 1945, ten Jews were killed and others seriously injured when a synagogue was set on fire, and on 4 July 1946 forty-two Jews were murdered, and many others injured, in a pogrom in the city of Kielce.[25] Following other violent episodes, approximately 100,000 Jews were forced to flee post-war Poland.[26]

Throughout eastern Europe, Jews found Christian families living in their homes or their homes totally plundered and left in a filthy condition, and encountered suspicion and unease at their return. Olga Barsony Verrall, who had been deported from her home in Szarvas in 1944, states that in post-war Hungary:

There was greater antisemitism [after the war] than had ever existed before, and our best neighbours and former friends would not even talk to us. The Christians in our town had never really exhibited strong antisemitism before the war, but they were fast learners.[27]

Etu Weisfried returned to her pre-war home in Hungary but soon left.[28] She and her new husband were forced to share her old family home with a Christian family, who resented their presence. She soon lost the baby she was carrying. She wrote to her two surviving sisters: 'It was foolish for us to

---

[24] Livia E. Bitton-Jackson, *My Bridges of Hope: Six Long Years to Freedom after Auschwitz* (London: Simon & Schuster, 1999), 8.

[25] See Thomas C. Fox, 'The Holocaust under Communism', in Dan Stone (ed.), *The Historiography of the Holocaust* (Basingstoke: Palgrave Macmillan, 2004), 420–39; and David Engel, 'Patterns of Anti-Jewish Violence in Poland, 1944–1946', *Yad Vashem Studies*, 26 (1998), 43–86.

[26] Jan Tomasz Gross argues that it was Polish guilt about their wartime actions that led to the Kielce pogrom. See his *Fear: Antisemitism in Poland after Auschwitz: An Essay in Historical Interpretation* (New York: Random House, 2007).

[27] Olga Verrall, *Missing Pieces: My Life as a Child Survivor of the Holocaust* (Calgary: University of Calgary Press, 2007), 64.

[28] For an excellent discussion of the post-war situation of Jews in Hungary, see Rita Horavitch, 'Jews in Hungary after the Holocaust: The National Relief Committee for Deportees, 1945–1950', *Journal of Israeli History*, 19 (1998), 69–91.

think that we could build new lives on top of smouldering ashes.'[29]
Weisfried and her husband later immigrated to Israel.

By the end of 1946, more than 150,000 eastern European Jewish
refugees were forced to make dangerous and often illegal journeys to
gather in the DP camps in the Allied zones of Austria, Germany, and
Italy. They constituted a small but significant minority of the approximately ten million unrepatriatable persons including forced labourers and
prisoners of war.[30] At least initially the Allies did not recognize that the
Jewish survivors needed to be treated separately. In 1943 the UNRRA
(United Nations Relief and Rehabilitation Administration) took over
responsibility for DPs—overseeing the distribution of food, medicine,
and clothing to those who had nothing. After the end of the war, in
1945, this meant overseeing the work of hundreds of refugee and DP
camps. Most of the Jewish survivors were housed in camps either on the
grounds of the recently liberated concentration camps or close to them.
Others found themselves in hastily constructed quarters in hospitals,
castles, and private houses, and sometimes even in small apartment blocks.
The ad hoc nature of the arrangements meant that the Jewish survivors—
who referred to themselves as *She'erit hapletah* (the 'Surviving Remnant', a
biblical term from Ezra 9:14 and I Chron. 4:43)[31]—were inevitably
housed alongside Nazi collaborators from Hungary, the Ukraine, and
the Baltic States, and even their former concentration camp guards who
had managed to disguise themselves to get into the DP camps of all types.
In the Neustadt camp on the Baltic Sea, for example, only 800 of the
4,000 DPs were Jewish.[32] In some cases conditions were alarmingly

---

[29] Quoted in Aranka Siegal, *Grace in the Wilderness: After the Liberation 1945–1948*
(New York: Signet, 1985), 66.

[30] As Atina Grossmann points out, the figures, 'both those cited by historians and those
collected at the time, are stunningly variable and surely inaccurate, itself a sign of the chaos
that accompanied peace and the speed with which conditions changed'. See her 'Gendered
Perceptions and Self-Perceptions of Memory and Revenge: Jewish DPs in Occupied
Postwar Germany as Victims, Villains and Survivors', in Judith Tydor Baumel and Tova
Cohen (eds.), *Gender, Place and Memory in the Modern Jewish Experience: Re-Placing
Ourselves* (London: Vallentine Mitchell, 2003), 78. For details of the different types of
DP camps, see Zorach Warhaftig, *Uprooted: Jewish Refugees and Displaced Persons after
Liberation, from War to Peace* (New York: Institute of Jewish Affairs for the American Jewish
Congress & World Jewish Congress, 1946). Cf. Kurt R. Grossmann, *The Jewish DP
Problem: Its Origin, Scope, and Liquidation* (New York: Institute of Jewish Affairs, World
Jewish Congress, 1951).

[31] See Ze'ev Mankowitz, 'The Formation of *She'erith Hapleita* [Surviving Remnant]:
November 1944–July 1945', *Yad Vashem Studies*, 20 (1990), 337–70, and idem, 'The
Affirmation of Life in *She'erith Hapleita* [Surviving Remnant]', *Holocaust and Genocide
Studies*, 5 (1990), 13–21.

[32] Michael Brenner, *After the Holocaust: Rebuilding Jewish Lives in Postwar Germany*,
trans. Barbara Harshav (Princeton, NJ: Princeton University Press, 1997), 11.

reminiscent of those the survivors had been imprisoned in. The constant flux of people in and out of the camps contributed to a feeling of instability. They also experienced anti-Semitism—both explicit and implicit—from some of the Allied troops and aid workers, who found that as the Jewish survivors began to recover and grow stronger they became less and less grateful to their liberators and more difficult. Jane Leverson, a Jewish relief worker and member of the Quaker team, wrote:

> They are very often not grateful for that which is done for them. They are extremely fussy about the clothes with which they are issued. They grumble about their food; they complain if they are asked to eat their meat and vegetable course from their soup plates. They will not take 'no' for an answer, and will beg in an irritatingly 'whiney' voice, for preferential treatment; they will bribe one in a most pathetic way . . . If they are like this now, so soon after liberation, one wonders how they will react when once again they are really free.[33]

Extreme suffering had left its mark on the survivors and they understandably felt they had little to be grateful about.

Although desperate to make their homes in other countries—in particular, the United States or British-controlled Palestine[34]—many were to stay in the camps for years. Zalman Grinberg, chairman of the Central Committee of Liberated Jews for the American Zone in Germany, stated in a public address in Munich in October 1945: 'The remnant of Jewry is gathered here. This is its waiting room. It is a shabby room, so we hope the day will come when the Jews will be taken to a place they can call their own.'[35] Whilst not all survivors wanted to make their home in Israel, to their great disappointment they soon found that the West did not want them either. Ruth Klüger writes:

[33] Cited in Johannes-Dieter Steinert, 'British Relief Teams in Belsen Concentration Camp: Emergency Relief and the Perception of Survivors', in Bardgett and Cesarani (eds.), *Belsen 1945*, 70–1.

[34] Although there was immigration during the two years before the establishment of the State of Israel in 1948, it was an option only for those young and energetic enough to feel able to overcome the hardships and restrictions of British Mandate rule. Of the 70,000 Jews who arrived during this time, mainly through immigration arranged by the semi-clandestine Jewish organization *Bricha* (Hebrew for 'flight') and often after internment by the British authorities in Cyprus, many were Holocaust survivors. See Hanna Yablonka, 'The Formation of Holocaust Consciousness in the State of Israel: The Early Days', in Efraim Sicher (ed.), *Breaking Crystal: Writing and Memory after Auschwitz* (Urbana, IL: Chicago University Press, 1998), 120. For work specifically concerned with the DPs and *Bricha*, see Yehuda Bauer, *Flight and Rescue: Bricha* (New York: Random House, 1970), and Ephraim Dekel, *B'riha: Flight to the Homeland* (New York: Random House, 1973).

[35] Cited in Angelika Königseder and Juliane Wetzel, *Waiting for Hope: Jewish Displaced Persons in Post-World War II Germany*, trans. John A. Broadwin (Evanston, IL: Northwestern University Press, 2001), 4.

The free world didn't welcome us as brothers and sisters, long lost but found again, liberated from evil forces and not to be jubilantly included in the Family of Man. That was the picture my childish yearning had painted. In reality we were a burden, a social problem.[36]

To get to countries such as Britain, the United States, Canada, or Australia, survivors needed birth certificates proving their age and place of birth and a whole range of other documents that they no longer possessed. Survivors who were suffering from illnesses such as tuberculosis found it almost impossible to find a country that would accept them. Instead, they were forced to stay in the often oppressive atmosphere of the DP camps.

In Dachau a football game between Jewish and non-Jewish DPs ended in someone being stabbed when the Jewish team won. Frightened for their lives in these hostile environments, many of the Jewish DPs refused to leave their barracks even to seek food or medical help. American servicemen, as well as the American Jewish Joint Distribution Committee (AJDC or 'Joint'), were so shocked at the treatment of the Jewish survivors that in July 1945 President Truman commissioned Earl G. Harrison, dean of the University of Pennsylvania Law School and American envoy to the Inter-Governmental Committee on Refugees, to investigate conditions in the camps in the American occupation zones of Germany and Austria. Harrison, who was accompanied by Joseph Schwartz, head of the AJDC in Europe, visited over thirty camps and found that many of the Jewish survivors were so mentally and physically damaged by their wartime experiences that they were unable to work or keep their living quarters in good order. Not only did many of the DP camps have only limited water and power supplies, but many were not even supplied with working latrines. Survivors also mostly lived in overcrowded conditions with limited food rations. Men and women often had to share sleeping quarters with only a sheet for privacy. Some of them were still in their concentration camp uniforms, and others were naked much of the time. Although Jewish, they came from different places, spoke different languages, and had different wartime experiences. Whilst some of the Jewish survivors were resolutely secular, others continued to be extremely religious.

What they all had in common, however, was that their freedom continued to be severely restricted. Many Jews had to seek written permission to leave the camps and were subject to strict curfews. The justification was that the German population needed to be protected from potentially vengeful—and possibly criminal—Jewish survivors, and that the survivors

---

[36] Klüger, *Landscapes of Memory*, 181.

needed to be protected from the still murderous Germans. Some survivors ran away as they could not bear to be imprisoned in camps again. Many also needed to travel to find their loved ones. Polish Auschwitz survivor and renowned writer and journalist Tadeusz Borowski tells a supposedly fictional story—but one that is probably based on events he actually experienced—of how an American soldier shot and killed a young Jewish girl who was trying to leave camp Allach (near Dachau), ignoring orders. When other DPs surrounded the dead body, an American lieutenant driving a jeep stops and asks, 'What's happened? Who harmed these people? Why do they shout so?' He is quietly informed, 'Nothing, sir. Nothing happened. You ['you guys', you plural] have just shot and killed a girl from the camp.' It is revealing that this episode is left out of the English translation of Borowski's work.[37]

Harrison's envoy recognized that the Jewish survivors needed not only better living conditions, but also moral support. His report, which Truman relayed to Eisenhower, and which was published in the *New York Times*, stated that:

> We appear to be treating the Jews as the Nazis treated them except that we do not exterminate them. They are in concentration camps in large numbers under our military guard instead of the SS troops. One is led to wonder whether the German people seeing this are not supposing that we are following or a least condoning Nazi policy.[38]

The result was the establishment of separate camps for Jews—Feldafing, Landsberg, and Föhrenwald in the US zone—and in the spring of 1946 a special advisor on Jewish affairs was appointed. Ultimately, Harrison wanted the Jewish DPs resettled if possible in Palestine, which was still a British protectorate with restricted Jewish immigration, or, if not there, in the United States (which until 1948 had strict immigration quotas), the British Empire, or countries in South America. Until this was possible, Jewish voluntary agencies such as the AJDC took over the running of the internal administration of the camps in the US zone, including sanitation, education, and religious and cultural activities while, in the British zone, the Jewish Relief Unit (JRU) took over welfare matters.

Although both men and women suffered in this situation, for women the situation in the DP camps had the potential to be particularly

[37] Tadeusz Borowski, 'The Battle for Grunwald', from the short story collection by Janusz Nel Siedlecki et al., *We Were in Auschwitz* (New York: Welcome Rain Publishers, 2000), cited in Tadeusz Debski, *A Battlefield of Ideas: Nazi Concentration Camps and their Political Prisoners* (New York: Columbia University Press, 2001), 246.

[38] Harrison Report, quoted in Leonard Dinnerstein, *America and the Survivors of the Holocaust* (New York: Columbia University Press, 1982), 300–1.

precarious. It is difficult to give precise figures on the sexual composition of the DP camps but it is reasonable to assume that fewer women than men survived the Holocaust. As we have seen, conditions in the women's camps had been worse and women—unlike men—were driven to their deaths with their children. As a result, in most of the DP camps, it is estimated that women made up about 40 per cent of the population. Moreover, they were treated and perceived very differently. At Belsen, which was in the centre of the British zone and the largest of the DP camps, Lieutenant-Colonel M.W. Gonin observed how differently the female survivors started to behave once they were given make-up. Belsen had received a consignment of red lipsticks. Gonin wrote:

> Women lay in bed with no sheets and no nightie but with scarlet lips, you saw them wandering about with nothing but a blanket over their shoulders, but with scarlet lips . . . At least someone had done something to make them individuals again; they were someone, no longer merely the number tattooed on the arm. At least they could take an interest in their appearance. That lipstick started to give them back their humanity.[39]

Whilst an interest in physical appearance is often interpreted positively as a sign of rehabilitation, Gonin's comments point to the fact that for these women survivors becoming human again meant asserting—enacting or performing—their gendered identities.[40] It also meant that women who had been until recently emaciated, bald, and sexually powerless suddenly found themselves the object of what seemed like positive male attention. For women from religious backgrounds this was often their first introduction to make-up and western ideals of femininity. All this made them extremely vulnerable. At liberation Livia Bitton-Jackson was mistaken for a woman of 62, when she was only 14.[41] In her testimony she bemoans the fact that whilst she 'remained skinny and unattractive', 'other girls blossomed into shapely young women', attracting male attention.[42] The sexual vulnerability of Jewish women in the post-war area remains a sensitive—and somewhat unexplored—topic in the afterlife of the Holocaust.

That the Red Army's seizure of Germany was accompanied by the mass rape of German women is widely known.[43] However, Jewish women were

---

[39] Cited in Steinert, 'British Relief Teams in Belsen Concentration Camp', 73.
[40] See Judith Butler, *Gender Trouble: Feminism and the Subversion of Identity* (New York: Routledge, 1990).
[41] Bitton-Jackson, *Elli*, 168.   [42] Ibid., 233.
[43] See, for example, Norman M. Naimark, *The Russians in Germany: A History of the Soviet Zone of Occupation, 1945–1949* (Cambridge, MA: Harvard University Press, 1995).

also clearly exposed to sexual violence and abuse—and this from the men who liberated them. There are many testimonies of Jewish girls who were raped or suffered attempted rape on their way from the camps.[44] In addition, they risked unwanted sexual advances by the American and British troops who were tempted to exploit the power they had over the DPs.

This can be understood as part of the depressingly familiar pattern of liberating armies who expect women not only to be grateful to them but to express that gratitude in sexual ways. It also meant a resumption of exchanging food for sex which had, for some, characterized life in the ghettoes and even in the camps. In that sense, this was less liberation than business as usual. Hungarian-born writer and director Edith Bruck survived Auschwitz, Dachau, Christianstadt, and Bergen-Belsen. She writes that in the latter DP camp,

> [T]he Americans would offer us chocolate or white bread, but only in exchange for a walk. At Bergen the most popular words were: *promenade, chocolate*! Many accepted, and many ended up pregnant during a promenade . . . Many women would give themselves for a dressing gown or for a few cans of meat.[45]

Polish Holocaust survivor Chava Rosenfarb wrote a diary in the DP camp at Belsen, excerpts of which were first published in Yiddish in 1948. In a diary entry dated 28 June she wrote:

> Two girls from our barrack did not come back to sleep last night. They arrived in time for lunch, bringing with them cigarettes and chocolates. They are not yet twenty years old. The Englishmen with whom they spent the night are the first men to admire their fresh, newly budding femininity. They are not the only ones in the camp. The forest is full of amorous couples. One meets them strolling along all the roads and pathways. One can hear again the almost-forgotten sound of women's laughter, a laughter meant specifically for men.
>
> Sometimes when I hear this laughter I have the impression that it will suddenly turn into a wild cry, into the painful longing wail of a woman's soul, a woman who tries to find in the eyes, hands, and smiles of a stranger some small trace of the beloved man she once knew. From all the corners of the yard, from all the rooms, I can hear the sounds of gaiety and laughter.

---

[44] Interpreting these testimonies is not easy. Often the experience of rape is attributed to a third person—a friend or companion; still more often sexual abuse is obscured or merely alluded to. See, for example, the oblique references in Sara Selver-Urbach, *Through the Window of My Home: Recollections from the Lodz Ghetto*, trans. Siona Bidansky (Jerusalem: Yad Vashem, 1971).

[45] Edith Bruck, *Who Loves You Like This* (Philadelphia, PA: Paul Dry, 2001), 57.

'Look, I have forgotten!' the cheerful voices call. But it is enough to look into the women's eyes to know something different.

The eighteen- and nineteen-year-old girls laugh earnestly and unaffectedly. How clever and wonderful life is! As if afraid that the nightmare they have just lived through might destroy their tender, young, newly awoken bodies. Life has taught them to forget. Easy, pleasant forgetfulness. Is it their fault that in their dreams they see the reflections of their parents' faces, or the smiles of their sisters and brothers, or shudder at the horrors they have so recently survived? During the day the girls flutter busily about singing, drawn from every barrack and courtyard to those who will teach them for the first time the language of love. The words may be strange, but they understand the gestures and the kisses. And then there is the sweetness of chocolate to bring back memories of their distant and yet not-so-distant childhoods.

Some women sell themselves to the soldiers simply and knowingly, just for the taste of a slice of white bread.[46]

In view of the above, it will not be surprising to learn that most of the abortions carried out at this time in the Allied zones were probably the result of impregnations by British and American soldiers.[47] Precise figures are impossible to come by as abortion was illegal in Germany (in both the Allied and Soviet zones) at this time unless it was for medical reasons or if a woman could prove rape by a foreigner.[48] Instead—again, just as in the ghettoes or even in the camps—women were forced into secret abortions which they procured on the black market. Although there was now, of course, no death sentence for pregnancy, a birth was a life sentence and neither the US nor the British Army agreed to take responsibility for illegitimate children.[49] Ultimately, one cannot gauge how many women were raped, coerced into having sex, or both—for the boundaries were, and are, not clear—by the liberating troops. Women were understandably reluctant to report such experiences, especially at the hands of those they were supposed to be grateful to. Moreover, as survivors of the Holocaust,

[46] Rosenfarb's daughter, Goldie Morgentaler, translated her mother's diary and published excerpts of it in *Tablet Magazine* (27 January 2014). See Chava Rosenfarb, <http://www.tabletmag.com/jewish-arts-and-culture/books/160640/rosenfarb.bergen.belsen.diary> (accessed 1 September 2016).

[47] Margarete Myers Feinstein, *Holocaust Survivors in Postwar Germany, 1945–1957* (Cambridge, MA: Cambridge University Press, 2014), 128.

[48] This was a temporary exception to Germany's strict abortion laws, brought about chiefly by the mass rape of German women by Red Army troops: see Atina Grossmann, *Reforming Sex: The German Movement for Birth Control and Abortion Reform, 1920–1950* (New York: Oxford University Press, 1995), 193–4, 195.

[49] See Barbara Smith Scibetta and Elfrieda Berthiaume Shukert, *War Brides of World War II* (New York: Penguin, 1989), and Myers Feinstein, *Holocaust Survivors in Postwar Germany*, 128.

many felt that these experiences paled in comparison with those who had not survived. Even so, testimonies suggest that sexual predators could be found everywhere. In that way, at least, surprisingly—alarmingly—little had changed.

Of course, some of the relationships that developed between the British and American servicemen and the Jewish survivors were based on genuine affection. Gerda Weissmann Klein married one of the German-Jewish American soldiers who had liberated her. When they first met he asked her if she had been sterilized. The relationship moved forward when she replied that she had not, although initially she found it hard to believe that he could be interested in her:

> I certainly couldn't look pretty to him. I recalled the pictures of beautiful American girls in the magazines he had brought me. Those were the girls he knew. Surely I could never compare with those girls. Besides, he must always remember me the way I looked when he met me, more like an animal than a human being.[50]

She later moved with him to Buffalo, New York, and found that: 'The greatest relief from the burdens of my past . . . was when death truly turned into life and the ultimate question was answered: Yes, I could have a healthy, normal child.'[51] Judith Magyar Isaacson also married an American soldier and moved with him to the United States, where she had a family and pursued a successful career.[52] For these women American men represented the possibility of a future far removed from the death and destruction of eastern Europe and the chance to bear children and bring them up in a land of freedom and plenty.

Nevertheless, it was partly because of their sexual vulnerability that many young women married quickly, eager for male protection. Celia K. married her husband just three weeks after meeting him, because 'everyone was out there raping girls'.[53] Subsequently, some women became mothers very young. It is estimated that in Belsen alone there were over a thousand marriages between 1945 and 1947.[54] In the first year after liberation as many as seven weddings were held daily. The newly founded Yiddish newspapers were soon filled with notices of weddings.[55]

[50] Gerda Weissmann Klein, *All But My Life* (New York: Hill & Wang, 1975), 231.

[51] Ibid.

[52] See Judith Magyar Isaacson, *Seed of Sarah: Memoirs of a Survivor* (Chicago, IL: University of Illinois Press, 1991).

[53] Cited in Beverley Chalmers, *Birth, Sex and Abuse: Women's Voices under Nazi Rule* (Guildford: Grosvenor House, 2015), 115.

[54] Cited in Brenner, *After the Holocaust*, 26.

[55] See Margarete Myers Feinstein, 'Hannah's Prayer: Jewish Women as Displaced Persons, 1945–1948', in Marcia Sachs Littell (ed.), *Women in the Holocaust: Responses,*

The AJDC built *mikvehs* (ritual baths) and produced wedding rings as well as wigs for Haredi brides. Few had any surviving family members at the weddings.

Often the grooms were men already known to the young brides— former neighbours or distant family members. The DP administrations as well as American Jewish organizations circulated lists of survivors which were scanned obsessively for surviving family members. In the inevitable absence of loved ones, survivors searched instead for people from their home towns, and sometimes men and women were brought together in this way. In such cases women could feel that their families had actually known their new husbands and might have approved of their unions. Edith Bruck fell in love with a fellow Hungarian survivor who reminded her of her brother. He evoked feelings of trust and a shared past.[56]

Ashkenazi Jews from Orthodox communities fleeing from eastern Europe were keen to find partners they could speak Yiddish with and who understood their religious traditions. They were seeking to rediscover 'Yiddishkeit' ('Jewishness') and all the religious commandments, customs, behaviours, and familial relationships associated with it.[57] However, survivors were sometimes so eager to feel a sense of closeness that they overlooked factors that in pre-war life might have proved important, such as socio-economic and educational status, age, and mutual attraction. Moreover, as was observed by Anton Gill, the British writer who interviewed over 120 survivors in the 1980s, it was impossible for the survivor to return to the person he or she had once been, no matter how desperately they desired to do so.[58]

Sometimes women married men who really were strangers—and who turned out to be highly unsuitable—within days of meeting them. Edith Horowitz stated that there were 'so many marriages, sometimes really strange marriages that never would have happened before the war'.[59] Most survivors wanted to rebuild their lives as quickly as possible and therefore the period between engagement and marriage was usually extremely brief. Newly married couples admitted with some irony that

Insights and Perspectives (Selected Papers from the Annual Scholars' Conference on the Holocaust and the Churches 1990–2000) (Merion Station, PA: Merion Westfield Press, 2001), 173–85.

[56] Bruck, *Who Loves You Like This.*

[57] See Michal Shaul, 'Testimonies of Ultra-Orthodox Holocaust Survivors', *Yad Vashem Studies*, 35/2, 143–85.

[58] Anton Gill, *The Journey Back from Hell: Conversations with Concentration Camp Survivors* (London: HarperCollins, 1994), 9–16.

[59] Cited in Atina Grossmann, 'Living On: Remembering Feldafing', in Jürgen Matthäus (ed.), *Approaching an Auschwitz Survivor: Holocaust Testimony and Its Transformations* (Oxford: Oxford University Press, 2009), 78.

'Hitler married us.'[60] What most couples had in common were terrible experiences and a desperate desire not to be alone. Psychiatrists such as Yael Danieli, who work specifically with Holocaust survivors, have described such partnerships as 'marriages of despair',[61] suggesting that these marriages were intended to compensate for all the suffering survivors had been forced to endure and to form the basis for a new, often idealized, future.

In addition, religious leaders in the DP camps encouraged young Jewish couples to get married as quickly as possible. This was partly out of a commitment to a Jewish future and was partly an attempt to curtail the sexual activity—and even sexual promiscuity—that they saw as being rife in the DP camps. Just as Jewish men in the ghettos lamented the inappropriate behaviour of young Jewish women, so too in the DP camps they continued to comment on the dubious morality of young girls. In other words, Jewish women were being protected not only from potential sexual predators but also from themselves. It was felt that female promiscuity might prevent a woman from getting married and—still more importantly for some men—it was hard to witness the scorn of the Allied officials, social workers, psychologists, and medical personnel at the 'undignified' behaviour of Jewish women.

Many of the relief workers and social workers who worked with the DPs observed that 'after the years of repression, gloom, terror and want', what psychoanalysts have called the almost 'hypersexuality' of the DP camps was an attempt to satisfy the 'pent-up desire to live'.[62] In other words, the young Jewish survivors wanted affection, sexual gratification, and proximity to another human being. After the war Czech-Hungarian Auschwitz survivor Aranka Siegal was sent to a school in Sweden for child survivors. She entered into a romantic relationship with another young survivor called David. She describes how one evening: 'His hands moved toward my hair because he knew I loved the sensation of his fingers moving through the long strands. It was still a novelty, after having had it all shaved off.' She continues, 'Stroking my hair just naturally led to kissing, and soon David's body was trembling... Signals went off in my head and I brought everything to an abrupt stop.'[63] Aranka's friend Dora, however, became pregnant and, lacking financial and emotional support, felt forced to give the baby up for adoption.

---

[60] Ibid., 79.

[61] Yael Danieli, 'The Heterogeneity of Postwar Adaptation in Families of Holocaust Survivors' in Randolph L. Braham (ed.), *The Psychological Perspectives of the Holocaust and of its Aftermath* (New York: Columbia University Press, 1988), 109–27.

[62] Cited in Grossmann, *Jews, Germans, and Allies*, 187.

[63] Siegal, *Grace in the Wilderness*, 49.

Whilst Aranka and Dora became involved with young Jewish survivors like themselves, other young Jews—both male and female—had romantic and sexual relationships with non-Jewish Germans. Such 'close encounters', to use Atina Grossmann's term,[64] were certainly of concern to many Jews and it made sense to encourage the young Jewish survivors to enter into Jewish marriages as quickly as possible. A Jewish woman who sustained any sort of relationship with a German man provoked all sorts of ambiguities, issues, and risks. Germans were responsible for the destruction of their people and entering into such a relationship meant exclusion from the community of survivors.[65] Although there is evidence to suggest that Jewish men also became involved with Gentile—and especially German—women, survivors claim that 'Jewish men did not *go out with* German women, they *slept* with them!'[66] Indeed, Jew Samuel Pisar, who after liberation engaged in black marketeering in the American occupation zone of Germany, writes that 'The nights passed with an assortment of German women':[67] many Germans lived in dire poverty in the immediate post-war period, and Jewish men who had access to American foodstuffs and luxury items such as cigarettes and nylons proved attractive prospects. While some Jewish men might actively have sought paid sex from German women, in other cases the relationships were more complex. Young male survivors, like their female counterparts, were lonely and seeking physical proximity to another human being. What is more, they may have felt that non-Jewish women offered a more 'carefree introduction to sex'.[68] Most male prisoners in the concentration camps experienced loss of their libido and therefore entering into physical relationships represented a process of sexual recovery. Furthermore, as Margarete Myers Feinstein writes, 'Untouched by the years of deprivation and persecution that had afflicted Jewish women and men, the German woman represented life. Sex with her affirmed his new life as a free man.'[69] Edith Bruck makes an oblique reference to this when she explains of the man she fell in love with after liberation: 'He went to [the nearby town of] Bergen when he needed a woman...We loved each other, but our love was confined to a kiss or holding hands.'[70] While civil marriages between Jewish men and German women did take place, there were also half-Jewish illegitimate children who were left with their German mothers.[71] Samuel Pisar's friend Niko became involved with a young married German woman whose husband

---

[64] Grossmann, *Jews, Germans, and Allies. Close Encounters in Occupied Germany.*
[65] Myers Feinstein, *Holocaust Survivors in Postwar Germany*, 120.
[66] Cited in Grossmann, 'Living On', 90.   [67] Pisar, *Of Blood and Hope*, 99.
[68] Grossmann, 'Living On', 90.
[69] Myers Feinstein, *Holocaust Survivors in Postwar Germany*, 117.
[70] Bruck, *Who Loves You Like This*, 58.   [71] Grossmann, 'Living On', 90–1.

had not yet returned from the war. When she became pregnant, Pisar writes that 'She was ready to abandon everything for him but he shied away from the responsibility and lived with her only intermittently.'[72] She was forced to move town and reunite with her husband. Amongst many Jews, the idea of Jewish men having sexual relations with German women was taboo. Kibbutz Buchenwald, an agricultural collective in post-war Germany formed to prepare Jews for emigration to Palestine, for example, threatened to expel any man found to be having sexual relations with a German woman.[73]

Some of the sexual encounters between the Jewish men and German women were no doubt non-consensual. Sex, it is widely acknowledged, is a powerful tool of revenge. There are, however, almost no references to the idea of sex as a means of retribution in either survivors' testimonies or accounts by German women. German women were raped by the DPs, but may have been reluctant to identify Jewish perpetrators; certainly, the legal cases which resulted were mostly focused on non-Jewish eastern European former prisoners.[74] One of the only explicit references to the rape of German women by Jewish men comes from Elie Wiesel's first autobiographical account, *Un di velt hot geshvign* (And the World Stayed Silent), written in Yiddish in 1955, ten years after he was liberated from Buchenwald. He writes of the newly liberated Buchenwald prisoners: 'Early the next day Jewish boys ran off to Weimar to steal clothing and potatoes. And to rape German girls [*un tsu fargvaldikn daytshe shikses*].'[75] However, not only has this disappeared from Wiesel's later publications, but he has staunchly refused to comment further.

It is unclear whether or not Dora, whom we discussed above, consciously decided to become pregnant (she was the sole survivor of her family). Certainly, she and her boyfriend Hershi found the reality of the pregnancy too difficult to deal with and Hershi in particular became distant and withdrawn.[76] Many of the young survivors were not only ignorant about birth control or unable to obtain contraceptives but they lacked even a basic education in matters to do with relationships and sexuality. In particular, they lacked parental supervision and struggled to negotiate their newly found freedom, resulting in what Samuel Pisar has

---

[72] Pisar, *Of Blood and Hope*, 102.

[73] See Judith Tydor Baumel, *Kibbutz Buchenwald: Survivors and Pioneers* (New Brunswick, NJ: Rutgers University Press, 1997).

[74] See Grossmann, 'Victims, Villains, and Survivors', 310. Cf. Naomi Seidman, 'Elie Wiesel and the Scandal of Jewish Rage', *Jewish Social Studies: History, Culture, and Society*, 3/1 (Fall 1996), 1–19.

[75] Grossmann, 'Victims, Villains, and Survivors', 310.

[76] Siegal, *Grace in the Wilderness*.

termed 'a kind of postwar juvenile delinquency'.[77] Other young survivors literally grew up in the DP camps.

It is estimated that 51,307 children under the age of 14 were living in DP camps in February 1946, of whom 27,185 were under the age of 6.[78] Some children had either survived the concentration camps because they looked older than they were, or had been living in forests and other open places, or had been retrieved from the Gentiles hiding them.[79] Some of these children were smuggled illegally by Zionist groups to Palestine between 1945 and 1950 or sent by Jewish charities to the United States to be looked after by extended family members. Restrictive American quota systems prevented other children from being adopted by American families—both Jewish and non-Jewish—even though many were shocked at the plight of the Jewish orphans and desperate to help them.[80] Thus, unable to escape, the children stayed in the camps, often attaching themselves to adult survivors from their former homelands, or forming surrogate families with other children until they were placed in orphanages and suchlike institutions.[81] A wave of Jewish refugees from the Soviet Union—whole families who had managed to survive the war in Russia—arrived in the DP camps in mid-1946. Nurseries, kindergartens, and schools soon sprang up in the DP camps. The AJDC also arranged additional supplies of fruit, butter, milk, meat, and vegetables, for the often under-nourished children.

It was not just children who found themselves alone, isolated, and desperately hoping for a family. Older women too—for example, those in their forties—who had previously been married but whose husbands were considered lost sometimes wished to start new unions. This was problematic, as according to Halakhic (Jewish religious) law, proof of death was required if they were to be permitted to form religiously sanctioned marriages. The few rabbis to have survived had to issue *heterim* (permissions to marry) for those who found themselves in this predicament. These marriages were particularly challenging. Many older women had lost not only their parents, their siblings, and wider family, but also

---

[77] Pisar, *Of Blood and Hope*, 104.

[78] Cited in Gitta Sereny, *The German Trauma: Experiences and Reflections 1938–2000* (London: Allen Lane, 2000), 27.

[79] For a recent survey of the subject, see Stone, *Liberation of the Camps*. Specifically on children's experiences, see Mark Wyman, *DPs: Europe's Displaced Persons, 1945–1951* (Ithaca, NY: Cornell University Press, 1989), Chapter 4.

[80] See Beth Cohen, *Case Closed: Holocaust Survivors in Postwar America* (New Brunswick, NJ: Rutgers University Press, 2007).

[81] The Central Committee of Jews in Poland collected a large number of testimonies of children in the immediate post-war years. See Laura Jockusch, *Collect and Record! Jewish Holocaust Documentation in Early Postwar Europe* (Oxford: Oxford University Press, 2012).

their children, who had either been murdered or hidden with Christians and lost forever. Almost no adult survivors had children who had survived with them. For men and women who survived whilst their children did not, the challenges of starting new lives were almost insurmountable. Whilst they desperately wanted to bring healthy children into a free world, new spouses and children often served to reinforce their guilt and feelings of loss. Men and women who had lost their children in the Holocaust often found it hard to connect emotionally with their children born after the war. Lawrence Langer cites a male survivor who, in a videotaped testimony, absent-mindedly referred to his children born after the war by the names of his children who perished with his first wife during the Holocaust.[82] Other parents did not allow themselves to express—or even feel—intense emotions towards their children, such was their fear of losing them.

As we have noted already, there was a widespread belief that it was the survivors' duty to have children as quickly as possible in an attempt to affirm the continuation of Jewish existence. Fania Fénelon, born Fanja Goldstein in Paris and a singer with the Women's Orchestra of Auschwitz, wrote that when women ceased menstruating they prayed to be freed from 'this curse the Germans were holding over us: sterility'.[83] After she was liberated from Auschwitz Kitty Hart declared: 'A family of my own—that is what I must build.'[84] The return of their menses and in particular of ovulation signalled recovery from the German curse.

As Atina Grossmann observed, '[i]n some kind of supreme historical irony', far from being *judenrein* (cleansed of Jews), occupied Germany in 1946 boasted the highest Jewish birth rate in the world.[85] While many German women put off becoming pregnant in the unstable post-war period, Jewish women were eager for motherhood. What is more, the babies were born in German hospitals serviced by German doctors and nurses. Hadassah Bimko Rosensaft's first husband was murdered in Auschwitz together with her parents and her 5-and-a-half-year-old son, Benjamin. After the war she married Josef Rosensaft, chairman of the Central Committee of Liberated Jews in the British Zone and of the Jewish Committee of the Bergen-Belsen DP camp. It was very important for them that their son be born in the camp hospital. Jewish life was

[82] Lawrence Langer, *Holocaust Testimonies: The Ruins of Memory* (New Haven, CT: Yale University Press, 1991), 74.

[83] Fania Fénelon, *Playing for Time*, trans. Judith Landry (New York: Atheneum, 1977), 89.

[84] Kitty Hart[-Moxon], *Return to Auschwitz: The Remarkable Story of a Girl who Survived the Holocaust* (London: Grafton, 1983), 16.

[85] Grossmann, 'Victims, Villains, and Survivors', 302.

re-emerging in the very country that had sought to extinguish it. It is irrefutable that there was a sudden Jewish baby boom in the DP camps between 1946 and 1947, at a time of a declining birth-rate amongst the non-Jewish population of Europe; this 'must be understood, therefore, as a specific and direct response to the catastrophic losses of the Holocaust'.[86] One of the first children to be born in the Föhrenwald DP camp, on 24 October 1945, was to a couple from Matzeev, Ukraine, who had lost their 2-year-old son and many other members of their families when the Nazis took control in 1939. The baby's father said:

> The birth of our son marked a new era and was a symbol of our life to be, of our continuation. Eva and I along with Rabbi Friedman decided to name our baby *Chaim Shalom Dov*. The initials represented some of the descendants of both of our families, and *Chaim* in Hebrew means 'life'. Chaim truly did bring hope and a new life to all of us... The newborn meant a new beginning. Our love for our child was mixed with sadness, because of the fact that there was no family with which to share our cherished moments. But, with all the suffering we had experienced from being Jewish, we were now proud to introduce our son into the world in a Jewish religious ceremony.[87]

Traditional Jewish rites of passage such as the *brith milah* (circumcision) of newborn boys symbolized the continuity of Jewish life and tradition, but also reminded families of how the Nazis had been able to identify Jewish males.

A survey carried out by the AJDC found that approximately 750 babies were born each month in the DP camps in the US zone. By the end of 1946 the number of Jewish babies had reached 8,000 and nearly a third of all Jewish women between the ages of 18 and 45 had either given birth or were pregnant.[88] Orthodox Jews in particular sought to have as many children as possible. The birth of healthy children was a source of much individual and communal pride. In February 1948, the DP journal *Yiddische Bilder* ran a competition for 'The Most Beautiful *She'erit Hapletah* Baby' and proud parents were encouraged to send in photographs of their offspring.[89] Photographs in DP publications showed mothers happily pushing healthy babies in prams whilst strong-looking fathers watched with pride. After a period of such enforced passivity and intense humiliation many men were desperate to affirm their masculinity, and proof of male fertility and the ability to look after a family was an important sign of this. Also, of course, having a child *was* a source of

[86] Grossmann, *Jews, Germans, and Allies*, 191.
[87] Cited in Königseder and Wetzel, *Waiting for Hope*, 103.
[88] Grossmann, *Jews, Germans, and Allies*, 188.   [89] Ibid., 191.

genuine happiness. Regardless of their tragic pasts, new parents experienced the exquisite pleasure of all-encompassing love for the children they had brought into the world. The pictures of their children were particularly important to people who had few, if any, remaining photographs of family members before the war. Indeed, many of the children were named in memory of the dead. It is the custom of Ashkenazi (east European) Jews to name their children after a deceased relative in an act of commemoration. Sometimes the children were given the names of siblings who had died. Eva Hoffman was born in Poland just two months after the end of the war. Her younger sister Alina was named after her mother's sister, who was murdered in the Holocaust. Reflecting on her experience as a child of survivors, she writes: '[M]y mother often feels a strange compassion for her younger daughter, as if with the name, she had bestowed on her some of fate's terrible burden.'[90]

For both men and women, having babies signalled a re-entry into the 'normal' life that had seemed lost forever. It was an attempt at a quasi-normalcy, a chance to regain some stake in the world. Being a mother or father—even more so than being a husband or wife—bestows a certain status on a person who has hitherto been robbed of all that makes them human. Furthermore, many of the survivors had no sense of how long they would be forced to languish in the DP camps awaiting their immigration papers or of the life they would lead when they reached their long-imagined destinations. Some did not even know where they would eventually be allowed to emigrate to. In a very real sense they were trapped between their past and the future. Starting a family was one way of gaining agency and looking to the future. They tried to make their living quarters as home-like as possible, but at the same time this underscored the fact that they had no home. The desperate desire to rebuild their shattered lives was necessarily fraught with frustration.

Furthermore, the experience of the Holocaust was so profound that relationships with other people proved extremely difficult. Women who had been raped in the ghettos, in hiding, in the concentration camps, or even by their liberators were left with feelings of shame and memories they did not know how to share. Rape was yet another terrible experience amidst a litany of other horrific events. Nevertheless it left a specific imprint on women's post-war lives. Nechama Tec interviewed a woman who was raped by a partisan when in hiding. The woman, Lidia Brown-Abramson, told Tec:

---

[90] Eva Hoffman, *Lost in Translation: A Life in a New Language* (London: Vintage, 1998), 7. Cf. idem, *After Such Knowledge: A Meditation on the Aftermath of the Holocaust* (London: Secker & Warburg, 2004).

Inside me something broke. I was sick. This feeling stayed and stayed, for years. I could not look at men... I had some kind of inner conflict. I did not like the physical part of sex. I did not put sex in an important place. I am glad I don't need it... I imagine that many women had similar experiences... shocking, this rape... horrible.[91]

Other women who had not experienced the agony of rape had nevertheless been violated: shaved of their hair, the most intimate parts of their bodies brutally searched for hidden objects, and again and again made to parade naked until this had become a routinized assault on their selves. What is more, such experiences were perceived to be so commonplace that they were not even recognized as sexual violence. Now, these women struggled to regain a sense of individual agency. Women who had—or were still— engaged in prostitution or what we might call 'sex for survival' were especially likely to suffer from feelings of depression, guilt, and even self-revulsion. Aranka Siegal was taken to a makeshift hospital immediately after liberation. She describes a young girl named Mindi pleading for an abortion: 'I'm not taking an SS bastard child home with me... I'm only twenty. I want to start a new life.'[92]

The intense focus on the large number of babies born in the DP camps can detract attention from the women who struggled to get pregnant. Some women took longer than others to recover from severe malnutrition and the amenorrhoea which accompanied it. Their past sufferings also meant that it was sometimes difficult to carry a pregnancy to term. Moreover, while women now had access to more food it was not always of a sufficiently nutritious nature to support a vulnerable pregnancy.[93] Hilda Mantelmacher, for example, states that 'Even when I was pregnant I never got an egg, never got any vitamins, never got milk... They just gave us bread and soup and maybe coffee.'[94] Furthermore, many of these very young women were too fearful of doctors or in some cases too embarrassed by their pregnancies (and the sexuality they implied) to seek medical help. Jewish doctors were scarce and some women were reluctant to see German doctors whom they often suspected of being former Nazis or Nazi sympathizers. The experience of the concentration camps had also taught women to hide at all costs any illness and pain and not draw attention to such things. It was hard for many to trust that they

[91] Nechama Tec, *Resilience and Courage: Women, Men, and the Holocaust* (New Haven, CT: Yale University Press, 2003), 311.

[92] Siegal, *Grace in the Wilderness*, 12.

[93] See Myers Feinstein, 'Hannah's Prayer', 177.

[94] Furthermore, although most of the new mothers wanted to breast-feed, their recent history of malnutrition meant that they did not always have adequate breast milk, and additional baby formula milk rations were not easy to come by (ibid., 178).

would now be looked after. Poor health put women at risk of miscarriage, as well as of stillbirths and increased maternal mortality.

Other women were ambivalent about motherhood. While some, regardless—or perhaps because—of their wartime experiences, never wanted to have children, the focus on Jewish renewal and 'Life Reborn' placed a great deal of pressure on women to have families.[95] Pregnancy had been until recently associated with death, and it was difficult to overcome the fear that a Jewish child could not possibly survive. At times the past and the present became muddled. Halina Birenbaum writes that:

> When my first son was born, I thought, with how much suffering does a man buy his entry into the world; and with how much ease did the barbarians kill millions of people. When I, with pride and emotion, like all young mothers, looked at the mouth of my child, wide-open, greedily seeking nourishment, I recalled with horror the thousands of unfortunate mothers in the ghetto who had nothing with which to feed their starving infants...So it is that always, involuntarily, at almost every step, scenes, memories and comparisons with those other days are mixed with my present life...[96]

Dina Wardi is an Israeli psychotherapist who has worked extensively with the children of survivors. She believes that many female survivors struggled with motherhood as they had not yet overcome the experience of losing their own mothers, many of whom were selected for death or even killed in the presence of their daughters.[97] Certainly this was the case for Birenbaum, who lost the mother she adored when she was selected for death on their arrival at Majdanek. It was true, too, for many other women who had never imagined being pregnant without the support of their mothers. When Hungarian Isabella Leitner, who survived Auschwitz and a death march to Bergen-Belsen, was carrying her first child, Peter, she wrote: 'Mama, I'm pregnant! There is another heart beating within that very body that was condemned to ashes...[We've] started the birth of a new six million.'[98] Other survivors felt anger at their parents for failing to protect them. This was the case for both men and women. Elie Wiesel, for

[95] Menachem Rosensaft (ed.), *Life Reborn: Jewish Displaced Persons 1945–1951: Conference Proceedings, Washington DC, January 14–17, 2000* (Washington, DC: United States Holocaust Memorial Museum, 2001).

[96] Halina Birenbaum, *Hope is the Last to Die: A Personal Documentation of Nazi Terror*, trans. David Welsh (New York: Twayne, 1967), 244.

[97] Dina Wardi, *Memorial Candles: Children of the Holocaust* (London: Routledge, 1992).

[98] Isabella Leitner, *Fragments of Isabella: A Memoir of Auschwitz* (New York: Thomas Y. Crowell, 1978), 96.

example, writes: 'The failure of my father and of all he symbolized long made me fear having a child.'[99]

In the almost obsessively pronatalist climate of the DP camps it is not surprising that the women who struggled to become pregnant experienced severe feelings of worthlessness. Infertility—whether a difficulty in conceiving or the inability to carry a pregnancy to term—was experienced as a further layer of humiliation and the ultimate *coup de grâce* of the Nazis. Both allegorically and literally it spelt the death of hope. Psychoanalyst Dinora Pines writes:

> Infertility, painful as it is for most women, was almost unbearable for them, since the next generation also concretely replaced those who had been killed and enabled the survivors to avoid the recognition of loss and mourning.[100]

In confronting a childless future, survivors mourned anew the families that they knew could never be carried on. For many couples, the decision to get married was inextricably bound to the desire to have children and they had hoped to conceive as quickly as possible following their weddings. Some marriages could not cope with the strain and broke down. Other couples lived together but did not actually commit to marriage until pregnancy.[101] For couples who were forced to endure the death of their dreams of children month after month the situation was often intolerable.

Some women who had a first child in the DP camps found that after all they had been through the experience of becoming a mother again was too overwhelming. Therefore some were reluctant to become pregnant again. Alina Bacall-Zwirn gave birth to her first child—a boy—in Auschwitz. The Gentile midwife who helped her give birth persuaded her to let the child die so that she might live. After the war she was reunited with the husband she had married in the Warsaw ghetto. When she discovered she was pregnant, she remembered:

> And I was so afraid to have a child. He [her husband Leo Bacall] wants family, and I said, for what? Again going to happen, again they're going to kill our children. I was so afraid. I got my son. I was pregnant with a second child and I didn't want it. I was afraid, again.

[99] Elie Wiesel, *And the Sea is Never Full*, trans. Marion Wiesel (New York: Knopf, 1999), 43. See also Maddy Carey, 'Jewish Masculinity in the Holocaust' (Ph.D. thesis, Royal Holloway, University of London, 2014).

[100] Dinora Pines, *A Woman's Unconscious Use of Her Body: A Psychoanalytical Perspective* (London: Virago, 1993), 178.

[101] Many couples lived together in the DP camps without being married. As well as wanting to wait to have children, men and women needed to leave enough time to pass to confirm the death of their former spouses.

> And I said to my husband, I don't want to have a child anymore. I hate to be in Germany, I hate all the Germans, I can't stand the stones, it's covered with blood, everything is in blood.

> If he was thinking to have a baby, I was angry at him. And I said, fine, I'm going to go and look how to get rid of the baby, and I went, and I got rid.[102]

Another effect of the importance placed on bearing Jewish children and thereby thwarting the Nazi policy of total annihilation of the Jews, together with the deep desire of Jewish men and women to honour their pre-war lives and traditions, was to cast women once again in their traditional roles. Indeed, in the DP camps, with the important exception of Hadassah Bimko Rosensaft, there were very few women in positions of leadership. Instead, women's existence continued to revolve around their lives as wives and mothers—or potential mothers. Most women abandoned any ambitions of employment outside the home when their children were born, whilst men—even in the camps—sought to obtain work that would enable them to support their families.[103] Experience of war, overwhelming loss, and displacement did not encourage a search for social transformation and a new understanding of gender. Rather, following the catastrophe of the Holocaust and continued hardship in the DP camps, the old values of pre-war gender roles became an ideal to which both Jewish men and women hoped to return.

This is why women's sexuality was controlled through marriage and motherhood. In the DP camps women made homes in provisional, sparsely furnished living quarters. Honouring the memory of their pre-war homes meant retaining the values of their parents and devoting all their energies to the raising of healthy Jewish children. They stretched limited rations to provide meals and hauled water from communal locations to wash their family's clothes. Orthodox women tried their best to recreate the Sabbath meals of their youth and to maintain the respective Jewish festivals. By doing so they were able to make important connections between the world of their childhood and the world they now found themselves in.[104] It also, of course, meant another victory over the Nazis. However, to achieve such things entailed many challenges, especially for the younger women who lacked not only home-making experience but also the mothers, aunts, and grandmothers who might have helped them.

---

[102] Alina Bacall-Zwirn and Jared Stark, *No Common Place: The Holocaust Testimony of Alina Bacall-Zwirn* (Lincoln, NE: University of Nebraska Press, 1999), 112.

[103] For a brilliant survey of these themes, see Grossmann, *Jews, Germans, and Allies*, Chapter 5.

[104] See Shaul, 'Testimonies of Ultra-Orthodox Holocaust Survivors', 163–4.

Ironically this caused some women—particularly those who had grown up in middle-class Jewish homes—to employ local German domestic help.[105] Other women found that being part of a traditional nuclear family again renewed rather than dispelled their feelings of loss.

The raising of healthy Jewish children was soon seen as a communal responsibility and DP camp leaders, administrators, and relief workers dedicated themselves to improving standards of hygiene and providing an effective medical system. Yiddish posters appeared in the camps urging pregnant women to take seriously the health of their unborn children.[106] This served to reinforce women's identities as mothers and caregivers and also, of course, subjected them to surveillance and discipline as they were brought back within the norms of a patriarchal system.

The last DP camp—Föhrenwald in Germany—was in operation until February 1957, a full twelve years after the liberation of the concentration camps.[107] Indeed, many of the DP camps had been in existence for so long that they had become microcosms of civil and political life. Theatres, sports facilities, hospitals, fire brigades, *yeshivas* (Jewish religious schools), Yiddish newspapers, historical commissions, etc. also flourished in the camps, along with highly organized political committees. The camps were policed by a Jewish force and Jewish courts prosecuted both violations in the camp—including domestic violence—and survivors accused of collaborating with the Nazis. Former Jewish *Kapos* and ghetto police accused of mistreating their fellow Jews attempted to conceal their pasts but were sometimes identified in the DP camps, and in some cases even beaten to death.[108] In August 1949 the Ministry of Justice in Israel introduced the Act against Jewish War Criminals, and the Israeli parliament—the Knesset—passed the Nazi and Nazi Collaborators (Punishment) Law in 1950. However, even then the majority of investigations did not lead to indictments, and those accused were able to appeal against the stipulated death penalty and instead received prison sentences ranging from a few months to three years.[109]

---

[105] Myers Feinstein, *Holocaust Survivors in Postwar Germany*, 150.

[106] See Grossmann, 'Living On', 78–81.

[107] Königseder and Wetzel, *Waiting for Hope*, 95.

[108] During the war a small number of Jewish collaborators and informers, including members of the *Judenrat* and the ghetto police, had been assassinated by the Jewish underground in Poland.

[109] See Tom Segev, *The Seventh Million: The Israelis and the Holocaust*, trans. Haim Watzman (New York: Hill & Wang, 1993), 259–61. On this subject, see Hanna Yablonka, 'The Nazis and Nazi Collaborators (Punishment) Law: An Additional Aspect of the Question of Israelis, Survivors and the Holocaust', *Katedra*, 82 (1996), 132–52 [Hebrew].

Eventually, the last DPs were scattered across the globe: to Israel, Britain, the United States, Europe, Africa, and Latin America. However, due to draconian immigration laws, survivors attempting to gain entry to such countries as Britain, Canada, and the United States faced considerable hurdles. These states in particular were fearful of being swamped by Jewish immigrants, and established strict immigration quotas in response. They were also not necessarily equipped to deal with the needs of the Jewish survivors once they arrived, and the skills that had enabled the Jews to survive were not necessarily helpful to life after the Holocaust. Kitty Hart writes:

> It was difficult for me to be polite and deferential. In the world of the concentration camp there had been no courtesies. You fought for everything. If you lost, you cursed. Curses and blows were more common than even the slightest nod of friendship. Illness had to be very serious indeed before anyone paid any attention: and when it did get that serious, it usually meant instant despatch to the incinerators. From a world of ceaseless bullying and shouting, of beatings and hunger and hatred, it was hard to adjust to artificial politeness, manners and mannerisms.[110]

As well as bringing up children, the survivors had to start new careers in new countries that were completely different to those they had been born in, adapt to a new culture, and, often, learn a new language. Like many refugees, even those who had professional qualifications before the war were often prevented from practising because of their new country's licensing requirements. Lacking extended family and friends, they had to build new support systems, start new relationships, and form communities. Other survivors report being met with suspicion and unease in the early years after the war. Czech survivor Ruth Bondy (born Ruth Bondyová) writes: 'In Israel Jews wanted to know: How did you stay alive? What did you have to do in order to survive? And in their eyes, a glimmer of suspicion: Kapo? Prostitute?'[111] A young woman who went to stay with relatives in America's Midwest stated that 'People who came to my cousins' house used to ask me such things as whether I had been able to survive because, perchance, I had slept with an SS man.'[112]

It is not surprising, therefore, that many survivors have felt the need to specifically deny such accusations in their testimonies. We read in

---

[110] Hart, *Return to Auschwitz*, 17–18.

[111] Cited in Na'ama Shik, 'Sexual Abuse of Jewish Women in Auschwitz-Birkenau', in Dagmar Herzog (ed.), *Brutality and Desire: War and Sexuality in Europe's Twentieth Century* (Basingstoke: Palgrave Macmillan, 2009), 237.

[112] Cited in Aaron Hass, *The Aftermath: Living with the Holocaust* (Cambridge: Cambridge University Press, 1995), 18.

Chapter 3 about Gisella Perl, for example, who handed back a piece of string, vital for keeping her shoes on her feet, when she realized that it was intended as a way of buying sex. Olga Lengyel, too, wrote that she would rather die from starvation than take the food offered to her by a Polish prisoner in exchange for sex.[113]

In recent years there has been a marked tendency to portray survivors in an almost heroic light, to suggest that in surviving the unimaginable they have achieved some sort of moral authority. Yet whilst this was no doubt true of some exceptional men and women, it could not be true for all. For the most part, as Joan Ringelheim has wryly observed, 'oppression does not make people better; oppression makes people oppressed'.[114] The survivors themselves were acutely aware of this. For example, Primo Levi has written:

> You review your memories . . . No, you find no obvious transgressions, you did not usurp anyone's place, you did not beat anyone (but would you have had the strength to do so?), you did not accept positions (but none were offered to you . . .), you did not steal anyone's bread; nevertheless you cannot exclude it. It is no more than a suspicion, indeed the shadow of a suspicion: that each man is his brother's Cain, that each one of us (and this time I say 'us' in a much vaster, indeed, universal sense) has usurped his neighbour's place and lives in his stead.[115]

The Holocaust necessarily informed the post-war lives of its survivors. Some survivors were unable to adapt to their new lives and committed suicide. Others were haunted by nightmares and constant unbidden remembrances. Trudi Levi, who survived Auschwitz-Birkenau and Buchenwald, lost her only son Ilan to suicide. She resolutely states that:

> I blame Hitler for his death. Because of the Holocaust Ilan lacked the support which grandparents and an extended family normally provide . . . I am convinced that if I had been able to give him more security and a feeling of belonging, he would not have been driven to an early death.[116]

The lives of the so-called 'second generation' have certainly been profoundly influenced by their parents' wartime experiences. Hadassah Rosensaft's son, Menachem Zwi, named in memory of his two grandfathers, was born

---

[113] Olga Lengyel, *Five Chimneys: The Story of Auschwitz*, trans. Clifford Coch and Paul P. Weiss (Chicago, IL: Ziff-Davis, 1947), 60–4.

[114] See Joan Ringelheim, 'Women and the Holocaust: A Reconsideration of Research', in Carol Rittner and John K. Roth (eds.), *Different Voices: Women and the Holocaust* (New York: Paragon House, 1993), 387.

[115] Levi, *The Drowned and the Saved*, 81–2.

[116] Trudi Levi, *A Cat Called Adolf* (London: Vallentine Mitchell, 1995), 163.

in the DP camp at Bergen-Belsen. At the first American Gathering of Jewish Holocaust survivors in Washington, DC, in April 1983, he gave an address on behalf of the second generation. He stated:

> I was born in Bergen-Belsen. That is the essence of my being. My cradle stood only a few hundred yards from the mass graves in which Anne Frank and tens of thousands of other European Jews lie buried anonymously. My parents survived the horrors of Auschwitz; my grandparents did not. I am alive; my five-year-old brother perished in a gas chamber.
>
> We, the sons and daughters of the survivors of the Holocaust, are the bridge between two worlds. Many of us bear the names of grandparents whom we have never met. That is our heritage. For us, the Holocaust is not an abstract historical phenomenon. It is our past, our parents' lives, our grandparents' death. It is our families, multiplied, and multiplied, and multiplied...It is my mother's son, and more than one million Jewish children. It is shadows and echoes, nightmares and lullabies...Sometimes, when I am alone, I see, or imagine that I see, the fading image of a little boy named Benjamin. Forty years ago, on Friday, April 11, 1943, that little boy was alive in the ghetto of Sosnowiec, in southern Poland. On August 4, it will be precisely 40 years since my brother was murdered by the Germans at Auschwitz. I am haunted by his face, his eyes, and I listen to a voice I never heard. But do I see him, or is it merely my own reflection? Are my tears mine, or are they his? I do not know. I shall never know...[117]

Although many survivors decided to have their tattoos removed,[118] it has proved impossible to leave the past behind. As Isabella Leitner writes, 'Bye, Auschwitz. I will never see you again. I will always see you.'[119] This ambivalence runs through the testimonies of those who survived the Holocaust. It speaks of an incomplete liberation—for, of course, they will never be truly free of their past and of the unspeakable experiences they have endured. This incomplete liberation also accounts for the experience of gender in the DP camps. In some ways, little changed. Women were still faced with sexual assault, and still forced to trade sex for food or simply for protection. In other ways, of course, much did change. The ability—the imperative—to marry, to conceive and bear children, to form families and plan futures: all this marked a new start for people who had lived under the shadow of death for years, and who had watched their families—and in many cases, their own children—die. Yet even this new dispensation was not a new beginning. It marked, in fact, a self-conscious

---

[117] Rosensaft, *Yesterday*, 165.   [118] Bacall-Zwirn, *No Common Place*, 54.
[119] Leitner, *Fragments of Isabella*, 51.

attempt to reset the clock: to return to the gender norms and gender roles of a pre-Holocaust period. For those women unable to bear children, for those unable to function as mothers or to form successful relationships, this was a new burden to carry. Even for those who seemed more fortunate, there was no new Jerusalem here; no sense that the patriarchy and the old systems of sexual subordination and gender hierarchy could or should be challenged.

Conclusion

Towards a Feminist History of Genocide

Most books on the subject of women and the Holocaust, or gender and the Holocaust, observes Rochelle G. Saidel, 'begin or end their work with a justification or apologia for bringing up the issue'.[1] This one will not. Not only does an attempt to deepen the understanding of women's experiences during the Holocaust need no apology, but I wish to end this book by urging that every history of the Holocaust employ gender as a conceptual tool of analysis. In order to avoid a monolithic view of Jews and Jewish victims of Nazism, we need to understand the gendered nature both of their victimhood and of their sense of self as well as the pivotal role that gender played during the Holocaust. Learning more about both the women who survived and who did not survive the Nazi genocide not only increases our understanding of this terrible period in history, but necessarily makes us rethink our relationship to the gendered nature of knowledge itself. This is not something to apologize for: rather, it is fundamental to a proper understanding of the Holocaust itself.

Nor am I going to apologize for the fact that this is an explicitly *feminist* history of the Holocaust. In some ways, of course, it did not need to be a feminist history. The themes explored here are central to and should be part of any understanding of the Holocaust. Yet, in other ways, it could hardly not be feminist, seeking as it does not to challenge just the status quo of Holocaust studies, but also some broader assumptions about gender. As we have seen, for rather too long historians and other scholars of the Holocaust have either ignored issues of gender or relegated them to a footnote of history. This is partly out of a concern that an interest in gender will somehow downplay the atrocities, undermine the uniqueness of the Holocaust, or deny the specificity of the Jewish experience. These concerns are real and valid: the Holocaust, above all, was an attack on the whole Jewish

---

[1] Rochelle G. Saidel, 'Women's Experiences during the Holocaust—New Books in Print', *Yad Vashem Studies*, 28 (2000), 378.

people. But it is telling—and alarming—that the Jewish people should have been gendered male in most accounts, and that the experience of Jewish men has been regarded as normative by most historians. A feminist history by its very nature challenges these assumptions, insisting that women's experiences are equally valid, equally important, and equally worthy of study.

As such, this book has argued not just for women's Holocaust experiences to be integrated into the mainstream of Holocaust research, but for this rewriting to transform that research as a result. This means using knowledge gained about women's lives to deepen and challenge our understanding of all areas of Holocaust experience. Not to do so subordinates women's voices to an overwhelmingly male master narrative and risks overlooking potentially significant fields of further research. That the Holocaust was an appalling event of almost unimaginable suffering for all involved in its wake should be self-evident. As Joan Ringelheim has written: 'Every Jew, regardless of gender, was equally a victim in the Holocaust.'[2] However, it is worth noting, as does Sara R. Horowitz, that although scholars have insisted 'in their own work on marking important distinctions among Holocaust survivors and victims—such as nationality, religious traditions, or political ideology—they feared that a study that looked at gender as a factor would likely result in distortion or trivialities'.[3] A focus on women does not deny the experiences of the male victims of Nazism but rather allows us to look more closely at what happened to women as women as well as to men as men. Gender is, after all, a relational category. To repeat the words of Joan Wallach Scott cited in the Introduction to this work: 'gender is a constitutive element of social relationships based on perceived differences between the sexes, *and* gender is a primary way of signifying relationships of power', and operates in ways which are often unspoken.[4]

Moreover, as I have sought to show, far from being an undifferentiated or somehow gender-neutral attack on the Jewish people, the Holocaust was in its very nature gendered. It affected men and women differently, and male and female experiences were different. Just because gender is a universal category does not mean that it is undifferentiated through time, much less that it is stable. In that respect, the events of the Holocaust make a gendered analysis more, rather than less, vital. This book has been about the ways in which socially and culturally constructed gender roles

    [2] Cited in John K. Roth, 'Equality, Neutrality, Particularity', in Elizabeth R. Baer and Myrna Goldenberg (eds.), *Experience and Expression: Women, the Nazis, and the Holocaust* (Detroit, MI: Wayne State University Press, 2003), 9.
    [3] Sara R. Horowitz, 'Gender, Genocide and Jewish Memory', *Prooftexts*, 20/1&2 (Winter/Spring 2000), 180.
    [4] Joan Wallach Scott, *Gender and the Politics of History* (New York: Columbia University Press, 1988), 42.

were placed under extreme pressure; yet it is also about the fact that gender continued to operate as an important arbiter of experience. Indeed, extraordinarily enough, the extreme conditions of the Holocaust—even of the death camps—may have reinforced the importance of gender.

This may seem a surprising—even, to some, an offensive—conclusion. The Nazis, it might be argued, treated Jewish men and Jewish women in strikingly similar ways. Both sexes, after all, were violently uprooted from their homes, forced to endure the misery and deprivations of the ghettos, driven out of sheer desperation to entrust their children with Gentile strangers in the uncertain hope of their survival, and subjected to the relentless brutality of the concentration camps. Ultimately, too, both men and women for no greater reason than that of being born Jewish met their fate in the gas chambers. Moreover, some might assume that, by the summer of 1942 and the liquidation of the ghettos, gender in one sense became all but irrelevant under the Nazis' escalating and relentless policy of mass murder, as men, women, and children were all condemned to the same brutal fate.

However, in another—very important—sense, gender became altogether more important, more crucial. On arrival at the concentration camps women were far less likely to survive the initial selection. Pregnant women as well as women accompanied by young children or those deemed incapable of hard labour were sent straight to the gas chambers. Gender operated as a crucial signifier between life and death. Women who escaped death at this time proceeded to women-only camps and were targeted in three main ways: sexually, reproductively, and maternally. The very qualities which made them women were manipulated and exploited by the Nazis as a source of dehumanization. Moreover, women were less likely to survive the camps even if they were not selected for death. In that sense—in that purely empirical sense—gender became a matter of life and death.

Even for survivors, too, the importance of gender cannot be overstated. Precisely because of their experiences—experiences which were dictated by their gender—many female survivors of the Holocaust found it particularly difficult to rebuild their lives after the war, especially if their wartime life involved such experiences as rape, fear of rape, abortion, sterilization, childbirth, infanticide, the murder of their children, and prostitution. More than that, as Ronit Lentin, has argued, 'Not only did survivors find it hard to tell. In many cases there was no one listening.'[5]

---

[5] Ronit Lentin, '"A Howl Unheard": Women Shoah Survivors Dis-placed and Re-silenced', in Claire Duchen and Irene Bandhauer-Schöffman (eds.), *After the War Was Over: Women, War and Peace in Europe 1940–1956* (London: Leicester University Press, 2000), 182.

She continues: 'Sex and all experiences connected with sex—rape, abortion, sexual abuse, pregnancy—are intimate parts of women's lives and therefore never easy to ask questions about.'[6]

As a feminist historian, I believe that it is my duty to listen to these women; to listen and to ask questions. Without asking questions—even if they are hard questions; even, one might say, if they turn out to be the wrong questions—we will never come closer to a fuller picture of women's experiences under Nazism. This means turning again to the testimonies of the victims which, whilst sometimes fragmentary, offer multiple accounts of gendered experience. Such an approach, inevitably and uncomfortably, means moving away from a reverential treatment of testimony—a sense that the words of the survivors are somehow a sort of sacred text. It means being willing to risk offence. It means raising troubling issues that many would rather see ignored. As Paula Hyman has rightly argued: 'Several decades of social history have demonstrated that one can discover new sources by asking new questions of old material or by recognizing as historically significant experiences that were previously unseen even when documented.'[7] Whilst testimonies can never be representative of Holocaust experience—the vast majority of victims died without ever writing down their experiences—they do nevertheless help us learn more about the life of the victims and emphasize the individuality of lived experience. They remind us of the wide range of different experiences, not just between men and women, but even between prisoners within the same concentration camp. Revealing the multiple identities of the witnesses based on such factors as ethnicity, social and economic class, marital status, nationality, religiosity, and political leaning forces us to resist simplistic gendered stereotypes and shows instead how gender needs to be understood in conjunction with other analytical categories.

It was reading these scores of very different testimonies, from a huge variety of very different people, that led me to believe that this needed to be a feminist history and not just a history of women in the Holocaust. For what these people—whether adult or young women in their teens, married or single, religious or secular, eastern or western European—all articulated was not merely the ongoing importance of gender in the Holocaust, but also the remarkable resilience of gendered categories even at moments in which the lives of these Jewish victims were almost unrecognizable—just as the Nazis intended them to be. Whether it was

---

[6] Ibid.

[7] Paula E. Hyman, 'Feminist Studies and Modern Jewish History', in Lynn Davidman and Shelly Tenenbaum (eds.), *Feminist Perspectives on Jewish Studies* (New Haven, CT: Yale University Press, 1994), 132.

the women of the ghettos, condemned for their exaggerated femininity or exalted by men for their maternal devotion; whether it was the women raped in hiding or struggling to form familial bonds in the camps; whether it was the women condemned to death for their pregnancies or propelled into hasty marriages after the war: all these women had their identities and their experiences defined above all by their gender. More than this—and still remarkably more than this—they too chose to emphasize their femininity and their feminine roles. So strong were conventions—so irresistible were ideas about gender—that even the cataclysm of the Holocaust was not a significant enough event to shake the fundamentals of a patriarchal society.

Such a conclusion begs many questions and my book is surely far from the last word on the subject. In most general terms, gender and the Holocaust is an area of research still ripe for interpretation. Whilst Joan Ringelheim and the early pioneers of women's Holocaust history such as Dalia Ofer and Lenore J. Weitzman were met with much hostility, today the study of gender in historical research is widely accepted. Even sceptics like Yehuda Bauer have come to accept that 'the Holocaust engendered a special fate for Jewish women, to be sure, just as it did for men'.[8] Whilst this statement from an important and hugely influential Jewish historian marks an important break from much of the scepticism which came before it, there is still work to be done. Clearly, writing gender—and especially writing women—back into the history of the Holocaust remains an ongoing process and demands further sustained attention. Issues of gender—rape and sexual abuse, women's potential for brutality, the monumental task of rebuilding lives after the war—remain under-researched and need to be properly addressed.

Moreover, although this—as a feminist history—has insisted on the need to listen to women's voices and value women's experiences, there is still much work to be done on men. So far research on masculinity and the Holocaust has largely restricted itself to the domain of the perpetrators. Yet precisely because it was gendered, the Holocaust was an attack on Jewish masculinity as well as on Jewish femininity. If Jewish women were, above all, feared as mothers, then Jewish men were reviled by the Nazis as fathers. More than this, the events of the Holocaust were experienced by Jewish men as an assault on their gendered identity. They ceased to be able to support their families, to be able to protect them. In the end, many were separated from them. Precisely because gender has been downplayed, this aspect of Holocaust history has been all but ignored. Yet, as we have

---

[8] Yehuda Bauer, 'The Problem of Gender: The Case of Gisi Fleischmann', in *Rethinking the Holocaust* (New Haven, CT: Yale University Press, 2001), 184–5.

noted, there is strong evidence that the attack on Jewish masculinity was understood and felt at the time. It also helps to account for the aftermath of the Holocaust: the rush to marry and reproduce; and, perhaps too, the insistence of many (male) survivors that they were not passive victims, but rather active resisters, fulfilling in this way some sort of positive masculine role.

This book also poses some troubling questions for all those who seek to make the world a more equal, fairer place. The Holocaust, I have suggested, was a gendered experience because it was an attack on Jewish men and women as the fathers and mothers of Jewish children and—still more importantly—because the experience of these men and women differed significantly. Gender was therefore inescapable. Far from being erased or becoming irrelevant, gender distinctions and gendered ideologies became more important for perpetrator and victim alike. For the survivors, too, a resumption of 'normal' gendered roles was proof of their survival, evidence that 'normal' life could begin again.

This is a remarkable—if previously unremarked—outcome of a uniquely horrific and almost unimaginably enormous historical event. If even the Holocaust—even the murder of six million Jews alongside the murder and displacement of millions of non-Jews—could not challenge, much less overturn, long-standing patriarchal assumptions, then what could? What can? Historians are rightly wary of politicizing the history they write, fearing the distorting effects of an explicit agenda. Yet there comes a moment when scholars must come clean and admit that they are motivated not merely by a disinterested search for truth. My feminist history of the Holocaust is, I hope, true; certainly I have laboured to produce a text which uses the words of those who experienced these terrible events to recapture something of their lives and deaths. It should, as a work of history, be judged by its success in so doing. Nonetheless, it is also motivated by the belief that listening to these women might provoke action as well as sadness; hope as well as despair.

The age of genocide is not over; nor are the brutal, discriminatory ideas about women which give genocide much of its power and ensure that it is women and children who are most often its victims. We owe it to them to challenge the deep-rooted ideologies, the underlying patriarchal assumptions, the violent, murderous sexism which was made manifest in the Holocaust and can be seen at work today. Only when we are willing to understand and to challenge the profoundly poisonous and unequal society in which we live—and in which most people live—will something like freedom and peace be possible.

Bibliography

Abrams, Lynn, *The Making of Modern Woman* (London: Longman, 2002).

Abzug, Robert H., *Inside the Vicious Heart: Americans and the Liberation of Nazi Concentration Camps* (New York: Oxford University Press, 1985).

Adelsberger, Lucie, *Auschwitz: A Doctor's Story*, trans. Susan Ray (London: Robson, 1996).

Adler, Rachel, 'A Question of Boundaries: Toward a Jewish Feminist Theology of Self and Other', *Tikkun*, 6/3 (1991), 43–6.

Adler, Stanisław, *In the Warsaw Ghetto 1940–1943: An Account of a Witness* (Jerusalem: Yad Vashem, 1982).

Ainsztein, Reuben, *Jewish Resistance in Nazi Occupied Eastern Europe* (London: Elek, 1974).

Aleksiun, Natalia, 'Gender and Nostalgia: Images of Women in Early "Yizker Bikher"', *Jewish Culture and History*, 5/1 (2002), 69–90.

Aleksiun, Natalia, 'Gender and the Daily Life of Jews in Hiding in Eastern Galicia', *Nashim: A Journal of Jewish Women's Studies and Gender Issues*, 27 (2014), 38–61.

Allen, Ann Taylor, 'The Holocaust and the Modernization of Gender: A Historiographical Essay', *Central European History*, 30/3 (1997), 349–64.

Améry, Jean, *At the Mind's Limits: Contemplations by a Survivor on Auschwitz and its Realities*, trans. Sidney Rosenfeld and Stella P. Rosenfeld (Bloomington, IN: Indiana University Press, 1980).

Aolain, Fionnuala Ni, 'Sex-Based Violence and the Holocaust—A Reevaluation of Harms and Rights in International Law', *Yale Journal of Law and Feminism*, 12/1 (2000), 43–84.

Apenszlak, Jacob (ed.), *The Black Book of Polish Jewry: An Account of the Martyrdom of Polish Jewry under the Nazi Occupation* (New York: American Federation for Polish Jews, 1943).

Appelman-Jurman, Alicia, *Alicia: My Story* (New York: Bantam, 1990).

Arad, Yitzhak, *Ghetto in Flames* (New York: Holocaust Library, 1982).

Arad, Yitzhak, *Belzec, Sobibór, Treblinka: The Operation Reinhard Death Camps* (Bloomington, IN: Indiana University Press, 1987).

Auerbach, Rachel, *Oyf difelder fun Treblinke* [In the Fields of Treblinka] (Warsaw: Żydowska Komisja Historyczna, 1947).

Auerbach, Rachel, *Bi'hutsot Varsha* [The Streets of Warsaw] (Tel Aviv: Israel Book, 1954).

Auerbach, Rachel, *Varshever tsavoes: Bagegenishn, aktiviten, goyroles* [Warsaw Testaments: Meetings, Activities, Fates], *1933–1943* (Tel Aviv: Israel Book, 1974).

Auerbach, Rachel, *Baym letstn veg: In geto Varshe un oyf der arisher zayt* [At Road's End: In the Warsaw Ghetto and on the Aryan Side] (Tel Aviv: Am Oved, 1977).

Bacall-Zwirn, Alina and Stark, Jared, *No Common Place: The Holocaust Testimony of Alina Bacall-Zwirn* (Lincoln, NE: University of Nebraska Press, 1999).

Bacon, Gershon C., 'The Missing 52 Percent: Research on Jewish Women in Inter-War Poland and its Implications for Holocaust Studies', in Dalia Ofer and Lenore J. Weitzman (eds.), *Women in the Holocaust* (New Haven, CT: Yale University Press, 1998), 55–67.

Baer, Elizabeth R. and Goldenberg, Myrna (eds.), *Experience and Expression: Women, the Nazis and the Holocaust* (Detroit, MI: Wayne State University Press, 2003).

Baldwin, Annabelle, 'Sexual Violence and the Holocaust: Reflections on Memory and Witness Testimony', *Holocaust Studies: A Journal of Culture and History*, 16/3 (2010), 112–34.

Ballinger, Pamela, 'The Culture of Survivors: Post-Traumatic Stress Disorder and Traumatic Memory', *History and Memory*, 10/1 (Spring 1988), 99–131.

Banet, Chana Marcus, *They Called Me Frau Anna* (New York: CIS, 1990).

Bar-On, Dan, *Parenthood and the Holocaust* (Search and Research Lectures and Papers, 1) (Jerusalem: Yad Vashem, 2001).

Bardgett, Suzanne and Cesarani, David (eds.), *Belsen 1945: New Historical Perspectives* (London: Vallentine Mitchell, 2006).

Barrett, Michele and Phillips, Anne, *Destabilizing Theory: Contemporary Feminist Debates* (Cambridge: Polity Press, 1992).

Bartoszewski, Władysław and Lewin, Zofia, *Righteous among Nations. How Poles Helped the Jews. 1939–1945* (London: Earls Court Publications, 1969).

Bauer, Yehuda, *Flight and Rescue: Bricha* (New York: Random House, 1970).

Bauer, Yehuda, 'The Problem of Gender: The Case of Gisi Fleischmann', in *Rethinking the Holocaust* (New Haven, CT: Yale University Press, 2001), 167–85.

Bauer, Yehuda, *A History of the Holocaust* (London: Franklin Watts, 2002).

Bauman, Janina, *Winter in the Morning: A Young Girl's Life in the Warsaw Ghetto and Beyond 1939–1945* (London: Virago, 1991).

Bauman, Janina, *Beyond these Walls: Escaping the Warsaw Ghetto—A Young Girl's Story* (London: Virago, 2006).

Baumel, Judith Tydor, 'Gender and Family Studies of the Holocaust: A Historiographical Overview', *Women: A Cultural Review*, 7/2 (1996), 115–24.

Baumel, Judith Tydor, 'DP's, Mothers and Pioneers: Women in the *She'erit Hapletah*', *Jewish History*, 11/2 (1997), 99–110.

Baumel, Judith Tydor, *Kibbutz Buchenwald: Survivors and Pioneers* (New Brunswick, NJ: Rutgers University Press, 1997).

Baumel, Judith Tydor, *Double Jeopardy: Gender and the Holocaust* (London: Vallentine Mitchell, 1998).

Baumel, Judith Tydor, 'Women's Agency and Survival Strategies during the Holocaust', *Women's Studies International Forum*, 22/3 (1999), 329–47.

Beck, Birgit, *Wehrmacht und sexuelle Gewalt. Sexualverbrechen vor deutschen Militärgerichten 1939–1945* (Paderborn: Schöningh, 2004).

Beinfeld, Solon, 'Health Care in the Vilna Ghetto', *Holocaust and Genocide Studies*, 12/1 (1998), 66–98.

Ben-Sefer, Ellen, 'Sex and the City: Women, Sexuality, and Reproduction', in Zygmunt Mazur, Jay T. Lees, Arnold Krammer, and Władysław Witalisz (eds.), *The Legacy of the Holocaust: Women and the Holocaust* (Kraków: Jagiellonian University Press, 2005), 57–72.

Ben-Sefer, Ellen, 'Forced Sterilization and Abortion as Sexual Abuse', in Sonja M. Hedgepeth and Rochelle G. Saidel (eds.), *Sexual Violence against Jewish Women during the Holocaust* (Waltham, MA: Brandeis University Press, 2010), 156–73.

Benedict, Susan and George, Jane M., 'Nurses and the Sterilization Experiments of Auschwitz: A Postmodernist Perspective', *Nursing Inquiry*, 13/4 (2006), 277–88.

Berg, Mary, *Warsaw Ghetto: A Diary*, trans. Norbert Guterman and Sylvia Glass, ed. S. L. Shneiderman (New York: Fischer, 1945).

Bergen, Doris L., 'Sex, Blood and Vulnerability: Women Outsiders in Nazi-Occupied Europe', in Robert Gellately and Nathan Stoltzfus (eds.), *Social Outsiders in Nazi-Occupied Europe* (Princeton, NJ: Princeton University Press, 2001), 273–93.

Bergen, Doris L., 'Sexual Violence in the Holocaust: Unique and Typical?', in Dagmar Herzog (ed.), *Lessons and Legacies*, vol. 7: *The Holocaust in International Context* (Evanston, IL: Northwestern University Press, 2006), 217–28.

Berman, Adolf, 'The Fate of the Children in the Warsaw Ghetto', in Israel Gutman and Livia Rothkirchen (eds.), *The Catastrophe of European Jewry: Antecedents, History, Reflections* (Jerusalem: Yad Vashem, 1976), 400–21.

Bernard, Catherine A., '"tell him that I": Women Writing the Holocaust', *Other Voices: The (e)Journal of Cultural Criticism*, 2/1 (February 2000).

Bezwinska, Jadwiga and Czech, Danuta (eds.), *Amidst a Nightmare of Crime: Manuscripts of Members of* Sonderkommando (New York: Howard Fertig, 1992).

Biddescombe, Perry, 'Dangerous Liaisons: The Anti-Fraternization Movement in the US Occupation Zones of Germany and Austria, 1945–1948', *Journal of Social History*, 34/3 (2001), 611–47.

Birenbaum, Halina, *Hope is the Last to Die: A Personal Documentation of Nazi Terror*, trans. David Welsh (New York: Twayne, 1967).

Bitton-Jackson, Livia E., *Elli: Coming of Age in the Holocaust* (London: Grafton, 1984).

Bitton-Jackson, Livia E., *My Bridges of Hope: Six Long Years to Freedom after Auschwitz* (London: Simon & Schuster, 1999).

Blady-Szwajger, Adina, *I Remember Nothing More: The Warsaw Children's Hospital and The Jewish Resistance*, trans. Tasja Darowska and Danusia Stok (London: Collins Harvill, 1990).

Bock, Gisela, Review of Claudia Koonz, *Mothers in the Fatherland*, *Bulletin of the German Historical Institute London*, 11/1 (1989), 16–24.

Bondy, Ruth, 'Women in Theresienstadt and the Family Camp in Birkenau', in Dalia Ofer and Lenore J. Weitzman (eds.), *Women in the Holocaust* (New Haven, CT: Yale University Press, 1998), 310–26.

Borowski, Tadeusz, *This Way for the Gas, Ladies and Gentlemen*, trans. Barbara Vedder (Harmondsworth: Penguin, 1967).

Borwicz, Michal, *Arishe papirn* [Aryan papers], 3 vols. (Buenos Aires: Tsentral-Farband fun Poylishe Yidn, 1955).

Borzykowski, Tuvia, *Between Tumbling Walls*, trans. Mendel Kohansky (Tel Aviv: Hakkibutz Hameuchad), 1976.

Brenner, Michael, *After the Holocaust: Rebuilding Jewish Lives in Postwar Germany*, trans. Barbara Harshav (Princeton, NJ: Princeton University Press, 1997).

Bridenthal, Renate, Koonz, Claudia, and Stuard, Susan (eds.), *Becoming Visible: Women in European History* (Boston, MA: Houghton Mifflin, 1987).

Bridgman, Jon, *The End of the Holocaust: The Liberation of the Camps* (Portland, OR: Areopagitica Press, 1990).

Brownmiller, Susan, *Against our Will: Men, Women, and Rape* (New York: Simon & Schuster, 1975).

Bruck, Edith, *Who Loves You Like This* (Philadelphia, PA: Paul Dry, 2001).

Butler, Judith, *Gender Trouble: Feminism and the Subversion of Identity* (New York: Routledge, 1990).

Butler, Judith, *Undoing Gender* (New York: Routledge, 2004).

Caplan, Jane, 'Gender and the Concentration Camps', in Nikolaus Wachsmann and Jane Caplan (eds.), *Concentration Camps in Nazi Germany: The New Histories* (London: Routledge, 2010), 82–107.

Carey, Maddy, 'Jewish Masculinity in the Holocaust' (Ph.D. thesis, Royal Holloway, University of London, 2014).

Caruth, Cathy, *Unclaimed Experience: Trauma, Narrative, and History* (Baltimore, MD: Johns Hopkins University Press, 1996).

Cesarani, David, *Final Solution: The Fate of the Jews 1933–1949* (London: Macmillan, 2016).

Chalmers, Beverley, *Birth, Sex and Abuse: Women's Voices under Nazi Rule* (Guildford: Grosvenor House, 2015).

Chatwood, Kirsty, '(Re)-Interpreting Stories of Sexual Violence', in Esther Herzog (ed.), *Life, Death and Sacrifice: Women and the Family in the Holocaust* (Jerusalem: Gefen, 2008), 161–81.

Chatwood, Kirsty, 'Schillinger and the Dancer: Representing Agency and Sexual Violence in Holocaust Testimonies', in Sonja M. Hedgepeth and Rochelle G. Saidel (eds.), *Sexual Violence against Jewish Women during the Holocaust* (Waltham, MA: Brandeis University Press, 2010), 61–74.

Chelouche, Tessa, 'Doctors, Pregnancy, Childbirth and Abortion during the Third Reich', *Israel Medical Association Journal*, 9 (2007), 202–6.

Child Survivors' Association of Great Britain, *Zachor* [Remembrance]: *Child Survivors Speak* (London: Elliot & Thompson, 2005).

Chinkin, Christine M., 'Rape and Sexual Abuse of Women in International Law', *European Journal of International Law*, 5 (1994), 50–74.

Chodorow, Nancy, *The Reproduction of Mothering: Psychoanalysis and the Sociology of Gender* (Berkeley, CA: University of California Press, 1978).

Cixous, Hélène and Clément, Catherine, 'Sorties', in *The Newly Born Woman* (Minneapolis, MN: University of Minnesota Press, 1986).

Clendinnen, Inga, *Reading the Holocaust* (Cambridge: Cambridge University Press, 1999).

Cohen, Beth, *Case Closed: Holocaust Survivors in Postwar America* (New Brunswick, NJ: Rutgers University Press, 2007).

Cohen, Boaz, 'The Children's Voice: Postwar Collection of Testimonies from Child Survivors of the Holocaust', *Holocaust and Genocide Studies*, 21/1 (2007), 73–95.

Cohen, Nathan, 'Diaries of the *Sonderkommando* in Auschwitz: Coping with Fate and Reality', *Yad Vashem Studies*, 20 (1990), 273–312.

Cohen, Nathan, 'Diaries of the *Sonderkommando*', in Israel Gutman and Michael Berenbaum (eds.), *Anatomy of the Auschwitz Death Camp* (Bloomington, IN: Indiana University Press, 1994), 522–34.

Corni, Gustavo, *Hitler's Ghettos: Voices from a Beleaguered Society 1939–1944* (London: Arnold, 2002).

Culbertson, Roberta, 'Embodied Memory, Transcendence, and Telling: Recounting Trauma, Re-establishing the Self', *New Literary History*, 26/1 (1995), 169–95.

Czech, Danuta, *Auschwitz Chronicle, 1939–1945: From the Archives of the Auschwitz Memorial and the German Federal Archives*, trans. Barbara Harshav, Martha Humphreys, and Stephen Shearier (New York: Henry Holt, 1990).

Czerniaków, Adam, *The Warsaw Ghetto Diary of Adam Czerniakow: Prelude to Doom*, eds. Raul Hilberg, Stanisław Staron, and Josef Kermisz (New York: Stein & Day, 1982).

Danieli, Yael, 'The Impact of the Holocaust Experience on Survivors in the U.S.', in Israel Gutman and Avital Saf (eds.), *The Nazi Concentration Camps: Structure and Aim, The Image of the Prisoner, The Jews in the Camps: Proceedings of the Fourth Yad Vashem International Historical Conference—January 1980* (Jerusalem: Yad Vashem, 1984), 603–21.

Danieli, Yael, 'The Heterogeneity of Postwar Adaptation in Families of Holocaust Survivors', in Randolph L. Braham (ed.), *The Psychological Perspectives of the Holocaust and of its Aftermath* (New York: Columbia University Press, 1988), 109–27.

David, Janina, *A Square of Sky: Memoirs of a Wartime Childhood* (London: Eland, 1992).

Dawidowicz, Lucy, *The War against the Jews, 1933–1945* (New York: Holt, Rinehart & Winston, 1975).

de Beauvoir, Simone, *The Second Sex* (New York: Vintage, 1973).

Dean, Martin 'Life and Death in the "Gray Zone" of Jewish Ghettos in Nazi-Occupied Europe: The Unknown, the Ambiguous, and the Disappeared', in Jonathan Petropoulos and John K. Roth (eds.), *Gray Zones: Ambiguity and Compromise in the Holocaust and its Aftermath* (New York: Berghahn, 2005), 205–21.

Dean, Martin and Megargee, Geoffrey P. (eds.), *Ghettos in German-Occupied Eastern Europe* (vol. 2 of Center for Advanced Holocaust Studies, *The United States*

Holocaust Memorial Museum Encyclopedia of Camps and Ghettos, 1933–1945) (Bloomington, IN: Indiana University Press, 2012).

Debski, Tadeusz, *A Battlefield of Ideas: Nazi Concentration Camps and their Political Prisoners* (New York: Columbia University Press, 2001).

Dekel, Ephraim, *B'riha: Flight to the Homeland* (New York: Random House, 1973).

des Pres, Terrence, *The Survivor: An Anatomy of Life in the Death Camps* (Oxford: Oxford University Press, 1976).

Dinnerstein, Leonard, *America and the Survivors of the Holocaust* (New York: Columbia University Press, 1982).

Dobroszycki, Lucjan, 'Jewish Elites under German Rule', in Henry Friedlander and Sybil Mylton (eds.), *The Holocaust: Ideology, Bureaucracy and Genocide* (New York: Kraus, 1980), 221–30.

Dobroszycki, Lucjan (ed.), *The Chronicle of the Lodz Ghetto, 1941–1944*, trans. Richard Lourie, Joachim Neugroschel, et al. (New Haven, CT: Yale University Press, 1984).

Donat, Alexander, *The Holocaust Kingdom: A Memoir* (London: Corgi, 1967).

Dufournier, Denise, *Ravensbrück: The Women's Camp of Death* (London: Allen & Unwin, 1948).

Dwórk, Deborah, *Children with a Star: Jewish Youth in Nazi Europe* (New Haven, CT: Yale University Press, 1993).

Dwók, Debórah and van Pelt, Robert Jan, *Auschwitz: 1270 to the Present* (London: Norton, 1996).

Eichengreen, Lucille, *From Ashes to Life: My Memories of the Holocaust*, with Harriet Hyman Chamberlain (San Francisco, CA: Mercury House, 1994).

Einhorn-Susułowska, Maria, 'Psychological Problems of Polish Jews Who Used Aryan Documents', in Antony Polonsky (ed.), *Polin. Studies in Polish Jewry*, vol. 13: *Focusing on the Holocaust and its Aftermath* (London: Littman Library, 2000), 104–11.

Elias, Ruth, *Triumph of Hope: From Theresienstadt and Auschwitz to Israel*, trans. Margot Bettauer Dembo (New York: John Wiley, 1998).

Engel, David, 'Patterns of Anti-Jewish Violence in Poland, 1944–1946', *Yad Vashem Studies*, 26 (1998), 43–86.

Engelking, Barbara, *Holocaust and Memory: The Experience of the Holocaust and its Consequences: An Investigation Based on Personal Narratives*, trans. Emma Harris, ed. Gunnar S. Paulsson (London: Leicester University Press, 2001).

Fein, Helen, 'Genocide and Gender: The Uses of Women and Group Destiny', *Journal of Genocide Research*, 1/1 (1999), 43–63.

Felman, Shoshana and Laub, Dori, *Testimony: Crises of Witnessing in Literature, Psychoanalysis, and History* (New York: Routledge, 1992).

Fénelon, Fania, *Playing for Time*, trans. Judith Landry (New York: Atheneum, 1977).

Ferderber-Salz, Bertha, *And the Sun Kept Shining* (New York: Holocaust Library, 1980).

Fine, Ellen S., 'Women Writers and the Holocaust: Strategies for Survival', in Randolph L. Braham (ed.), *Reflections of the Holocaust in Art and Literature* (New York: City University of New York Press, 1990), 79–98.

Fine, Ellen S., 'Intergenerational Memories: Hidden Children and Second Generation', in John K. Roth and Elizabeth Maxwell (eds.), *Remembering for the Future: The Holocaust in an Age of Genocide*, vol. 3 (New York: Palgrave, 2001), 78–92.

Fink, Ida, *The Journey*, trans. Johanna Weschler and Francine Prose (London: Hamish Hamilton, 1992).

Fishman, David, *Embers Plucked from the Fire: The Rescue of Jewish Cultural Treasures in Vilna* (New York: YIVO Institute for Jewish Research, 2009).

Flaschka, Monika J., '"Only Pretty Women Were Raped": The Effect of Sexual Violence on Gender Identities in Concentration Camps', in Sonja M. Hedgepeth and Rochelle G. Saidel (eds.), *Sexual Violence against Jewish Women during the Holocaust* (Waltham, MA: Brandeis University Press, 2010), 77–93.

Fodor, Renée, 'The Impact of the Nazi Occupation of Poland on the Jewish Mother–Child Relationship', *YIVO Annual of Jewish Social Science*, 11 (1956/7), 270–85.

Fogelman, Eva, *Conscience and Courage: Rescuers of Jews during the Holocaust* (New York: Anchor, 1994).

Fox, Thomas C., 'The Holocaust under Communism', in Dan Stone (ed.), *The Historiography of the Holocaust* (Basingstoke: Palgrave Macmillan, 2004), 420–39.

Friedländer, Saul, *When Memory Comes*, trans. Helen R. Lane (New York: Noonday, 1991).

Friedländer, Saul, 'The Holocaust', in Martin Goodman (ed.), *The Oxford Handbook of Jewish Studies* (Oxford: Oxford University Press, 2002), 412–44.

Friedländer, Saul, *Nazi Germany and the Jews*, vol. 1: *The Years of Persecution, 1933–1939* (London: Weidenfeld & Nicolson, 2007).

Friedländer, Saul, *Nazi Germany and the Jews 1939–1945*, vol. 2: *The Years of Extermination* (London: Weidenfeld & Nicolson, 2007).

Friedman, Jonathan, 'Togetherness and Isolation: Holocaust Survivor Memoirs of Intimacy and Sexuality in the Ghettos', *Oral History Review*, 28/1 (Winter/Spring 2001), 1–16.

Frister, Roman, *The Cap: The Price of a Life* (New York: Continuum, 1999).

Fromer, Rebecca Camhi, *The Holocaust Odyssey of Daniel Bennahmias, Sonderkommando* (Tuscaloosa, AL: University of Alabama Press, 1993).

Gafny, Emunah Nachmany, *Dividing Hearts: The Removal of Jewish Children from Gentile Families in Poland in the Immediate Post-Holocaust Years* (Jerusalem: Yad Vashem, 2009).

Gershon, Karen (ed.), *We Came as Children: A Collective Autobiography of Refugees* (London: Macmillan, 1966).

Gilbert, Martin, *Auschwitz and the Allies* (London: Michael Joseph, 1981).

Gilbert, Martin, *The Holocaust: The Jewish Tragedy* (London: Fontana, 1987).

Gilbert, Martin, *The Day the War Ended: VE-Day 1945 in Europe and around the World* (London: HarperCollins, 1995).

Gilbert, Shirli, *Music in the Holocaust: Confronting Life in the Nazi Ghettos and Camps* (Oxford: Oxford University Press, 1995).

Gill, Anton, *The Journey Back from Hell: Conversations with Concentration Camp Survivors* (London: HarperCollins, 1994).

Glenn, Susan A., *Daughters of the Shtetl: Life and Labor in the Immigrant Generation* (Ithaca, NY: Cornell University Press, 1995).

Goldenberg, Myrna, 'Different Horrors/Same Hell: Women Remembering the Holocaust', in Roger Gottlieb (ed.), *Thinking the Unthinkable: Human Meanings of the Holocaust* (New York: Paulist Press, 1990), 150–66.

Goldenberg, Myrna, 'Lessons Learned from Gentle Heroism: Women's Holocaust Narratives', *Annals of the American Academy of Political and Social Sciences*, 548 (1996), 78–93.

Goldenberg, Myrna, 'Food Talk: Gendered Responses to Hunger in Concentration Camps', in John K. Roth and Elizabeth Maxwell (eds.), *Remembering for the Future: The Holocaust in an Age of Genocide* (Basingstoke: Palgrave, 2001), 248–57.

Goldenberg, Myrna, 'Rape during the Holocaust', in Zygmunt Mazur, Jay T. Lees, Arnold Krammer, and Władysław Witalisz (eds.), *The Legacy of the Holocaust: Women and the Holocaust* (Kraków: Jagiellonian University Press, 2007), 159–69.

Gottesfeld Heller, Fanya, *Strange and Unexpected Love: A Teenage Girl's Holocaust Memoirs* (Hoboken, NJ: Ktav, 1993).

Gradowski, Jan, *Rescue for Money. Paid Helpers in Poland, 1939–1945* (Search and Research Series 13) (Jerusalem: Yad Vashem, 2008).

Greenfield, Henry, *The Hidden Children* (New York: Ticknor & Fields, 1993).

Greenspan, Henry, *On Listening to Holocaust Survivors* (New York: Praeger, 1998).

Greif, Gideon, 'Between Sanity and Insanity: Spheres of Everyday Life in the Auschwitz-Birkenau *Sonderkommando*', in Jonathan Petropoulos and John K. Roth (eds.), *Gray Zones: Ambiguity and Compromise in the Holocaust and its Aftermath* (New York: Berghahn, 2005), 37–60.

Greif, Gideon, *We Wept without Tears: Testimonies of the Jewish* Sonderkommando *from Auschwitz* (New Haven, CT: Yale University Press, 2005).

Gringauz, Samuel, 'The Ghetto as an Experiment of Jewish Social Organization', *Jewish Social Studies*, 11/1 (1949), 3–20.

Gringauz, Samuel, 'Some Methodological Problems in the Study of the Ghetto', *Jewish Social Studies*, 12/1 (1950), 65–72.

Gross, Jan Tomasz, *Fear: Antisemitism in Poland after Auschwitz: An Essay in Historical Interpretation* (New York: Random House, 2007).

Gross, Jan Tomasz, with Grudzińska, Irena, *Golden Harvest: Events at the Periphery of the Holocaust* (Oxford: Oxford University Press, 2012).

Grossman, Mendel, *With a Camera in the Ghetto*, eds. Zvi Szner and Alexander Sened (New York: Schocken, 1977).

Grossmann, Atina, 'Trauma, Memory, and Motherhood: Germans and Jewish Displaced Persons in Post-Nazi Germany, 1945–1949', *Archiv für Sozialgeschichte*, 38 (1981), 215–39.

Grossmann, Atina, 'Feminist Debates about Women and National Socialism', *Gender and History*, 3/3 (1991), 350–8.

Grossmann, Atina, *Reforming Sex: The German Movement for Birth Control and Abortion Reform, 1920–1950* (New York: Oxford University Press, 1995).

Grossmann, Atina, 'Victims, Villains, and Survivors: Gendered Perceptions and Self-Perceptions of Jewish Displaced Persons in Occupied Postwar Germany', *The Journal of the History of Sexuality*, 11/1–2, Special Issue: Sexuality and German Fascisms (January/April 2002), 291–318.

Grossmann, Atina, 'Women and the Holocaust: Four Recent Titles', *Holocaust and Genocide Studies*, 16 (Spring 2002), 94–108.

Grossmann, Atina, 'Gendered Perceptions and Self-Perceptions of Memory and Revenge: Jewish DPs in Occupied Postwar Germany as Victims, Villains and Survivors', in Judith Tydor Baumel and Tova Cohen (eds.), *Gender, Place and Memory in the Modern Jewish Experience: Re-Placing Ourselves* (London: Vallentine Mitchell, 2003), 78–108.

Grossmann, Atina, *Jews, Germans, and Allies: Close Encounters in Occupied Germany* (Princeton, NJ: Princeton University Press, 2007).

Grossmann, Atina, 'Living On: Remembering Feldafing', in Jürgen Matthäus (ed.), *Approaching an Auschwitz Survivor: Holocaust Testimony and its Transformations* (Oxford: Oxford University Press, 2009), 73–94.

Grossmann, Kurt R., *The Jewish DP Problem: Its Origin, Scope, and Liquidation* (New York: Institute of Jewish Affairs, World Jewish Congress, 1951).

Gurewitsch, Brana (ed.), *Mothers, Sisters, Resisters: Oral Histories of Women Who Survived the Holocaust* (Tuscaloosa, AL: University of Alabama Press, 1998).

Gutman, Israel, *The Jews of Warsaw, 1939–1943, Ghetto, Underground, Revolt*, trans. Ina Friedman (Brighton: Harvester, 1982).

Gutman, Israel, 'Social Stratification in the Concentration Camps', in Israel Gutman and Avital Saf (eds.), *The Nazi Concentration Camps: Structure and Aims, The Image of the Prisoner, The Jews in the Camps: Proceedings of the Fourth Yad Vashem International Historical Conference—January 1980* (Jerusalem: Yad Vashem, 1984), 143–76.

Gutman, Israel, *Resistance: The Warsaw Ghetto Uprising* (Boston, MA: Houghton Mifflin, 1994).

Hájková, Anna, 'Sexual Barter in Times of Genocide: Narrating the Sexual Economy of the Theresienstadt Ghetto', *Signs: Journal of Women in Culture and Society*, 38/3 (Spring 2013), 503–33.

Halkin, Hillel, 'Feminizing Jewish Studies', *Commentary*, 105/2 (February 1998), 39–45.

Hanson, Joanna K. M., *The Civilian Population in the Warsaw Uprising of 1944* (Cambridge: Cambridge University Press, 1982).

Hardman, Anna, 'Women and the Holocaust', *Holocaust Educational Trust Research Papers*, 1/3 (1999–2000).

Hardman, L. H. and Goodman, Cecily, *The Survivors: The Story of the Belsen Remnant* (London: Vallentine Mitchell, 1958).

Hart[-Moxon], Kitty, *Return to Auschwitz: The Remarkable Story of a Girl who Survived the Holocaust* (London: Grafton, 1983).

Hass, Aaron, *The Aftermath: Living with the Holocaust* (Cambridge: Cambridge University Press, 1995).

Hausner, Gideon, *Justice in Jerusalem* (New York: Harper & Row, 1966).

Hedgepeth, Sonja M. and Saidel, Rochelle G. (eds.), *Sexual Violence against Jewish Women during the Holocaust* (Waltham, MA: Brandeis University Press, 2010).

Heineman, Elizabeth D., *What Difference Does a Husband Make? Women and Marital Status in Nazi and Postwar Germany* (Berkeley, CA: University of California Press, 1999).

Heineman, Elizabeth D., 'Sexuality and Nazism: The Doubly Unspeakable?', *Journal of the History of Sexuality*, 11/1–2 (2002), 22–46.

Heineman, Elizabeth D., 'Gender, Sexuality, and Coming to Terms with the Nazi Past', *Central European History*, 38/1 (2005), 41–74.

Heinemann, Marlene E., *Gender and Destiny: Women Writers and the Holocaust* (Westport, CT: Greenwood Press, 1986).

Helm, Sarah, *If This Is a Woman: Inside Ravensbrück, Hitler's Concentration Camp for Women* (London: Little, Brown, 2015).

Henry, Patrick, 'Banishing the Coercion of Despair: Le Chambon-sur-Lignon and the Holocaust Today', *Shofar: An Interdisciplinary Journal of Jewish Social Studies*, 20/2 (2001), 69–84.

Herchel, Susannah, 'Does Atrocity Have a Gender? Feminist Interpretations of Women in the SS', in Jeffry M. Diefendorf (ed.), *Lessons and Legacies*, vol. 6: *New Currents in Holocaust Research* (Evanston, IL: Northwestern University Press, 2004), 300–21.

Herman, Judith Lewis, *Trauma and Recovery* (New York: Basic Books, 1992).

Hertzog, Esther (ed.), *Life, Death and Sacrifice: Women and the Family in the Holocaust* (Jerusalem: Gefen, 2008).

Herzog, Dagmar (ed.), *Sexuality and German Fascism* (New York: Berghahn, 2005).

Herzog, Dagmar (ed.), *Brutality and Desire: War and Sexuality in Europe's Twentieth Century* (New York: Palgrave Macmillan, 2009).

Hilberg, Raul, *The Destruction of the European Jews*, 3 vols. (Chicago, IL: Quadrangle, 1961).

Hilberg, Raul, *Perpetrators, Victims, Bystanders: The Jewish Catastrophe, 1933–1945* (London: HarperCollins, 1993).

Hodara, Raquel, 'The Polish Jewish Woman from the Beginning of the Occupation to the Deportation to the Ghettos', *Yad Vashem Studies*, 32 (2004), 397–432.

Hoffman, Eva, *Lost in Translation: A Life in a New Language* (London: Vintage, 1998).

Hoffman, Eva, *After Such Knowledge: A Meditation on the Aftermath of the Holocaust* (London: Secker & Warburg, 2004).

Hogan, David J. (ed.), *The Holocaust Chronicle* (Lincolnwood, IL: Publications International, 2007).

Holden, Wendy, *Born Survivors* (London: Little, Brown, 2015).

Holliday, Laurel (ed.), *Children's Wartime Diaries: Secret Writings from the Holocaust and World War II* (London: Piatkus, 1995).

Horavitch, Rita, 'Jews in Hungary after the Holocaust: The National Relief Committee for Deportees, 1945–1950', *Journal of Israeli History*, 19 (1998), 69–91.

Horowitz, Sara R., 'Memory and Testimony of Women Survivors of Nazi Genocide', in Judith R. Baskin (ed.), *Women of the Word: Jewish Women and Jewish Writing* (Detroit, MI: Wayne State University Press, 1994), 258–82.

Horowitz, Sara R., 'Gender, Genocide and Jewish Memory', *Prooftexts*, 20/1&2 (Winter/Spring 2000), 158–90.

Höss, Rudolf, *Commandant of Auschwitz: The Autobiography of Rudolf Hoess*, trans. Constantine FitzGibbon and Joachim Neugroschel (London: Phoenix, 2001).

Huberband, Shimon, *Kiddush Hashem* [Sanctification of the Name]: *Jewish Religious and Cultural Life in Poland during the Holocaust*, trans. David E. Fishman, eds. Jeffrey S. Gurock and Robert S. Hirt (Hoboken, NJ: Ktav, 1987).

Hyman, Paula E., 'The Modern Jewish Family: Image and Reality', in David Kraemer (ed.), *The Jewish Family: Metaphor and Memory* (Oxford: Oxford University Press, 1989), 179–93.

Hyman, Paula E., 'East European Jewish Women in an Age of Transition, 1880–1930', in Judith R. Baskin (ed.), *Women of the Word: Jewish Women and Jewish Writing* (Detroit, MI: Wayne State University Press, 1994), 270–86.

Hyman, Paula E., 'Feminist Studies and Modern Jewish History', in Lynn Davidman and Shelly Tenenbaum (eds.), *Feminist Perspectives on Jewish Studies* (New Haven, CT: Yale University Press, 1994), 120–39.

Hyman, Paula E., *Gender and Assimilation in Modern Jewish History: The Roles and Representation of Women* (Seattle, WA: University of Washington Press, 1995).

Hyman, Paula E., 'Gender and the Jewish Family in Modern Europe', in Dalia Ofer and Lenore J. Weitzman (eds.), *Women in the Holocaust* (New Haven, CT: Yale University Press, 1998), 25–34.

Irigary, Luce, *This Sex Which is Not One* (Ithaca, NY: Cornell University Press, 1985).

Isaacson, Judith Magyar, *Seed of Sarah: Memoirs of a Survivor* (Chicago, IL: University of Illinois Press, 1991).

Iwaszko, Tadeusz, Kubica, Helena, Piper, Franciszek, Strzelecka, Irena, and Strzelecki, Andrzej, *Auschwitz 1940–1945: Central Issues in the History of the Camp*, vol. 2 (Oświęcim: Auschwitz State Museum, 1995).

Jewish Black Book Committee, *The Black Book: The Nazi Crime against the Jewish People* (New York: Duell, Sloan & Pearce, 1946).

Jockusch, Laura, *Collect and Record! Jewish Holocaust Documentation in Early Postwar Europe* (Oxford: Oxford University Press, 2012).

Jones, Adam, *Gendercide and Genocide* (Nashville, TN: Vanderbilt University Press, 2004).

Kangisser Cohen, Sharon, *Child Survivors of the Holocaust in Israel: 'Finding Their Voice': Social Dynamics and Post-War Experiences* (Brighton: Sussex Academic Press, 2005).

Kaplan, Chaim A., *Scroll of Agony: The Warsaw Diary of Chaim A. Kaplan*, trans. and ed. Abraham I. Katsh (Bloomington, IN: Indiana University Press, 1999).

Kaplan, Marion, 'Jewish Women in Nazi Germany: Daily Life, Daily Struggles, 1933–1939', *Feminist Studies*, 16/3 (1990), 579–606.

Kaplan, Marion, *Between Dignity and Despair: Jewish Life in Nazi Germany* (New York: Oxford University Press, 1998).

Karay, Felicia, 'Women in the Forced Labor Camps', in Dalia Ofer and Lenore J. Weitzman (eds.), *Women in the Holocaust* (New Haven, CT: Yale University Press, 1998), 285–309.

Kassow, Samuel, *Who Will Write Our History? Emanuel Ringelblum, the Warsaw Ghetto, and the Oyneg Shabes Archive* (Bloomington, IN: Indiana University Press, 2007).

Kassow, Samuel, 'Oyerbach Rokhl [Auerbach, Rachel]', in *The YIVO Encyclopaedia of Jews in Eastern Europe*, vol. 2 (New Haven, CT: Yale University Press, 2008), 1301–2.

Katz, Esther, and Ringelheim, Joan Miriam (eds.), *Proceedings of the Conference: Women Surviving the Holocaust* (New York: Occasional Papers from The Institute for Research in History, 1983).

Keren, Nili, 'The Family Camp', in Israel Gutman and Michael Berenbaum (eds.), *Anatomy of the Auschwitz Death Camp* (Bloomington, IN: Indiana University Press, 1994), 428–41.

Kermish, Joseph, 'Introduction', in Adam Czerniaków, *Yoman geto Varhsa* [Warsaw Ghetto Diary]: *6.9.1939–23.7.1942* (Jerusalem: Yad Vashem, 1968).

Kermish, Joseph, 'The Activities of the Council for Aid to Jews (Żegota) in Occupied Poland', in Israel Gutman and Efraim Zuroff (eds.), *Rescue Attempts during the Holocaust: Proceedings of the Second Yad Vashem Conference* (Jerusalem: Yad Vashem, 1977), 367–98.

Kermish, Joseph, 'Daily Entries of Hersh Wasser', in *Yad Vashem Studies*, 15 (1983), 201–82.

Kermish, Joseph (ed.), *To Live with Honor and Die with Honor! Selected Documents from the Warsaw Ghetto Underground Archives 'O.S.' ['Oneg Shabbath']* (Jerusalem: Yad Vashem, 1986).

Klajman, Jack, *Out of the Ghetto* (London: Vallentine Mitchell, 2000).

Klein, Gerda Weissmann, *All But My Life* (New York: Hill & Wang, 1975).

Klonicki-Klonymus, Aryeh and Klonicki, Malwina, *The Diary of Aryeh Klonicki (Klonymus) and his Wife Malwina, with Letters Concerning the Fate of their Child Adam*, trans. Avner Tomaschaff (Tel Aviv: Ghetto Fighters House, 1973).

Klüger, Ruth, *Landscapes of Memory: A Holocaust Girlhood Remembered* (London: Bloomsbury, 2003).

Königseder, Angelika and Wetzel, Juliane, *Waiting for Hope: Jewish Displaced Persons in Post-World War II Germany*, trans. John A. Broadwin (Evanston, IL: Northwestern University Press, 2001).

Koonz, Claudia, *Mothers in the Fatherland: Women, the Family and Nazi Politics* (London: Jonathan Cape, 1987).

Koonz, Claudia, 'Consequences: Women, Nazis and Moral Choice', in Carol Rittner and John K. Roth (eds.), *Different Voices: Women and the Holocaust* (New York: Paragon House, 1993), 287–308.

Kornreich Gelissen, Rena (with Heather Dune Macadam), *Rena's Promise: A Story of Sisters in Auschwitz* (London: Weidenfeld and Nicolson, 1996).

Krasnopёrko, Anna, *Briefe meiner Erinnerung. Mein Überleben im jüdischen Ghetto von Minsk 1941/42* (Frankfurt: Villigst, 1991).

Krell, Robert, 'Therapeutic Value of Documenting Child Survivors', *Journal of the American Academy of Child Psychiatry*, 24/4 (1985), 397–400.

Kristeva, Julia, 'Women's Times', *Signs: Journal of Women in Culture and Society*, 7/1 (1981), 13–35.

Kruk, Herman, *Togebukh fon Vilner geto* [Diary of the Vilna Ghetto] (New York: YIVO, 1961).

Kruk, Herman, 'Diary of the Vilna Ghetto', trans. Shlomo Noble, *YIVO Annual of Jewish Social Sciences*, 13 (1965), 9–78.

Kruk, Herman, *The Last Days of the Jerusalem of Lithuania*, trans. Barbara Harshav (New Haven, CT: Yale University Press, 2002).

Kubica, Helen, 'Children', in Israel Gutman and Michael Berenbaum (eds.), *Anatomy of the Auschwitz Death Camp* (Bloomington, IN: Indiana University Press, 1994), 412–28.

Lagerwey, Mary D., *Reading Auschwitz* (London: Sage, 1998).

Lancman, Abram, Jonah, Edmund, and Bartoszewski, Wladyslaw, *Youth in the Time of the Holocaust* (Warsaw: Rytm, 2005).

Landes, Joan B., 'The Public and the Private Sphere: A Feminist Reconsideration', in Johanna Meehan (ed.), *Feminists Read Habermas: Gendering the Subject of Discourse* (New York: Routledge, 1993), 91–116.

Langbein, Hermann, *People in Auschwitz*, trans. Harry Zohn (Chapel Hill, NC: University of North Carolina Press, 2004).

Langer, Lawrence, *Holocaust Testimonies: The Ruins of Memory* (New Haven, CT: Yale University Press, 1991).

Langer, Lawrence, 'Gendered Sufferings? Women in Holocaust Testimonies', in Dalia Ofer and Lenore J. Weitzman (eds.), *Women in the Holocaust* (New Haven, CT: Yale University Press, 1998), 351–63.

Langer, Lawrence, *Preempting the Holocaust* (New Haven, CT: Yale University Press, 1998).

Lasik, Aleksander, Piper, Franciszek, Setkiewicz, Piotr, and Strzelecka, Irena (eds.), *Auschwitz 1940–1945: Central Issues in the History of the Camp*, vol. 1 (Oświęcim: Auschwitz-Birkenau State Museum, 2000).

Laska, Vera, *Women in the Resistance and in the Holocaust: The Voices of Eyewitnesses* (Westport, CT: Greenwood Press, 1988).

Laska, Vera, 'Women in the Resistance and in the Holocaust', in Carol Rittner and John K. Roth (eds.), *Different Voices: Women and the Holocaust* (New York: Paragon House, 1993), 250–69.

Lavsky, Hagit, 'The Day After: Bergen-Belsen from Concentration Camp to the Centre of the Jewish Survivors in Germany', *German History*, 11/1 (1993), 36–59.

Lavsky, Hagit, *New Beginnings: Holocaust Survivors in Bergen-Belsen and the British Zone in Germany, 1945–1950* (Detroit, MI: Wayne State University Press, 2002).

Leitner, Isabella, *Fragments of Isabella: A Memoir of Auschwitz* (New York: Thomas Y. Crowell, 1978).

Lengyel, Olga, *Five Chimneys: The Story of Auschwitz*, trans. Clifford Coch and Paul P. Weiss (Chicago, IL: Ziff-Davis, 1947).

Lentin, Ronit, '"A Howl Unheard": Women Shoah Survivors Dis-placed and Re-silenced', in Claire Duchen and Irene Bandhauer-Schöffman (eds.), *After the War Was Over: Women, War and Peace in Europe 1940–1956* (London: Leicester University Press, 2000), 179–93.

Lerner, Gerda, *The Majority Finds its Past: Placing Women in History* (Oxford: Oxford University Press, 1981).

Lerner, Gerda, *The Creation of Patriarchy* (Oxford: Oxford University Press, 1986).

Leszczyńska, Stanisława, 'Raport położnej z Oświęcimia' [Report of a Midwife from Auschwitz], in *Przęglad Lekarski* [Overview of Medicine], 1 (1965) (available at <http://www.wmpp.org.pl/pl/pielegniarki-na-frontach/ii-wojna-%C5%9Bwiatowa/stanis%C5%82awa-leszczy%C5%84ska.html>, site accessed 2 September 2016).

Levenkron, Nomi, 'Death and the Maidens: "Prostitution", Rape, and Sexual Slavery during World War II', in Sonja M. Hedgepeth and Rochelle G. Saidel (eds.), *Sexual Violence against Jewish Women during the Holocaust* (Waltham, MA: Brandeis University Press, 2010), 13–28.

Leverton, Bertha and Lowensohn, Shmuel (eds.), *I Came Alone: The Stories of the Kindertransports* (Lewes: Book Guild Publishing, 1990).

Levi, Primo, *The Drowned and the Saved*, trans. Raymond Rosenthal (London: Abacus, 1988).

Levi, Trudi, *A Cat Called Adolf* (London: Vallentine Mitchell, 1995).

Levin, Nora, *The Holocaust: The Destruction of European Jewry 1933–1945* (New York: Schocken, 1973).

Lewin, Abraham, *A Cup of Tears: A Diary of the Warsaw Ghetto*, trans. Christopher Hutton, ed. Antony Polonsky (Oxford: Blackwell, 1988).

Lewis, Helen, *A Time to Speak* (Belfast: Blackstaff, 1992).

Lifton, Robert J., *The Nazi Doctors: Medical Killing and the Psychology of Genocide* (London: Macmillan, 1986).

Lilly, Robert J., *Taken By Force: Rape and American GIs in Europe during World War II* (New York: Palgrave, 2007).

Linden, R. Ruth, *Making Stories, Making Selves: Feminist Reflections on the Holocaust* (Columbus, OH: Ohio State University Press, 1993).

Lingens-Reiner, Ella, *Prisoners of Fear* (London: Gollancz, 1948).

Longerich, Peter, *Heinrich Himmler* (Oxford: Oxford University Press, 2002).

Lower, Wendy, '"Anticipatory Obedience" and the Nazi Implementation of the Holocaust in the Ukraine: A Case Study of Central and Peripheral Forces in the Generalbezirk Zhytomyr, 1941–1944', *Holocaust and Genocide Studies*, 16/1 (2002), 1–22.

Lupton, Deborah, *The Emotional Self* (London: Sage, 1998).

MacKinnon, Catherine, 'Rape, Genocide, and Women's Human Rights', *Harvard Women's Law Journal*, 17/5 (1994), 5–16.

MacKinnon, Catherine (ed.), *Are Women Human? And Other Dialogues* (Cambridge, MA: Harvard University Press, 2006).

Mankowitz, Ze'ev, 'The Affirmation of Life in *She'erith Hapleita*', *Holocaust and Genocide Studies*, 5 (1990), 13–21.

Mankowitz, Ze'ev, 'The Formation of *She'erit Hapleita*: November 1944–July 1945', *Yad Vashem Studies*, 20 (1990), 337–70.

Mankowitz, Ze'ev, *Life between Memory and Hope: The Survivors of the Holocaust in Occupied Germany* (Cambridge: Cambridge University Press, 2002).

Mark, Ber (ed.), *Megiles Oyshvits* [The Scrolls of Auschwitz] (Tel Aviv: Am Oved, 1977).

Mark, Ber (ed.), *The Scrolls of Auschwitz* (Tel Aviv: Am Oved, 1985).

Marks, Jane, *The Hidden Children: The Secret Survivors of the Holocaust* (London: Piatkus, 1993).

Marrus, Michael R., *The Unwanted: European Refugees in the Twentieth Century* (New York: Oxford University Press, 1985).

Marrus, Michael R., *The Holocaust in History* (Harmondsworth: Penguin, 1993).

Marshall, Robert, *In the Sewers of Lvov: The Last Sanctuary from the Holocaust* (London: Fontana, 1991).

Mazor, Michael, 'The House Committees in the Warsaw Ghetto', in Yehuda Bauer and Nathan Rotenstreich (eds.), *The Holocaust as Historical Experience* (New York: Holmes & Meier, 1981), 95–108.

Meed, Vladka, *On Both Sides of the Wall: Memoirs from the Warsaw Ghetto*, trans. Benjamin Meed (Tel Aviv: Hakibutz Hameuchad, 1973).

Michalczyk John J., *Filming the End of the Holocaust: Allied Documentaries, Nuremberg and the Liberation of the Concentration Camps* (London: Bloomsbury, 2014).

Michlic, Joanna Beata, *Jewish Children in Nazi-Occupied Poland: Survival and Polish–Jewish Relations during the Holocaust as Reflected in Early Postwar Recollections* (Search and Research: Lectures and Papers) (Jerusalem: Yad Vashem, 2008).

Michlic, Joanna Beata, 'Rebuilding Shattered Lives: Some Vignettes of Jewish Children's Lives in Early Postwar Poland', in Dalia Ofer, Françoise S. Ouzan, and Judy Baumel Schwartz (eds.), *Holocaust Survivors: Resettlement, Memories, Identities* (New York: Berghahn, 2011), 46–87.

Michlic, Joanna Beata, 'The War Began for Me after the War', in Jonathan Friedman (ed.), *The Routledge History of the Holocaust* (London: Routledge, 2011), 482–97.

Michman, Dan, 'Le-Verur ha-Tnaim le-Kiyyum Chayim Datiyim Tachat ha-Shilton ha-Naz' [An Appraisal of the Conditions for Religious Life under the Nazi Regime], *Sinai*, 91/5–6 (August/September 1982), 254–69.

Michman, Dan, 'Research on the Problems and Conditions of Religious Jewry under the Nazi Regime', in Israel Gutman and Gideon Greif (eds.), *The Historiography of the Holocaust Period* (Jerusalem: Yad Vashem, 1988), 737–48.

Milton, Sybil, 'Women and the Holocaust: The Case of German and German-Jewish Women', in Renate Bridenthal, Atina Grossmann, and Marion Kaplan (eds.), *When Biology Became Destiny: Women in Weimar and Nazi Germany* (New York: Monthly Review Press, 1984), 297–323.

Millu, Liana, *Smoke over Birkenau*, trans. Lynne Sharon Schwartz (Philadelphia, PA: Jewish Publications Society, 1991).

Moi, Toril, 'What Is a Woman? Sex, Gender and the Body in Feminist Theory', in *What Is a Woman? And Other Essays* (Oxford: Oxford University Press, 1999), 13–120.

Moore, Bob, *Victims and Survivors: The Nazi Persecution of the Jews in the Netherlands 1940–1945* (London: Hodder, 1997).

Mühlhäuser, Regina, *Eroberungen. Sexuelle Gewalttaten und intime Beziehungen deutscher Soldaten in der Sowjetunion, 1941–1945* (Hamburg: Hamburger Edition, 2010).

Müller, Fillip, *Eyewitness Auschwitz: Three Years in the Gas Chambers* (Chicago, IL: Ivan R. Dee, 1999).

Myers Feinstein, Margarete, 'Hannah's Prayer: Jewish Women as Displaced Persons, 1945–1948', in Marcia Sachs Littell (ed.), *Women in the Holocaust: Responses, Insights and Perspectives. (Selected Papers from the Annual Scholars' Conference on the Holocaust and the Churches 1990–2000)* (Merion Station, PA: Merion Westfield Press, 2001), 173–85.

Myers Feinstein, Margarete, 'Absent Fathers, Present Mothers: Images of Parenthood in Holocaust Survivor Narratives', *Nashim: A Journal of Jewish Women's Studies and Gender Issues*, 13 (2007), 155–82.

Myers Feinstein, Margarete, *Holocaust Survivors in Postwar Germany, 1945–1957* (Cambridge, MA: Cambridge University Press, 2014).

Naimark, Norman M., *The Russians in Germany: A History of the Soviet Zone of Occupation, 1945–1949* (Cambridge, MA: Harvard University Press, 1995).

Niewyk, Donald L. (ed.), *Fresh Wounds: Early Narratives of Holocaust Survival* (Chapel Hill, NC: University of North Carolina Press, 1998).

Nomberg-Przytyk, Sara, *Auschwitz: True Tales from a Grotesque Land*, trans. Roslyn Hirsch, eds. Eli Pfefferkorn and David H. Hirsch (Chapel Hill, NC: University of North Carolina Press, 1985).

Nyiszli, Miklos, *Auschwitz: A Doctor's Eyewitness Account*, trans. Tibère Kremer and Richard Seaver (New York: Arcade, 1993).

Ofer, Dalia, 'Cohesion and Rupture: The Jewish Family in East European Ghettos during the Holocaust', in Peter Y. Medding (ed.), *Coping with Life and Death: Jewish Families in the Twentieth Century* (Studies in Contemporary Jewry, 14) (New York: Oxford University Press, 1998), 143–65.

Ofer, Dalia, 'Gender Issues in Diaries and Testimonies of the Ghetto: The Case of Warsaw', in Dalia Ofer and Lenore J. Weitzman (eds.), *Women in the Holocaust* (New Haven, CT: Yale University Press, 1998), 143–69.

Ofer, Dalia, 'Her View through My Lens: Cecilia Slepak Studies Women in the Warsaw Ghetto', in Judith Tydor Baumel and Tova Cohen (eds.), *Gender, Place and Memory in the Modern Jewish Experience: Re-placing Ourselves* (London: Vallentine Mitchell, 2003), 29–50.

Ofer, Dalia, 'Motherhood under Siege', in Esther Hertzog (ed.), *Life, Death and Sacrifice: Women and the Family in the Holocaust* (Jerusalem: Gefen, 2008), 41–67.

Ofer, Dalia and Greenwood, Naftali, 'Everyday Life of Jews under Nazi Occupation: Methodological Issues', *Holocaust and Genocide Studies*, 9 (1995), 42–69.

Ofer, Dalia and Hyman, Paula E. (eds.), *Jewish Women: A Comprehensive Historical Encyclopaedia* (Philadelphia, PA: Jewish Publications Society, 2007).

Ofer, Dalia and Weitzman, Lenore J. (eds.), *Women in the Holocaust* (New Haven, CT: Yale University Press, 1998).

Owings, Alison, *Frauen: German Women Recall the Third Reich* (London: Penguin, 1993).

Paldiel, Mordecai, 'Fear and Comfort: The Plight of Hidden Jewish Children in Wartime-Poland', *Holocaust and Genocide Studies*, 6/4 (1992), 397–413.

Patterson, David, *Sun Turned to Darkness: Memory and Recovery in the Holocaust Memoir* (New York: Syracuse University Press, 1998).

Patterson, David, *Along the Edge of Annihilation: The Collapse and Recovery of Life in the Holocaust Diary* (Seattle, WA: University of Washington Press, 1999).

Paulsson, Gunnar S., 'The Demography of Jews in Hiding in Warsaw, 1943–1945', in Antony Polonsky (ed.), *Polin: Studies in Polish Jewry*, vol. 13: *Focusing on the Holocaust and its Aftermath* (London: Littman Library, 2000), 78–103.

Paulsson, Gunnar S., *Secret City: The Hidden Jews of Warsaw, 1940–1945* (New Haven, CT: Yale University Press, 2002).

Pawelczyńska, Anna, *Values and Violence in Auschwitz: A Sociological Analysis*, trans. Catherine S. Leach (Berkeley, CA: University of California Press, 1979).

Pentilin, Susan L, 'Holocaust Victims of Privilege', in Harry James Cargas (ed.), *Problems Unique to the Holocaust* (Lexington, KY: University of Kentucky Press, 1999), 25–42.

Perechodnik, Calel, *Am I a Murderer? Testament of a Warsaw Jewish Ghetto Policeman*, ed. Frank Fox (New York: Westview, 1996).

Perl, Gisella, *I Was a Doctor in Auschwitz* (New York: International Universities Press, 1948).

Person, Katarzyna, 'Sexual Violence during the Holocaust—The Case of Forced Prostitution in the Warsaw Ghetto', *Shofar*, 33/2 (2015), 103–21.

Pine, Lisa, *Nazi Family Policy 1933–1945* (Oxford: Berg, 1997).

Pine, Lisa, 'Gender and the Holocaust: Male and Female Experiences of Auschwitz', in Amy E. Randall (ed.), *Genocide and Gender in the Twentieth Century: A Comparative Survey* (London: Bloomsbury, 2015), 37–62.

Pines, Dinora, *A Woman's Unconscious Use of Her Body: A Psychoanalytical Perspective* (London: Virago, 1993).

Pisar, Samuel, *Of Blood and Hope* (London: Cassell, 1979).

Plank, Karl A., *Mother of the Wire Fence: Inside and Outside the Holocaust* (Louisville, KY: Westminster John Knox, 1994).

Podolsky, Anatoly, 'The Tragic Fate of Ukrainian Jewish Women under Nazi Occupation, 1941–1944', in Sonja M. Hedgepeth and Rochelle G. Saidel (eds.), *Sexual Violence against Jewish Women during the Holocaust* (Waltham, MA: Brandeis University Press, 2010), 94–108.

Polonsky, Antony, *The Jews in Poland and Russia*. vol. 3: *1914–2008* (London: The Littman Library of Jewish Civilization, 2012).

Preiss, Leah, 'Women's Health in the Ghettos of Eastern Europe', in Dalia Ofer and Paula E. Hyman, *Jewish Women: A Comprehensive Historical Encyclopaedia* (Philadelphia, PA: Jewish Publications Society, 2007).

Proctor, Robert N., *Racial Hygiene: Medicine under the Nazis* (Cambridge, MA: Harvard University Press, 2002).

Reilly, Joanne, 'Cleaner, Carer and Occasional Dance Partner? Writing Women Back into the Liberation of Bergen-Belsen', in Jo Reilly, Tony Kushner, David Cesarani, and Colin Richmond (eds.), *Belsen in History and Memory* (London: Frank Cass, 1997), 149–61.

Reilly, Joanne, *Belsen: The Liberation of a Concentration Camp* (London: Routledge, 1998).

Reiter, Andrea, *Children of the Holocaust* (London: Vallentine Mitchell, 2006).

Riley, Denise, *Am I That Name? Feminism and the Category of 'Women' in History* (Minneapolis, MN: University of Minnesota Press, 1988).

Ringelblum, Emanuel, *Notes from the Warsaw Ghetto: The Journal of Emanuel Ringelblum*, ed. and trans. Jacob Sloan (New York: Schocken, 1974).

Ringelblum, Emanuel, 'The Girl Couriers of the Underground Movement' (19 May 1942), Shoah Resource Center, <http://www.yadvashem.org/odot_pdf/ Microsoft%20Word%20-%202147.pdf>, site accessed 29 August 2016.

Ringelheim, Joan, 'The Unethical and the Unspeakable: Women and the Holocaust', *Simon Wiesenthal Center Annual*, 1 (1984), 69–87.

Ringelheim, Joan, 'Women and the Holocaust: A Reconsideration of Research', *Signs: Journal of Women in Culture and Society*, 10/4 (Summer 1985), 741–61.

Ringelheim, Joan, 'Thoughts about Women and the Holocaust', in Roger S. Gottlieb (ed.), *Thinking the Unthinkable: Meanings of the Holocaust* (New York: Paulist, 1990), 141–9.

Ringelheim, Joan, 'Women and the Holocaust: A Reconsideration of Research', in Carol Rittner and John K. Roth (eds.), *Different Voices: Women and the Holocaust* (New York: Paragon House, 1993), 374–418.

Ringelheim, Joan, 'Gender and Genocide: A Split Memory', in Ronit Lentin (ed.), *Gender and Catastrophe* (London: Zed Books, 1997), 18–33.

Ringelheim, Joan, 'The Split between Gender and the Holocaust', in Dalia Ofer and Lenore J. Weitzman (eds.), *Women in the Holocaust* (New Haven, CT: Yale University Press, 1998), 340–50.

Rittner, Carol and Myers, Sandra (ed.), *The Courage to Care: Rescuers of Jews during the Holocaust* (New York: New York University Press, 1989).

Rittner, Carol and Roth, John K. (eds.), *Different Voices: Women and the Holocaust* (New York: Paragon House, 1993).

Rogers, Annie G., Casey, Mary E., Ekert, Jennifer, Holland, James, Nakkula, Victoria, and Sheinberg, Nurit, 'An Interpretive Poetics of Languages of the Unsayable', in Ruthellen Josselson and Amia Lieblich (eds.), *Making Meaning of Narratives in the Narrative Study of Lives* (London: Sage, 1997), 77–106.

Roland, Charles G., 'An Underground Medical School in the Warsaw Ghetto', *Medical History*, 33 (1989), 399–419.

Roland, Charles G., *Courage under Siege: Starvation, Disease and Death in the Warsaw Ghetto* (Oxford: Oxford University Press, 1992).

Rolnikas, Macha, *Je Devais le Raconter* (Paris: Les Éditeurs Français Réunis, 1966).

Rosenfarb, Chava, <http://www.tabletmag.com/jewish-arts-and-culture/books/160640/rosenfarb.bergen.belsen.diary> (accessed 1 September 2016).

Rosensaft, Hadassah, *Yesterday: My Story* (Jerusalem: Yad Vashem, 2004).

Rosensaft, Menachem (ed.), *Life Reborn: Jewish Displaced Persons 1945–1951: Conference Proceedings, Washington DC, January 14–17, 2000* (Washington, DC: United States Holocaust Memorial Museum, 2001).

Roskies, David G., *The Jewish Search for a Useable Past* (Bloomington, IN: Indiana University Press, 1999).

Roskies, David G. (ed.), *The Literature of Destruction: Jewish Responses to Catastrophe* (Philadelphia, PA: Jewish Publications Society, 1989).

Roth, John K., 'Equality, Neutrality, Particularity', in Elizabeth R. Baer and Myrna Goldenberg (eds.), *Experience and Expression: Women, the Nazis, and the Holocaust* (Detroit, MI: Wayne State University Press, 2003), 5–23.

Rubenstein, Joshua and Altman, Ilya (eds.), *The Unknown Black Book: The Holocaust in the German-Occupied Soviet Territories* (Bloomington, IN: Indiana University Press, 2010).

Rupp, Leila J., *Mobilizing Women for War: German and American Propaganda, 1939–1945* (Princeton, NJ: Princeton University Press, 1978).

Saidel, Rochelle G., 'Women's Experiences during the Holocaust—New Books in Print', *Yad Vashem Studies*, 28 (2000), 368–78.

Saidel, Rochelle G., 'Integrating Ravensbrück Women's Concentration Camp into Holocaust Memorialization in the US', in Marcia Sachs Littell (ed.), *Women in the Holocaust: Responses, Insights and Perspectives (Selected Papers from the Annual Scholars' Conference on the Holocaust and the Churches 1990–2000)* (Merion Station, PA: Merion Westfield Press, 2001), 63–74.

Saidel, Rochelle G., *The Jewish Women of Ravensbrück Concentration Camp* (Madison, WI: University of Wisconsin Press, 2004).

Sakowska, Ruta (ed.), *Archiwum Ringelbluma: Konspiracyjna Archiwum Getta Warszawy* [Ringelblum Archive: Underground Warsaw Ghetto Archive]. vol. 2: *Dzieci—tajne nauczanie w getcie warzawskim* [Children—Secret Education in the Warsaw Ghetto] (Warsaw: Jewish Historical Institute, 2000).

Sax, Benjamin C. and Kunz, Dieter (eds.), *Inside Hitler's Germany: A Documentary History of Life in the Third Reich* (Lexington, KY: D.C. Heath, 1992).

Scarry, Elaine, *The Body in Pain: The Making and Unmaking of the World* (Oxford: Oxford University Press, 1985).

Schiessl, Christoph, 'An Element of Genocide: Rape, Total War, and International Law in the Twentieth Century', *Journal of Genocide Research*, 4/2 (2002), 197–210.

Schloss, Eva (with Evelyn Julia Kent), *Eva's Story: A Survivor's Tale by the Step-Sister of Anne Frank* (London: W.H. Allen, 1988).

Schoenfeld, Gabriel, 'Auschwitz and the Professors', *Commentary*, 105/6 (June 1998), 42–6.

Scibetta, Barbara Smith and Shukert, Elfrieda Berthiaume, *War Brides of World II* (New York: Penguin, 1989).

Scott, Joan Wallach, 'Gender: A Useful Category of Historical Analysis', *American Historical Review*, 91/5 (December 1986), 1053–75.

Scott, Joan Wallach, *Gender and the Politics of History* (New York: Columbia University Press, 1988).

Segev, Tom, *The Seventh Million: The Israelis and the Holocaust*, trans. Haim Watzman (New York: Hill & Wang, 1993).

Seidman, Naomi, 'Elie Wiesel and the Scandal of Jewish Rage', *Jewish Social Studies: History: Culture, and Society*, 3/1 (Fall 1996), 1–19.

Seidman, Naomi, 'Theorizing Jewish Patriarchy in Extremis', in Miriam Peskowitz and Laura Levitt (eds.), *Judaism since Gender* (New York: Routledge, 1997), 40–9.

Selver-Urbach, Sara, *Through the Window of My Home: Recollections from the Lodz Ghetto*, trans. Siona Bodansky (Jerusalem: Yad Vashem, 1971).

Sereny, Gitta, *The German Trauma: Experiences and Reflections 1938–2000* (London: Allen Lane, 2000).

Shaul, Michal, 'Testimonies of Ultra-Orthodox Holocaust Survivors', *Yad Vashem Studies*, 35/2, 143–85.

Shepard, Ben, *After Daybreak: The Liberation of Belsen, 1945* (London: Jonathan Cape, 2005).

Shik, Na'ama, 'Infinite Loneliness: Some Aspects of the Lives of Jewish Women in the Auschwitz Camps according to Testimonies and Autobiographies Written between 1945 and 1948', in Doris L. Bergen (ed.), *Lessons and Legacies*, vol. 8: *From Generation to Generation* (Evanston, IL: Northwestern University Press, 2008), 125–56.

Shik, Na'ama, 'Sexual Abuse of Jewish Women in Auschwitz-Birkenau', in Dagmar Herzog (ed.), *Brutality and Desire: War and Sexuality in Europe's Twentieth Century* (Basingstoke: Palgrave Macmillan, 2009), 221–47.

Siegal, Aranka, *Grace in the Wilderness: After the Liberation 1945–1948* (New York: Signet, 1985).

Sierakowiak, Dawid, *The Diary of Dawid Sierakowiak: Five Notebooks from the Łódź Ghetto*, trans. Kamil Turowksi, ed. Alan Adelson (London: Bloomsbury, 1997).

Sinnreich, Helene J., '"And It Was Something We Didn't Talk About": Rape of Jewish Women during the Holocaust,' *Holocaust Studies: A Journal of Culture and History*, 14/2 (December 2008), 1–22.

Sinnreich, Helene J., 'The Rape of Jewish Women during the Holocaust', in Sonja M. Hedgepeth and Rochelle G. Saidel (eds.), *Sexual Violence against Jewish Women during the Holocaust* (Waltham, MA: Brandeis University Press, 2010), 108–23.

Smith, Lynn, *Remembering: Voices of the Holocaust. A New History in the Words of the Men and Women Who Survived* (New York: Carroll & Graf, 2006).

Smith, Roger W., 'Women and Genocide: Notes on an Unwritten History', *Holocaust and Genocide Studies*, 8/3 (1994), 315–34.

Snyder, David Raub, *Sex Crimes under the Wehrmacht* (Lincoln, NE: University of Nebraska Press, 2007).

Sofsky, Wolfgang, *The Order of Terror: The Concentration Camp* (Princeton, NJ: Princeton University Press, 1997).

Stargardt, Nicholas, *Witnesses of War: Children's Lives under the Nazis* (London: Jonathan Cape, 2005).

Steinberg, Avraham, 'Induced Abortion according to Jewish Law', *Journal of Halacha [Jewish Law] and Contemporary Society*, 1/1 (1981), 29–52.

Steinert, Johannes-Dieter, 'British Relief Teams in Belsen Concentration Camp: Emergency Relief and the Perception of Survivors', in Suzanne Bardgett and David Cesarani (eds.), *Belsen 1945: New Historical Perspectives* (London: Vallentine Mitchell, 2006), 62–79.

Stephenson, Jill, *Women in Nazi Society* (London: Routledge, 1975).

Sternberg Newman, Judith, *In the Hell of Auschwitz: The Wartime Memoirs of J.S. Newman* (New York: Exposition, 1963).

Stola, Daniusz, 'Early News of the Holocaust from Poland', *Holocaust and Genocide Studies*, 11/1 (Spring 1997), 1–27.

Stone, Dan, 'The *Sonderkommando* Photographs', *Jewish Social Studies: History, Culture, and Society*, 7/3 (2001), 131–48.

Stone, Dan, *The Liberation of the Camps: The End of the Holocaust and its Aftermath* (New Haven, CT: Yale University Press, 2015).

Strzelecka, Irena, 'Women', in Israel Gutman and Michael Berenbaum (eds.), *Anatomy of the Auschwitz Death Camp* (Bloomington, IN: Indiana University Press, 1994), 393–412.

Szmaglewska, Seweryna, *Smoke over Birkenau*, trans. Jadwiga Rynas (New York: Henry Holt, 1947).

Szpilman, Władysław, *The Pianist: The Extraordinary Story of One Man's Survival in Warsaw, 1939–45*, trans. Anthea Bell (London: Victor Gollancz, 1999).

Taylor Allen, Ann, 'The Holocaust and the Modernisation of Gender: A Historiographical Essay', *Central European History*, 30/3 (1997), 349–64.

Tec, Nechama, 'Sex Distinctions and Passing as Christians during the Holocaust', *East European Quarterly*, 18/1 (March 1984), 113–23.

Tec, Nechama, 'Women among the Forest Partisans', in Dalia Ofer and Lenore J. Weitzman (eds.), *Women in the Holocaust* (New Haven, CT: Yale University Press, 1998), 223–34.

Tec, Nechama, *Resilience and Courage: Women, Men, and the Holocaust* (New Haven, CT: Yale University Press, 2003).

Tec, Nechama, *When Light Pierced the Darkness: Christian Rescue of Jews in Nazi-Occupied Poland* (New York: Oxford University Press, 1986).

Tedeschi, Giuliana, *There Is a Place on Earth: A Woman in Birkenau*, trans. Tim Parks (London: Lime Tree, 1993).

Temkin-Bermanowa, Bathia, *Dziennik z podziemia* [Official from the Underground], eds. Anka Grupińska and Pawél Szapiro (Warsaw: Jewish Historical Institute, 2000).

Tory, Avraham, *Surviving the Holocaust: The Kovno Ghetto Diary*, ed. Martin Gilbert (Cambridge, MA: Harvard University Press, 1991).

Trunk, Isaiah, *Judenrat: The Jewish Councils of Eastern Europe under Nazi Occupation* (New York: Macmillan, 1972).

Trunk, Isaiah, *Jewish Responses to Nazi Persecution* (New York: Stein & Day, 1982).

Unger, Michal, 'The Status and Plight of Women in the Łódź Ghetto', in Dalia Ofer and Lenore J. Weitzman (eds.), *Women in the Holocaust* (New Haven, CT: Yale University Press, 1998), 123–42.

Venezia, Shlomo, *Inside the Gas Chambers: Eight Months in the* Sonderkommando *of Auschwitz* (Malden, MA: Polity, 2009).

Verrall, Olga, *Missing Pieces: My Life as a Child Survivor of the Holocaust* (Calgary: University of Calgary Press, 2007).

Wachsmann, Nikolaus, *KL: A History of the Nazi Concentration Camps* (London: Little, Brown, 2015).

Walk, Joseph, 'Religious Leadership during the Holocaust', in Israel Gutman and Cynthia J. Haft (eds.), *Patterns of Jewish Leadership in Nazi Europe 1933–1945. Proceedings of the Third Yad Vashem International Conference* (Jerusalem: Yad Vashem, 1979), 377–91.

Wardi, Dina, *Memorial Candles: Children of the Holocaust* (London: Routledge, 1992).

Warhaftig, Zorach, *Uprooted: Jewish Refugees and Displaced Persons after Liberation, from War to Peace* (New York: Institute for Jewish Affairs for the American Jewish Congress & World Jewish Congress, 1946).

Waxman, Zoë, 'Unheard Testimony: Unheard Stories: The Representation of Women's Holocaust Experiences', *Women's History Review*, 12/4 (2003), 661–77.

Waxman, Zoë, *Writing the Holocaust: Identity, Testimony, Representation* (Oxford: Oxford University Press, 2006).

Waxman, Zoë, 'Rape and Sexual Abuse in Hiding', in Sonja M. Hedgepeth and Rochelle G. Saidel (eds.), *Sexual Violence against Jewish Women during the Holocaust* (Waltham, MA: Brandeis University Press, 2010), 124–35.

Waxman, Zoë, 'Testimony and Silence: Sexual Violence and the Holocaust', in Zoë Brigley Thompson and Sorcha Gunne (eds.), *Feminism, Literature and Rape Narratives: Violence and Violation* (New York: Routledge, 2010), 117–30.

Waxman, Zoë, 'Towards an Integrated History of the Holocaust: Masculinity, Femininity, and Genocide', in Christian Wiese and Paul Betts (eds.), *Years of Persecution, Years of Extermination: Saul Friedländer and the Future of Holocaust Studies* (London: Continuum, 2010), 311–21.

Waxman, Zoë, *Anne Frank* (Stroud, Gloucestershire: The History Press, 2015).

Weisblum, Giza, 'The Escape and Death of the "Runner" Mala Zimetbaum', in Yuri Suhl (ed.), *They Fought Back: The Story of the Jewish Resistance in Nazi Europe* (New York: Crown, 1967), 182–281.

Weitzman, Lenore J., 'Living on the Aryan Side in Poland: Gender, Passing, and the Nature of Resistance', in Dalia Ofer and Lenore J. Weitzman (eds.), *Women in the Holocaust* (New Haven, CT: Yale University Press, 1998), 187–222.

Weitzman, Lenore J., 'Women of Courage: The *Kashariyot* (Couriers) in the Jewish Resistance during the Holocaust', in Jeffry M. Diefendorf (ed.), *Lessons and Legacies*, vol. 6: *New Currents in Holocaust Research* (Evanston, IL: Northwestern University Press, 2004), 112–52.

Weitzman, Lenore J. and Ofer, Dalia, 'The Role of Gender in the Holocaust', in Dalia Ofer and Lenore J. Weitzman (eds.), *Women in the Holocaust* (New Haven, CT: Yale University Press, 1998).

Weitzman, Lenore J. and Ofer, Dalia, 'Women in the Holocaust: Theoretical Foundations for a Gendered Analysis of the Holocaust', in Marcia Sachs Littell (ed.), *Women in the Holocaust: Responses, Insights and Perspectives (Selected Papers from the Annual Scholars' Conference on the Holocaust and the Churches 1990–2000)* (Merion Station, PA: Merion Westfield Press, 2001), 1–24.

Wiesel, Elie, *Night/Day/Dawn*, trans. Stella Rodway (New York: Bantam, 1960).

Wiesel, Elie, *All Rivers Run to the Sea: Memoirs* (New York: Knopf, 1995).

Wiesel, Elie, *And the Sea is Never Full*, trans. Marion Wiesel (New York: Knopf, 1999).

Winick, Myron (ed.), *Hunger Disease: Studies by the Jewish Physicians in the Warsaw Ghetto*, trans. Martha Osnos (New York: Wiley, 1979).

Wittig, Monique, 'One is Not Born a Woman', in *The Straight Mind* (Hemel Hempstead: Harvester Wheatsheaf, 1992), 9–20.

Wolf, Diane L., *Beyond Anne Frank: Hidden Children and Postwar Families in Holland* (Los Angeles, CA: University of California Press, 2007).

Wollaston, Isabel, *A War against Memory?: The Future of Holocaust Remembrance* (London: SPCK, 1996).

Wyman, Mark, *DPs: Europe's Displaced Persons, 1945–1951* (Ithaca, NY: Cornell University Press, 1989).

Yablonka, Hanna, 'The Nazis and Nazi Collaborators (Punishment) Law: An Additional Aspect of the Question of Israelis, Survivors, and the Holocaust', *Katedra* 82 (1996), 132–52 [Hebrew].

Yablonka, Hanna, 'The Formation of Holocaust Consciousness in the State of Israel: The Early Days', in Efraim Sicher (ed.), *Breaking Crystal: Writing and Memory after Auschwitz* (Urbana, IL: Chicago University Press, 1998), 119–37.

Zuccotti, Susan, *The Holocaust, the French, and the Jews* (Lincoln, NE: University of Nebraska Press, 1993).

Index

Printed and bound by CPI Group (UK) Ltd, Croydon, CR0 4YY